THE COMING Millennial Kingdom

NATHAN E. JONES

HARVEST PROPHECY
AN IMPRINT OF HARVEST HOUSE PUBLISHERS

Cover design by Faceout Studio, Spenser Fuller

Cover images © sokolart / Shutterstock; Spencer Fuller / Faceout Studios

Interior design by KUHN Design Group

For bulk, special sales, or ministry purchases, please call 1-800-547-8979.
Email: CustomerService@hhpbooks.com

The Coming Millennial Kingdom

Published by Harvest House Publishers
Eugene, Oregon 97408
www.harvesthousepublishers.com

ISBN 978-0-7369-9166-7 (pbk)
ISBN 978-0-7369-9167-4 (eBook)

Library of Congress Control Number: 2024946099

Printed in the United States of America

25 26 27 28 29 30 31 32 33 / BP / 10 9 8 7 6 5 4 3 2 1

"*The Coming Millennial Kingdom* provides us with an advanced, comprehensive backstage pass to our future as believers. Expertly written and deeply rooted in Scripture, your understanding of prophecy will be greatly enhanced!"

—**Jeff Kinley**, host *The King Is Coming*; cohost *The Prophecy Pros Podcast*

"A masterful exploration of the millennial kingdom, uncovering its wonders through the lens of Scripture. Jones paints a vivid picture of Christ's righteous government, with Jerusalem as its capital, and a restored creation where peace reigns. This work is an invitation to marvel at God's redemptive plan and fix our eyes on the reign of King Jesus in His glorious kingdom."

—**Dr. Ron Rhodes**, author, *The End Times in Chronological Order*

"Sadly, the intricate details of our 1,000 years here on earth in Christ's kingdom are marginalized or misinterpreted by many Christians who think we're in the millennial kingdom now. When believers are not taught, they fall into serious doctrinal error and confusion. I was pleased to read Nathan's book about Christ's kingdom that is yet to come. It will open many eyes with an outstanding overview of premillennialism."

—**Jan Markell**, founder/director, Olive Tree Ministries

"This book breaks through the dark, tumultuous clouds of these end times with brilliant descriptive details about God's unfathomable promises to believers. The apostle Paul's words in 1 Corinthians 2:9-10 come alive in the reader's spiritual understanding: 'As it is written, Eye hath not seen, nor ear heard, neither have entered into the heart of man, the things which God hath prepared for them that love him. But God hath revealed them unto us by his Spirit: for the Spirit searcheth all things, yea, the deep things of God.'"

—**Terry James**, Raptureready.com

"*The Coming Millennial Kingdom* is incredibly thorough, taking readers on a tour through the Old and New Testaments to demonstrate the literal nature of God's unconditional prophetic promises about the future kingdom age. Jones points to the only hermeneutically sound conclusion: There is a literal future kingdom age coming, in which God's promises to Israel and the church will be beautifully fulfilled!"

—**Todd Hampson**, author, Non-Prophet's Guide series; cohost *The Prophecy Pros Podcast*

"This easy-to-read book on our coming future home and governmental responsibilities will be an encouragement to God's people. Readers will be inspired to serve the Lord with great anticipation of the fulfillment of our future rewards in the 1,000-year reign of Jesus our King."

—**Mondo Gonzales**, cohost at Prophecy Watchers

"Nathan guides the reader through various questions regarding the coming Davidic kingdom of Christ on the earth. His conclusions are encouraging, faithful to Scripture, and filled with hope. The book causes one to pray with even more passion for the kingdom of Jesus Christ to come soon."

—**Terry Cooper**, lead minister, Ninevah Christian Church, KY

"Christians too often think of the immediate over the eternal. With bills to pay, kids to raise, and sales quotas to meet, the earthly frequently trumps the eternal. *The Coming Millennial Kingdom* redirects our focus and answers pressing questions about our future. Nathan's approach is biblical without being mechanical, a perfect blend of futurist and biblical realist that every believer should read."

—**Joe Kerr,** ghostwriter, editor, White House Special Media Press Corps

"Few scholars can communicate important biblical truth in an easy-to-understand fashion. Nathan Jones is one of those scholars. In *The Coming Millennial Kingdom*, he skillfully explains intricate details about the future earthly reign of Christ in a way that fills the reader with vivid images of, and an earnest longing for, the glorious return of the King!"

—**J.B. Hixson, PhD**, president/founder, NBW Ministries

"*The Coming Millennial Kingdom* contains teaching and encouragement about the climax of all human history: the messianic kingdom of Christ. It is well organized and engaging and has treasures for every reader to discover. Best of all, it provides comfort and hope in what the Lord has yet to do with this world—causing believers to long for Christ's return."

—**Bradley W. Maston, PhD**, pastor, Fort Collins Bible Church, CO

"With such darkness, death, and destruction on this earth, how exciting to read, in detail, what the future will look like during the reign of Jesus Christ, when the government is finally on His shoulders! *The Coming Millennial Kingdom* is sure to bring a sense of relief, encouragement, and perspective to believers everywhere."

—**David Fiorazo,** author, podcaster, host of *Worldview Matters*

"Nathan's treatment of the coming kingdom is well outlined, well written, and well rounded. It covers every vital aspect of the kingdom—from the promises to the tribulation to the kingdom blessings—on a level that is within the reach of the student, yet rich enough for the theologian."

—**Lee W. Brainard**, Soothkeep Ministry

"Nathan Jones's depth and knowledge of Bible prophecy is a truly a gift from the Lord. *The Coming Millennial Kingdom* is an example of the simple yet profound way that he communicates biblical truth along with down-to-earth applications. The information he provides here makes this a must-have resource that will bless everyone who reads it!"

—**Dr. Victoriano Batista, PhD**, Calvary Chapel pastor and evangelist; coauthor of *The Mighty Angels of Revelation*

This book is dedicated to my loving parents,
Edward and Joyce Jones,
who have faithfully been teaching their children since the cradle to
"watch…and pray always that you may be counted worthy"
(Luke 21:36).

ACKNOWLEDGMENTS

I would like to think that this book stands as the pinnacle of my lifetime studying the Bible, particularly that wonderfully endearing doctrine called eschatology. But, alas, as a wise old professor once so sagely pointed out, we students of the Bible merely stand on the shoulders of close to 2,000 years' worth of interpreters and interpretations. Therefore, of those on whose shoulders I am now standing, I must start my acknowledgments by crediting the source of all divine knowledge—my Lord and Savior, Jesus Christ. Thank You, Lord Jesus, for revealing Yourself through Your Holy Scriptures and guiding Spirit. I so long to see Your radiance emanating from the throne of David and to worship You as the worthy King of kings. Long live the kingdom of Christ!

I would also like to acknowledge the theologians and scholars of past church history, many of whom have been lost and forgotten by time, but in glory we will at long last become acquainted. I would also like to acknowledge the theologians and scholars of present church history, many of whom have taught, lectured, or mentored me in my journey to better understand "our great God and Savior" (Titus 2:13). These paragons of my Bible college and seminary years poured their passion for the Lord, His Word, and His Great Commission into each of their lessons. And, to the many colleagues and mentors during my ministry career, way too numerous to name here, thank you.

And, finally, much appreciation to the good folks at Harvest House Publishers, whose passion for disseminating God's Word continually motivates their readers to prayerfully attain that long-anticipated affirmation, "Well done, good and faithful servant" (Matthew 25:21, 23).

CONTENTS

FOREWORD

Back in 2007, God gave me a vision to transform the Lamb & Lion Ministries website into a web ministry. Up until that time, the website had simply been an archive of our publications and videos. I felt the Lord wanted us to develop it into a dynamic, interactive tool for evangelism and a communication hub for the discussion of Bible prophecy. What I needed to accomplish this was an Internet evangelist.

Trying to find the right person to take on this task seemed next to impossible. Ideally, I wanted a person who was technically qualified in all aspects of website creation and maintenance. But the person also needed to be trained theologically and have an in-depth knowledge of Bible prophecy. Needless to say, that combination of qualifications was not going to be easy to find. In fact, I doubted that such a person even existed!

But I kept praying, and once again, God proved that with Him all things are possible (Matthew 19:26). Nathan Jones, who at the time was serving at a megachurch in Kentucky, applied for the position, explaining that he had both a heart for Bible prophecy and extensive technical knowledge in communicating over the Internet. I was astounded and delighted.

After Nathan was brought on board, I discovered that God had blessed our ministry with a highly gifted person who could do much more than just present the gospel over the Internet and answer questions about Bible prophecy. Also serving as my cohost on our ministry's television program *Christ in Prophecy*, I watched Nathan over the years develop into a very talented teacher, preacher, and writer. He has become a much-requested conference speaker, and the books he's written are full of spiritual insights.

Furthermore, he has been gifted by God to explain the difficult concepts of Bible prophecy in down-to-earth, understandable terms that the people in the pews can comprehend. He shares my belief that God wants to communicate with the average person and not just scholars.

Regarding the interpretation of Bible prophecy, Nathan believes that God truly means what He says. Therefore, his explanations of prophecies always seek the plain-sense meaning. He studiously avoids spiritualization and sensationalism—two of the worst abuses of Bible prophecy in the church today.

Because the spiritualization of Scripture prevails in most denominations, causing them to deny any future earthly reign of Jesus, most Christians know little or nothing about the many prophecies concerning the coming kingdom of Christ—a reign promised to bring peace, righteousness, and justice to the earth for 1,000 years. Nor are they aware of the promise that Christians will participate in that kingdom, and that during the millennium, Jesus will also fulfill all the promises He has made to the Jewish people. To rectify this tragic oversight, Nathan, in this book, will reveal to you the glorious "forgotten" promises God has made about the future kingdom of Christ that is soon coming to the earth.

Knowing Christ's coming victory—and your role in it—will equip you with an eternal perspective that will enable you to cope with life's challenges in the here and now. And, as this world grows increasingly dark, I believe you will agree with me: Hope is needed now more than ever. Knowledge about God's marvelous promises concerning the near future will provide you with that much-needed hope in the present.

So prepare yourself for a spiritual feast of God's prophetic Word and turn the page.

Maranatha!

Dr. David R. Reagan
Founder of Lamb & Lion Ministries

CHAPTER 1

NATIONS IN FREEFALL

My mother used to tell me of a millennium that was coming, when Christ should reign, and all men should be free and happy. And she taught me, when I was a boy, to pray, "Thy kingdom come." Sometimes I think all this sighing, and groaning, and stirring among the dry bones foretells what she used to tell me was coming. But who may abide the day of His appearing?[1]

Harriet Beecher Stowe, *Uncle Tom's Cabin*

Let's gather around the coffee table as if playing a round of Trivia Night. First question: *What would you say have been the greatest empires in world history?*

So you can best answer this question, let's quickly define what an empire is: "an extensive group of states or countries ruled over by a single monarch, an oligarchy, or a sovereign state."[2] The criteria for determining greatness is based on the enduring impact the empire has made on the world overall, either through its military domination, scientific advancements, or cultural achievements. The greatest empires have the biggest impact on global society, thereby controlling the destinies of millions of people. These are the far-reaching history changers that charted the course of overall human development for generations to come.

Which empires did you choose? If you are thinking along the same lines as I am, I chose the following nine as being the greatest:

1. Egypt for its pharaohs and pyramids
2. Babylon for its pivotal role in the Old Testament
3. the Persian Empire for its sciences
4. the Macedonian-Greek kingdom for its culture
5. the Roman Empire for its military strength
6. the British Empire for its vast colonization of every continent
7. the Soviet Union for the fear it so long hung over the world
8. the United States for the freedoms it provides
9. the European Union for the amazing achievement of unifying long-warring nations

(Though, as an American, I am, of course, guilty of being Western-centric in my choices.)

Alas, I answered wrong. According to the historical-geographical experts at *WorldAtlas*, the following eight empires check all the criteria boxes as being the truly greatest of the world-impacting dominions.[3]

THE EIGHT GREAT EMPIRES

1. The Akkadian Empire

The Akkadian Empire is the great-granddaddy of all subsequent empires, stretching as far back as nearly one step away from Noah's ark. Established around 2334 BC by the esteemed Sargon of Akkad, this empire ruled over 310,000 square miles of ancient Mesopotamia, which was truly an amazing mass of land at a time when the world was so thinly populated. At its zenith, the Akkadian Empire was the model of strength due to its centralized government, well-ordered administration, and well-managed infrastructure.

But like all rulers who taste too much success and amass too much power, Sargon's grandson Naram-Sin developed a "deity-sized ego" and so proclaimed himself "king of the four corners of the universe" and a god equal to any other in the Mesopotamian pantheon.[4] Thus the Akkadian decline began around 2154 BC due to a combination of revolts against Naram-Sin, political instability, economic decline, a devastating drought, and invasions by the rival Gutians. All of these factors contributed to the collapse of this once-impressive forerunner empire.

2. The Persian Empire (Achaemenid Empire)

Established by Cyrus the Great and dominating the Middle East between 550 to 330 BC, ancient Persia at its peak spread remarkably over three continents: Asia, Africa, and Europe. The Persian Empire is remembered for its deeply educated society that adhered to codified laws, was run by an efficient bureaucracy, boasted one of the first postal systems, and constructed the 1,553-mile Royal Road that facilitated trade and military dominance. The Medo-Persians even showed respect for the customs and religions of its conquered people.

The empire's fourth king, Xerxes (486–465 BC), likely King Ahasuerus from the book of Esther, lived by the maxim, "A wise ruler listens to the counsel of his advisors before making decisions."[5] And indeed, Xerxes did listen to his advisors' advice when it came to making an example out of his absent wife, Queen Vashti, who had refused to parade herself naked around his drunken friends. The first chapter of the book of Esther exposed how Xerxes' fearful advisors worried such insolence would put all the empire's men at risk of having their wives despise their husbands. Nip it in the bud, they begged, and so the king banished his own wife. All it took to bring down this "enlightened" empire was the arrival of the unstoppable Alexander the Great and his Macedonian armies in 334 BC, who were enraged over Xerxes' earlier victory at the famous Battle of Thermopylae.

3. The Roman Empire

Birthed out of the Roman Republic in 27 BC by its first emperor, Julius Caesar, the Roman Empire stands apart as the geopolitical juggernaut that profoundly shaped the future of Western civilization. To this very day, Western societies model Roman law and governance, continue to utilize Roman infrastructure and architecture, speak languages that find their origins in Latin, have practiced Christianity since Constantine I, and long for the return of Rome's Pax Romana period, which for centuries brought its citizens prosperity and stability. At its zenith, the might of the Roman military spread its iron control over three whole continents.

Unfortunately, Rome's emperors earned their fame as notorious lunatics and self-proclaimed gods who grew increasingly mad from drinking lead-laced wine. Case in point, the brutal Caligula (AD 37–41) fed prisoners to wild beasts, held conversations with the moon, and legend says he appointed his beloved horse Incitatus as Rome's first equine official.[6] The Roman Empire died a slow and painful death as it crumbled into pieces due to military overreach, economic instability, societal decadence, and an open-border policy that led to barbarian invasions until its inevitable fall in AD 476.

4. The Mongol Empire

Eurasia was blitzkrieged by the mighty Mongol warlord Genghis Khan in AD 1206. His exceptional military strategy and his successors' strong organizational skills established the largest contiguous empire ever forged. Having developed advanced communications and trade systems to facilitate the empire's control over such a vast amount of territory, the Mongol Empire linked East to West along the Silk Road to produce an unprecedented cultural exchange.

Such rapid expansion came at an unfathomable cost, as the sheer brutality of Khan's conquests caused the mass killing of one-tenth of the world's known population—a staggering 50 million deaths![7] For Genghis Khan, his "greatest happiness" was "to vanquish your enemies, to chase them before you, to rob them of their wealth, to see those dear to them bathed in tears, [and] to clasp to your bosom their wives and daughters."[8] Way too vast an empire to maintain control over, by the late thirteenth century, the Mongol Empire became fractured and plagued by domestic conflicts, succession issues, and frequent rebellions.

5. The Ottoman Empire

Birthed out of the Turkish tribes under Osman I in AD 1299 and reaching its peak under Suleiman the Magnificent (1520–1566), the Ottoman Empire dominated the old Roman lands for an incredible 600 years (1299–1922). Strategically situated between Europe and Asia, this superpower was hailed for its multiethnic and multicultural society, religious tolerance, well-established laws, and long-running social stability.

The Ottoman Empire was also infamous for its shady style of leadership. History recorded that the rulers in Turkey were so criminally corrupt that their primary interest was robbing their own people blind. They were also too lazy to run the affairs of the empire at the local level, so neglected their municipalities.[9] Like the Mongols, the Ottomans engaged in genocide. Of the estimated two million Armenians living in the empire at the onset of World War I, the Ottomans deported well over a million, and hundreds of thousands more were summarily massacred. The rise in power of the Western nations caused this empire's bitter defeat, and by the end of World War I, most of its lands were divvied up among its enemies.

6. The British Empire

From the sixteenth to the mid-twentieth century, the sun never set on the lands controlled by the British Empire, which, during that time, was considered the world's most extensive geopolitical power. This imperialistic empire mastered maritime exploration and trade to colonize practically every continent. The British Empire influenced much of the world's cultures, governments, and systems of law, and made English the dominant trade language to this day.

The first king of Great Britain, James VI (1566–1625), led a very long line of sovereigns who smugly believed in the divine right of kings as being superior to any mere man. As James stated, "The estate of monarchy is the supremest thing upon earth; for kings are not only God's lieutenants upon earth, and sit upon God's throne, but even by God Himself they are called gods."[10] However, globalizing the world came at a steep price, for the British Empire of today is practically an empire in name only due to many of its colonies having declared their independence, the rise of rival powers, and the horrific losses it suffered over two world wars.

7. The Russian-Soviet Empire

Founded in Moscow under Ivan I in the twelfth century and evolving into the Russian Empire under Peter the Great in 1721, the latter's autocratic tsarist rule resulted in massive territorial expansion, leading Russia to control the largest single landmass of any country in history. Social class unrest led to the horrifically bloody Communist October Revolution of 1917. The Soviet Union devoured the Russian Empire and then meteorically rose to superpower status during the Cold War.

In its attempt to construct a socialist utopia, the Soviet Union—under the monstrously violent Joseph Stalin, who led the country from 1924 to 1953—purged more than 20 million of his people and starved millions of Ukrainians to death. He once bragged to Winston Churchill, "The devil is on my side. Because, of course, everyone knows that the devil is a Communist—and God, no doubt, is a good Conservative."[11] Inherent defects within the Communist system of government inevitably led to the Union's economy collapsing in 1991. Though Russia subsequently lost its superpower status, it remains a formidable global threat under President Vladimir Putin.

8. The United States of America

While the United States wouldn't categorize itself as an empire, many other nations do so because of the USA's unchallenged military, political, and cultural influence over the entire world. Having declared its independence in 1776 from the British Empire, the US has stood on one leg by its faith in Judeo-Christian values and on the other by the ideals of the Enlightenment concerning liberty and democracy. Swelled in population not by conquest but by immigration, fueled by seemingly endless resources, and almost unbeatable in technological innovation, the US emerged from World War II as a global power and claims the title as today's only recognized superpower.

Ever since President Harry Truman tasked Congress in late 1945 with the charge, "We must relentlessly preserve our superiority on land and sea and in the air," the US has planted some 750 bases in about 80 foreign countries and territories, leading one author to label the US as "a pointillist empire that spans the globe."[12] Today, the US has abandoned its foundational beliefs, been stricken by internal divisions, is teetering on bankruptcy due to reckless deficit spending, and has been losing its influence on the world stage. For these reasons, many historians classify the US as an empire in swift decline.

THE COMMONALITY

Why did I just give you a brief survey of the world's most influential empires? Because this leads to the second question of our trivia night: *What do all of these empires have most in common?*

Your answer might span the spectrum from raw political power, to vast military might, to long-standing cultural influences, to economic superiority, and even to longevity. And you would be right, though only to some degree.

The sole shared characteristic, once revealed, should appear blindingly apparent, much like a buoy light bobbing in a storm at sea. It's a characteristic historically and repeatedly proven again and again. And it is this:

> Every one of these mighty empires became an absolute, total failure, either consummately in the past or is currently in a state of decline now and so is heading toward an inevitable collapse.

THE FAILURE OF HUMAN GOVERNMENT

Why is failure alone the most significant common trait? Why have these and every other mighty empire or nation been stamped in red with *Failure*? The reason is because they have been unable to fulfill the primary reason for why human governments exist.

Because we all live out our days under some flavor of political *ism*, and so benefit from or suffer under them, let's identify the primary reason why human governments exist. As the US is considered by many to be the pinnacle of all human governments in the freedoms it enjoys, the influence that it extends, and the wealth it generates, let's look to the nation's Founding Fathers for the answer to the reason why every empire or nation inevitably fails.

While laying the groundwork for the prenatal US, the Founding Fathers held fast to the biblical revelation that government under human control has been divinely purposed. The God of this logical and orderly universe is the very One who instituted government by revealing Himself and His will for its establishment in the Bible.

Case in point: In the Old Testament, the prophet Daniel wrote that God is the very One who "changes the times and the seasons; He removes kings and raises up kings" (Daniel 2:21). In speaking to Babylon's potentate, Daniel exclaimed, "The God of heaven has given you a kingdom, power, strength, and glory...and has made you ruler over them all" (verses 37-38). God does so "in order that the living may know that the Most High rules in the kingdom of men, gives it to whomever He will, and sets over it the lowest of men" (Daniel 4:17).

In the New Testament, the Son of God revealed that the power of authority originates from heaven when He told Pilate, "You could have no power at all against Me unless it had been given you from above" (John 19:11). The apostle Paul echoed Christ's revelation: "There is no authority except from God, and the authorities that exist are appointed by God" (Romans 13:1). Even when it comes to the painful chore of paying taxes, Paul instructed us as to why we should pay up, noting (somewhat to our reluctance) that our leaders "are God's ministers" who are "attending continually to this very thing" (verse 6). The apostle Peter echoed this divine calling, instructing every person to

> submit yourselves to every ordinance of man for the Lord's sake, whether to the king as supreme, or to governors, as to those who are sent by him for the punishment of evildoers and for the praise of those who do good (1 Peter 2:13-14).

What exactly was the Most High attempting to accomplish by placing and empowering certain people to govern over other people? One of America's Founding Fathers, Thomas Paine, believed the purpose as "security being the true design and end of government."[13] Another Founding Father, Thomas Jefferson, declared, "The most sacred of the duties of a government is to do equal and impartial justice to all its citizens."[14] And, when both security and justice reign, then as John Adams noted, "the form of government, which communicates ease, comfort, security, or in one word happiness to the greatest number of persons, and in the greatest degree, is the best."[15]

In summary, security instead of enslavement, justice instead of corruption, virtue instead of vice, and the preservation of the happiness of its people rather than the cause of their suffering—these are the godly ideals upon which these men founded a nation. They understood that to these ends rest the primary reason for why God has instituted human government.

America's Founding Fathers also learned from their burdens living in a vassal territory suffering under a control-freak British king that such an idealized form of government would be, with a God-fearing citizenship, tenuous to maintain at best, and without a God-fearing people, an inevitable failure. Why so? Because the Founding Fathers understood from the hard lessons they'd learned in life, as well as from the Bible's warnings that human governments will always remain inherently evil because mankind is inherently evil, and in sore need of a redeemer (Romans 3:23).

In his essay on Alexander Hamilton, historian Forrest McDonald echoed the sentiment of the Founding Fathers when he wrote, "Men are inherently evil, governed by greed and lust and love of power and a host of even less endearing passions."[16] And, as America's first president, George Washington, with no small amount of fear, spoke his fabled warning about the true nature of any government ruled over by fallen men: "Government is not reason. Government is not eloquence. It is force. And, like fire, it is a dangerous servant and a fearful master."[17] Paine went so far as to call government, even in its best state, a "necessary evil," and in its worst state, an "intolerable one"![18]

Even secularists have peered down the long corridor of history and come to the same conclusion. As author Cory Price remarked, "Given the nature of humankind, no organization seems capable of permanence; for better or worse."[19] Empires demonstrate time and time again that they will eventually become unsustainable because "the constant interplay of internal and external pressures inevitably introduces too many fractures, overwhelming these consolidations of power, and leading to their eventual collapse."[20] In other words, people do not get along very well with each other, making lasting national unity an impossibility.

In drafting the US Constitution, the authors alertly understood that as long as human governments exist as a necessary evil, their administrators will be prone to fall into villainy and corruption. The Founding Fathers knew that as long as a government is composed of people, and because people are inherently fallen and evil, the more corrupt a government will become, causing more and more of its people to suffer. Lawlessness and crime will run rampant, natural disasters will go unaided, poverty and hunger will be the norm, disease and misery will be their citizens' inheritance, war and strife will define their existence, and human suffering will know no end.

So, to stem the inescapable tide of unscrupulous behavior expected from its elected leaders, the Founding Fathers wisely espoused that governmental power must be limited.[21] They did this by dividing power into separate branches to create a balance of power among those branches. A government must constantly be checked and watched and questioned by the population so that it can extract only the least amount of taxes necessary to perform the most limited of functions, that of providing security for its people. A government not constantly monitored, they believed, would inevitably grow into a monster—one that, to feed its endless thirst for power, would consume its people's money and trample on their God-given inalienable rights.

A NEW EMPIRE RISING

Unfortunately, the Founding Fathers are long dead, and Western nations increasingly no longer hold to the Fathers' firm beliefs in

God-given inalienable rights and religious freedom. Cries are erupting from all points of the compass, calling for a new form of government to replace what's considered old and broken. What we are now witnessing—with no small trepidation—is the formation of a global government. A whole new empire is on the rise!

Knowing what we do about the Bible's teachings concerning mankind's fallen nature, and likewise its failings in bringing about a secure and just government, this begs our third question: *Will this prenatal global government, once established, be benevolent or destructive?*

At first glance, it would be uncharitable to claim that no nation has ever strived to benefit its people. During the twentieth century, the leaders of the free world made an unprecedented attempt to unify all governments—first under the banner of the League of Nations and then under the United Nations (UN)—assumedly to seek altruistic outcomes. For example, in December 1948, the UN adopted the Universal Declaration of Human Rights (UDHR), a document that lists 30 basic human rights.[22] In this document, the UN exhorted every person in every society to promote respect for these freedoms. Those who penned the UDHR believed that educated people make morality-based decisions that contribute toward the common good of all in a society.[23] A global body that governs from a belief in human rights sounds great, utopian even, and right in line with the purpose for why governments exist.

And yet, in the decades since the UDHR was created, the record of human rights abuses throughout the world has been growing at an alarming rate. In response, in 1993, the UN General Assembly set aside the following decade to focus on promoting a universal culture of human rights. But, just ten years later, the UN announced that its efforts were making no noticeable difference in promoting world peace.[24] After all, how could the UN possibly promote peace when, at the same time, it militarizes its humanitarian actions under its Responsibility to Protect Doctrine?[25] As ethicist Esther Reed pointed out, when a government attempts altruism, it always "risks blundering into the proverbial china shop and knocking over everything not nailed firmly to the floor."[26]

We can only conclude, then, from the United Nations' unending failures, that a truly global government birthed out of the UN will only and inevitably result in becoming just as much a force of destruction as the nationalistic empires ever were. God have mercy!

GOVERNMENT AS THE CAUSE OF A CRISIS OF FAITH

People take notice when their government fails their expectations to protect them from lawlessness and crime, natural disasters, poverty and hunger, disease and misery, war and strife, and the deluge of human sufferings that ravage the world. Despite all the positive propaganda spewing from tech-censored mainstream media, we know for a fact that today's governments are failing because they cannot keep the peace, but rather, often remain in a perpetual state of war. We can only lament when a government fails to put an end to our sufferings, which limits our pursuit of happiness. At some point in our lives, no matter how pro-big government some of us might be, we awaken to the realization that government has at some level failed to achieve its primary purpose—true security and justice for its people.

The abject failure of the God-ordained institution that is human government has led many to experience a crisis of faith in God Himself. Bob Wenz, formerly with the National Association of Evangelicals, identified this very problem. He noted that the failures of government have long resulted in a crisis of faith for many who believe in God, and for those who do not believe in God, creates a major obstacle to their coming to salvation.[27]

Hence the meteoric rise in our day of the "nones." Individuals who could be properly labeled "practical atheists," their disillusioned souls have forsaken the belief in a sovereign Creator and a theistic worldview. In the process of a society increasingly transitioning from theism to atheism, these nones have transferred onto the government—what they see as a most imposing institution seemingly bigger than life—the divine qualities of a great being who is all-knowing, all-powerful, and all-good. In doing so, these practical atheists expect that government will somehow be able to anticipate and prevent all evils from ever happening. Wenz called this a "false premise" because the practical atheist is wrongly expecting their government to possess all the divine qualities and abilities that no person, let alone any government, could ever possess.[28] The unbeliever's faith is misplaced when making a god out of government, and so that faith remains unfulfilled and perpetually in crisis.

And to those who do believe in God and have been raised with a Judeo-Christian upbringing, Sunday school taught us what America's Founding Fathers long espoused—that bad things happen in our world because humanity is inherently sinful. While God necessarily chooses to not directly intervene in restraining all of humanity's evil tendencies, He has ordained human government to function in His place, at least to a limited degree, in a restraining capacity and to punish evildoers.

Wenz pointed out that when those who believe in God likewise see a human government fail, their crisis of faith becomes twofold.[29] When seriously evil leaders succeed in their corrupted pursuit of happiness, dismayed believers are left asking, "Why didn't God exercise His divine power and prevent 'this' from happening?" They know that God has established human governments, and when they fail to live up to their unrealistic expectations, they join the practical atheists in crying out, "Why didn't the government stop 'this'?"

For centuries on end, believers in God have struggled with the inclination to blame the Almighty for not preventing every bad thing that's ever happened, while at the same time also projecting that same blame onto their God-ordained human government. Wenz concluded that his experiences in ministry have proven to him that many of the once-faithful had abandoned their faith in God because they couldn't find a "satisfactory answer" to this dilemma.[30]

THE PROBLEM OF EVIL

"God has failed us."

"Government has failed us."

"How then can there be a God?"

This dilemma has been identified by the defenders of the Christian faith—the apologists—as the problem of evil as it relates to failed human government. And, as we have come to learn, it creates a crisis of faith for two groups. The first are those who hold to theism, meaning those who believe in the existence of an all-powerful, all-knowing, eternally living, perfectly good, and all-loving being who created the world. And second, there are their atheistic counterparts, meaning those who deny the existence of any sort of divine being or supernatural reality.[31]

Many worldly philosophers and faithful theologians have attempted to tackle this conundrum, each from their point of view. Speaking for the atheists, philosopher J.L. Mackie concluded that the belief in a God who is omnipotent and wholly good conflicts with the presence of evil (which he defined as suffering) in the world, and because God and suffering cannot possibly coexist, theistic belief must then be positively irrational.[32]

Speaking for the theists, professor Donna Divine explained what happens when a theistic person's faith is challenged by the perceived failure of God to prevent evil from winning:

> When one's ideology, once taken for granted as a narrative of the past and a projection for the future, cannot explain what is happening in the present, it will create a difference

> between what is imagined and what is real, resulting in a deep feeling of loss.[33]

Or, as songwriter David Grossman sang in "The Sticker Song," such a feeling of loss leads the burdened theist to plead with the Almighty over how much evil they can swallow and to beg their heavenly Father to show mercy.[34]

A day doesn't go by that I haven't prayed that prayer. I'm sure that you have, too, as we reel at the bewildering chaos ravaging this evil world around us. Christians throughout the centuries have shared in this heavenward plea.

How we respond to this faith struggle inevitably affects, in turn, our view of the origins of moral law. A struggling theist could end up shifting their worldview from what's called theonomy, meaning a belief in the cosmos originating in a personal Creator who set the universe's foundation and defines what moral law is, to a less monotheistic-centered heteronomy, meaning the cosmos originated in some deistic supernatural realm.[35] They could even shift so far as to embrace the fully atheistic perspective of autonomy with its belief that the cosmos and moral law originated from within itself.[36] Many in our society have adopted this latter, hopeless view.

Such vastly differing worldviews have sparked our divisive culture wars, polarized our societies against each other, and fractured our systems of morality. We clash over contradictory opinions on sociopolitical matters because we don't share common moral or political viewpoints.[37] With no shared value system, societies inevitably tear themselves apart at the seams. And when societies finally do descend into chaos, their governments yet again demonstrate their inability to create a unified belief system that can hold their nations together, even when increasing force is used.

Even the paragons of faith from the Bible, such as the minor prophets, faced the same faith crisis we experience today. For example, the prophet Micah, when he lamented over how failed and corrupt the nation of Judah's government had become, wailed:

> The faithful man has perished from the earth, and there is no one upright among men...The prince asks for gifts. The judge seeks a bribe. The great man utters his evil desires and so they scheme together (Micah 7:2-3).[38]

Another minor prophet, Habakkuk, staked himself out on a rampart to behold his beloved yet abased Jerusalem and lamented over the evils of his time. God responded to the frustrated prophet that he must wait for the Lord to act, for "the vision is yet for an appointed time," and so, in the meantime, "the just shall live by his faith" (Habakkuk 2:1-4). The spokesmen of God struggled in their misery, pining over whether there would ever be any hope that mankind would finally be freed from the failure that is flawed human government. They were told merely to wait patiently for God's will to be done, and in the expectant waiting, to keep the faith.

The prophets wondered, as we wonder today, our fourth question: *Is humanity destined to forever suffer under the weight of corrupted governments?*

THE VISION OF THE END OF HUMAN GOVERNMENT

Praise God, our heavenly Father has not left this long-pondered-over question unanswered! The Almighty's response to the problem of evil as it relates to failed human governments was at last given decades after Habakkuk's time, and to of all people, the head of the most powerful government of its era—Nebuchadnezzar, king of Babylon (605–562 BC).[39] God provided the world His answer via a dream imparted to Nebuchadnezzar, one that the young prophet Daniel interpreted and recorded for us in Daniel chapter 2.

The prophet divulged that the troubled king had marveled at a massive statue forged in the shape of a man. The statue's head was molded out of fine gold, its chest and arms of silver, its belly and thighs of bronze, it stood erect on two legs of iron, and its feet were comprised of a mixture of iron and clay. And, to his utter amazement, the king also witnessed a stone—described as "cut out without [human] hands" (verse 34)—careening like a meteor out of the sky to strike the statue at its feet. The great statue was subsequently obliterated, and its dust blew away in the wind. Suddenly, the sky-felled stone grew into a mighty mountain, until it filled the entire earth.

Daniel credited God alone for the revealing of what King Nebuchadnezzar had dreamed, as well as what the dream had meant—the prophesied end of all human empires. The prophet himself would later experience two of his own God-given visions that would reiterate this prophecy. The first was the vision of the four beasts as recorded in Daniel 7, and the second was the vision of a ram and a goat in Daniel 8.

When we lay these three messages from God side by side and compare them, we learn that the statue represented four temporal human kingdoms followed by a fifth divine kingdom.[40] The head of gold, corresponding to the lion (7:4), explicitly identified Nebuchadnezzar to be that head as king of the Babylonian Empire. The chest and arms of silver, corresponding to the bear (7:5) and the vision of the two-horned ram (chapter 8), represented the Medo-Persian Empire, which would decades later conquer Babylon. The belly and thighs of bronze, corresponding to the leopard (7:6) and the shaggy goat (chapter 8), represented the supplantation of the Medo-Persian Empire by Greece and its division after the death of Alexander the Great in 323 BC.[41] The legs of iron, corresponding to the composite beast (7:7, 19), would come to be identified as the Roman Empire. Rome's final, divided, weakened condition was represented by the two feet comprised of a mixture of iron and clay. The ten toes corresponded to the ten horns (7:24), indicating the final form of earthly human government would divide the world into ten regions, each one ruled by a powerful king.

Daniel also noted the metals that formed this behemoth statue increased in strength going from head to toes while, oddly, at the same time, they decreased in value. Jewish historian and theologian Arnold Fruchtenbaum explained that the Babylonian monarchy was known for its valuable gold and a king who stood above the law, the Medo-Persian monarchy for its love of silver and a king who was subject to the law, the Greek kings forged in brass held to no central dynastic or royal right to rule, and Rome tread fiercely as if iron but existed as a republic led by an imperial form of government.[42] The visions presented the power of each successive human government as growing less centralized, until the final one would comprise a power-sharing arrangement among ten kings and one "little horn" who would rise to rule the entire world, but only for a brief time (Daniel 7:8; 8:9-12).

Nebuchadnezzar's vision foretold how a day would come when human governments, in all their forms, would be wiped away by the arrival of that stone not cut by human hands. Fruchtenbaum emphasized the fact that the stone that came from the sky denotes a divine origin, with mountains in the Bible often symbolizing a king, kingdom, or throne.[43] So, in summary, Daniel had prophesied that a divine ruler would burst from the sky at the speed of a streaking meteor to obliterate all human governments and to establish His illustrious kingdom—one that will encompass the entire earth.

THE TIMING OF THE END OF HUMAN GOVERNMENTS

When can we expect the end of human governments to occur?

As for the timing of this coming divine kingdom, Jesus Christ said this event would occur after the trampling of Jerusalem by the

Gentiles has ended and "the times of the Gentiles are fulfilled" (Luke 21:24-28). The "times of the Gentiles" is that long period of history from the Jewish exile by the Babylonian Empire in 586 BC to the second coming of the Messiah, when Christ will personally liberate the city of Jerusalem, thereby ending the Gentile nations' influence over that city.[44]

Because the return of the Messiah will end the "time of the Gentiles," this coming divine king must be that metaphorical stone that smote Nebuchadnezzar's statue representing human governments and blew the remains away like dust. That means the end of Gentile rule can be achieved only by the second person of the Trinity. Jesus Christ Himself proclaimed that when He returns to the earth, it is He who will "strike the nations" (Revelation 19:15). And once that great deed is accomplished, the Messiah will establish His eternal and universal kingdom (Revelation 20-22).[45] On that glorious day, governments under human control will at long last become a relic of the past, replaced forevermore by Christ's kingdom.

WHY GOD TELLS US THE FUTURE

What are God's reasons for revealing the whys and hows of human governments ending and being replaced with Christ's coming earthly kingdom?

According to theologian Lit-Sen Chang, God's reasons involve both ultimate and immediate purposes.[46] First, let's look at the ultimate purpose. God provided special revelation through the prophets and the unique highest prophet—Jesus Christ, the source of all prophetic revelation (Revelation 19:10). Our Lord used words, visions, dreams, miracles, and theophanies so that He could "reveal His divinity to His creation, display His many excellencies, and declare His glory, especially in His work of redemption."[47] As we witness how God's plan for the ages unfolds, we're meant to be astounded more and more by our wonderful Creator, Redeemer, and King.

And second, the immediate purpose is achieved when God displays His awe-inspiring majesty. Doing so causes sinners to fall on their faces in repentance, become regenerate, and live on to fulfill their ultimate purpose of loving God and each other for all eternity. When the fallen become saved, their miraculous recreation and restoration into a right relationship with the heavenly Father reflects His glorious excellencies, which go on to lead even more of the lost to salvation.[48]

Did you know that a whopping 31 percent of the Bible is prophetic? God truly wants us to know the future! Knowing God's prophetic Word, therefore, becomes extremely vital to our lives.

How God reveals Himself and His will through the unfolding of biblical prophecies acts as an evangelistic beacon calling sinners to salvation and into a right relationship with the everlasting Father. And, for those who are already saved, Bible prophecy can also be wielded as a powerful apologetic, which, as Jude defined, allows Christians to "contend earnestly for the faith which was once for all delivered to the saints" (Jude 3). By the power of the Holy Spirit and through the study of God's Word, Christians can use prophecy as a spiritual weapon to expose the erroneous teachings and heresies that oppose the worship of the one true God and lead mankind astray. As Chang so eloquently described this epic battle for the truth, "It is theology at war!"[49]

God's revelation of Himself and His will through fulfilled Bible prophecy brings Him praise and glory, leads the lost to salvation, and provides an unassailable defense of the Christian faith. Those are the big-picture purposes.

God's little-picture purpose for revealing His future victories is directed at two different people groups. The first consisted of the prophets' immediate audience—the Israelites. After 70 years of exile to a pagan, foreign nation, the Jews in Daniel's time held very little hope of ever returning to their homeland. God's prophetic messages to Israel—both then and now—were meant to reassure the Jewish people that their time of exile from their homeland and His presence would indeed come to an end. Because God remains ever-faithful to His covenants, He then must restore His people—not only to Jerusalem but also into His everlasting kingdom. Prophecy provided the ancient Israelites with hope, and as you will soon see, is meant to give modern-day Israel great hope as well.

The second group to benefit from this little-picture purpose for why God has promised a divine, everlasting kingdom has been identified by biblical scholar Sidney Greidanus. He explained that God wanted to provide much-needed hope to His other chosen people—the church.[50] Ever since the church was founded at Pentecost and up to that wondrous day when Christ will call all His faithful up to heaven in the rapture—this era called the church age—Christians have suffered and will continue to suffer mightily under the oppression of failed human governments. Why, a staggering 45 million Christians were martyred in the twentieth century alone![51]

As we, the church, wait for Jesus to usher in His perfect kingdom, we groan unceasingly under the pains of persecution. We're oftentimes left dismayed that there appears to be no end in sight to our sufferings. The longer this promised kingdom is delayed, the easier it becomes for Christians to lose hope, and so risk losing faith in Jesus and His stated promise to return. To counter this malaise, God has revealed hope-filled prophecies about Christ's kingdom that are meant to confirm His faithfulness as a covenant-keeper who always keeps His promises. With that revelation, we Christians can take heart, shore up our faith, and persevere in our hope that infinitely better days lie ahead.

WHAT YOU ARE ABOUT TO LEARN

Each of us lives out our days under a dire predicament—failed human governments. Mankind's inability to overcome its fallen human nature and so properly provide security, justice, and peace has caused so much misery, hardship, and death over the past millennia. This human failure has perpetuated a crisis of faith for many who believe in the Almighty. And the fact that unbelievers have erected a false and futile god out of government has created a major roadblock that hinders many of them from coming to faith in Jesus Christ, thereby keeping them traveling along the broad road to hell.

But, my friends, God has not left us without hope! Look to the Bible. Our heavenly Father has provided His response to our crushing existential problem. The answer to failed human governments will be the institution of Christ's kingdom, better known as the millennial kingdom.

So, what exactly is this kingdom Christ will institute?

When is He going to establish His rule?

Will we actually live in this kingdom?

And, finally, what will everyday life be like for those dwelling in that new era?

These are the vital questions you and I are about to explore, and they're hardly trivial. So, in the next chapter, I will explain what the kingdom of Christ truly means. Then we will discover what prophecy has to say concerning the dire conditions that must come about before the kingdom arrives. Next, we will mine the Bible for the verses that teach us how Christ's kingdom will be established during the millennium, as well as what everyday life will be like (my favorite part).

And, finally, we will put to the test whether the millennial kingdom truly succeeds in bringing about the prophesied perfect society we all long for, or whether we should instead be looking toward the eternal state. We'll do so by diving into the various viewpoints the great theologians of the past have proposed about this future kingdom and compare them to what the Bible has to say. This is necessary because, as one commentator noted, "It may sound like a lot of quibbling over 1,000 years, but it goes to the heart of understanding God's glorious promises for the future."[52]

By the time you have finished this book, my heartfelt hope is that you will fully understand the *whats* and *hows* about the ways God will use the kingdom of Christ to provide the solutions failed human governments can never provide. I would also like to remove any hurdles you may be experiencing about placing or growing your faith in Jesus Christ due to lingering questions about why an all-good and all-powerful God would allow us to suffer under the weight of our fallen natures and inept authorities. And, most importantly, as you continue your life's journey, as if a stranger in a foreign land, I want to encourage you to join me as a fellow citizen of this coming glorious kingdom.

To accomplish these goals, I plan to use Scripture and Scripture alone to reveal what God wants us to know about His kingdom. We will take our stand on the critical beliefs that Scripture is the infallible Word of God and that God desires for mankind to know His great plan for the ages (1 Corinthians 2:10-16; 2 Timothy 3:16). With these two vital assumptions working as our guiding light, you will gain a clearer understanding of God's incredible plan for your life in the here and now, and for the future. You will then be able to defend what you have learned, becoming an equipped defender of the faith—an apologist. And lastly, you will be ready to go out into the world and proclaim Christ's kingdom, thereby leading the lost to salvation and the saved into having stronger faith and a renewed hope.

Sound good? Then let's get into it!

CHAPTER 2

THE KINGDOM OF CHRIST

The kingdom is coming, O tell ye the story,
God's banner exalted shall be!
The earth shall be full of His knowledge and glory,
As waters that cover the sea.[1]

MARY B. SLADE, *nineteenth-century hymnist*

So, what exactly is the kingdom of Christ again?

To address this very nuanced subject, let us turn to the great intellectual Puritan pastor, Cotton Mather (1663–1728), for the answer. In his discourse *Things to be look'd for*, Mather explained that the kingdom of Christ can be understood as "a three-fold kingdom with a fourth kingdom yet to come."[2] Fast-forward more than two centuries later, theologian Charles Ryrie would present his summary of the relationship of the church to this four-aspect kingdom in what I like to refer to as Ryrie's four kingdoms concept.[3] Let's take a brief look at each of these four folds of the kingdom of Christ.

THE FOUR FOLDS OF THE KINGDOM OF CHRIST

1. The Spiritual Kingdom

The first fold in the four kingdoms concept was identified by Mather as the Spiritual Kingdom, "wherein...His Word and Grace Rule over the Consciences of men."[4] A realm without land, borders, or walls, the only acreage ruled over in this first aspect is the human heart.

The Lord Jesus often taught of this first aspect of the kingdom in parables—earthly stories that have heavenly meanings—when referring to the kingdom of heaven. For example, Jesus likened the kingdom of heaven in the parable of the wheat and the tares to a man who plants the good seed that grows into an abundant harvest (Matthew 13:24-30, 37-43; Mark 4:26-29). In His parable of the mustard seed, Jesus compared the kingdom to a tiny seed that grows into a mighty tree that provides a magnificent home for all the birds (Matthew 13:31-32; Mark 4:30-32; Luke 13:18-19). In other parables, Jesus likened the kingdom to items of great value: hidden leaven (Matthew 13:33; Luke 13:21), found treasure (Matthew 13:44), and highly sought-after pearls (Matthew 13:45). In making these vivid comparisons, it's clear that Jesus emphatically wished to drive home just how valuable and sought-after His kingdom should be to us.

Jesus also illustrated the favorable attributes of the kingdom of heaven to the labor of sifting the good from the bad. In the parable of the dragnet, a net is cast into the sea in search of treasures, both old and new, revealing that only those considered "good" are gathered into "vessels," meaning enter His kingdom, while the bad are discarded into a fiery furnace, meaning hell (Matthew 13:47-50). The parables of the unforgiving servant, wedding feast, ten virgins, and great supper confirm how only the expectant faithful are granted entry into this favored realm (Matthew 18:23-35; 22:2-14; 25:1-13; Luke 14:16-24). And, for those faithful who already dwell in this realm, spiritual rewards also factor in, demonstrated by Christ's parables of the workers in the vineyard and the talents (Matthew 20:1-16; 25:14-30; Luke 19:12-27).

This spiritual aspect of the kingdom of Christ, Jesus explained, is presently "not of this world" (John 18:36). Those who populate this spiritual kingdom arrive at its "gates" with an innocent faith like that of little children (Matthew 18:3; 19:14; Mark 10:14; Luke 18:16). In contrast, and with an air of sadness, Jesus decried how the earthly riches of the wealthy become a stumbling block that prevents them access to true spiritual riches (Matthew 19:23-24; Mark 10:23-25; Luke 18:24-25, 29-30).

While Christ's representatives dwell on this earth, they are given the duty of carrying the "keys" to the kingdom of heaven to loosen and bound as they deem fit (Matthew 16:19). And, wherever the kingdom is preached, it will be received by its citizens as good news and with glad tidings (Luke 8:1). For those who dwell in this spiritual aspect of the kingdom of Christ, its mysteries are revealed by the Holy Spirit alone (Luke 8:10).

Clearly, an intangible element defines the Spiritual Kingdom. As the author of the book of Romans taught, this kingdom "is not [for] eating and drinking, but [for] righteousness and peace and joy in the Holy Spirit" (Romans 14:17).

2. *The Providential Kingdom*

The second fold of Cotton Mather's explanation of the four kingdoms concept concerns the Providential Kingdom, "wherein He governs all the affairs and motions of the world."[5] Though there is some overlap of labels in Scripture, the Lord Jesus often taught about this fold when referring synonymously to the kingdom of God. This aspect then concerns the sovereign rule of God over all of heaven and creation.[6]

The Providential Kingdom extends well into every realm in which the power of God's reign is experienced. This even includes the

Almighty's power over the demonic realm, as Christ emphasized His authority to wield such all-encompassing power when He declared, "If I cast out demons by the Spirit of God, surely the kingdom of God has come upon you" (Matthew 12:28).

The purified subjects of the Providential Kingdom are made manifest as the Almighty defeats His enemies, thereby gathering incrementally over the ages a purified people over whom God will eternally reign. These chosen citizens voluntarily submit to the rule of God over their lives through faith and the receiving of a second birth through God's Son.[7] Concerning humanity's role in entering this aspect of the kingdom, T.Z. Koo, an evangelist to China, clarified:

> The kingdom of God does not exist because of your effort or mine. It exists because God reigns. Our part is to enter this kingdom and bring our life under His sovereign will.[8]

3. *The Ecclesiastical Kingdom*

Cotton Mather labeled the third fold the Ecclesiastical Kingdom, "wherein He appoints and prospers the ordinances of a Church-State."[9] In other words, the second person of the Trinity rules over and through His "body"—the church.[10]

With supreme authority as the head over His church, Jesus likened Himself to "the stone which the builders rejected [that] has become the chief cornerstone" (Psalm 118:22; Matthew 21:42; Mark 12:10; Luke 20:17; 1 Peter 2:7). Christ's authority over the Ecclesiastical Kingdom fulfilled, in part—and yet awaiting final fulfillment in the future—many of the prophecies concerning the coming judge, lawgiver, and messianic king (Isaiah 33:22). Through this church "kingdom," Jesus holds preeminence as head, not only over the body of faithful believers who altogether are christened "the church," but through it over every person who has lived during the last 2,000 years (Romans 9:5; 1 Corinthians 11:3; Colossians 1:13, 18).[11]

The foundation for the Ecclesiastical Kingdom was established by the death, burial, and resurrection of Jesus Christ, and was inaugurated on the day of Pentecost (Acts 2; 1 Corinthians 3:11). Christ's love for the church as if for a bride was His motivation for establishing it (Ephesians 5:22-33). And, through this bride, the "Holder of the Seven Stars" empowers His church to speak in His name in its assigned work to bring the lost to their Savior, and so ever grow its ranks (Matthew 16:19; Revelation 2:1, 9, 13, 19).

Of note, Cotton Mather developed his understanding of the four kingdoms concept from the teachings of another great Puritan pastor, his equally famous father, Increase Mather (1639–1723).[12] While Increase agreed with Cotton and separated the Providential Kingdom from the other folds, with Increase defining the Providential aspect as "whereby He [God] governs the world in respect whereof He is called the King of nations" (Jeremiah 10:7; Matthew 28:18; John 5:27), the two men held divergent views as to the separation between the Spiritual and Ecclesiastical folds.[13] Increase saw these two folds as being merely one within the Spiritual fold "in respect whereof He [Christ] is styled the King of saints."[14] Increase saw the Spiritual Kingdom to be both "internal in the souls and hearts and consciences of men," and so fitly termed this internal aspect as the kingdom of Grace (Romans 14:17; Colossians 1:13), with the external aspect funneled through the work of the ecclesiastical movement, which he labeled personally as the kingdom of Ordinances (Acts 1:3).[15]

4. *The Davidical Kingdom*

Regardless of how the father-son theological team separated the Spiritual from the Ecclesiastical folds, they both were in agreement that the Bible taught of yet a fourth fold to the kingdom of Christ. Cotton labeled this final aspect the "fourth yet to come" while Increase labeled it Christ's "Davidical Kingdom," yet both credited this aspect as belonging solely unto our Lord Jesus Christ.[16] The fourth fold rests in the final culmination of a covenant and future fulfillment of the prophecies concerning the Davidical Kingdom, or more commonly today called the Davidic kingdom, wherein Jesus Christ physically, in person, rules and reigns over the entire earth from David's throne in Jerusalem.

Obviously, if we were to travel to Jerusalem today, we would not see Jesus there as king ruling in person over the earth. Seriously, I have traveled to Israel three times so far, and never once have I encountered as part of the tour a visit to Christ's home. Therefore, this fourth aspect of the kingdom of Christ still remains to be fulfilled, and so rests squarely in the future.

From his studies of the Bible, Cotton pinpointed when the Davidical Kingdom would be realized in the future. He said it would immediately follow a time of worldwide destruction by the prophesied Antichrist in a great conflagration, with the resulting need afterward for a brief time of refining and purifying of the earth.[17] Cotton noted:

> Yea, the final destruction of Antichrist seems the period at which it shall commence. Yet the world shall not be annihilated; it shall only be refined and purified, that it may be serviceable unto some glorious ends.[18]

Much confusion has come about over the centuries as to what constitutes the kingdom of Christ, all because people choose to believe there's only one, or two, or maybe even three of the folds, yet completely leave out this fourth fold—the Davidical Kingdom. When this fourth aspect is excluded, a complete and proper understanding of the kingdom of Christ cannot be made. And, because the Davidical Kingdom has been lost on so many Christians due to burying it within the other three folds, I think it would be better labeled the Forgotten Kingdom.

The likely reason for why so many Christians either overlook or outright dismiss the fourth fold can be identified by this witty statement made by the early-twentieth century clergyman S. Parkes Cadman, who quipped, "The kingdom of God will not come in a day; it will not be left with the morning milk."[19] This "fourth yet to come" kingdom—the Davidical Kingdom—has been millennia in the making, yet still awaits its realization. Alas, sadly, since the days of the Christians of the fourth and fifth centuries so long ago, most people have lacked patience for the Davidical Kingdom's arrival, and so have assumed it was never meant to come literally. As a result, they have spiritualized the messianic prophecies into meaningless imaginations. What a tragedy of lost hope!

GOD'S PROMISE TO KING DAVID

And, what a loss when it comes to our gaining a proper understanding of the Almighty! To rectify this grievous subtraction of the Davidic kingdom from the kingdom of Christ, we are now going to explore Christ's ages-long divine endeavor.

The Davidic kingdom was initially established on a promise—a covenant—God made with King David some 3,000 years ago. But wait—before we get into the facts that constitute this particular covenant, as students of the Bible, we must travel even further back, all the way to Genesis, and review God's other covenants so foundational to the subject of the Davidic kingdom.

1. The Noahic Covenant

It should be remembered that the initial dominion—meaning sphere of rule and authority—over this earth was given by the Creator to Adam and Eve, who were made in God's image (Genesis 1:26-28).[20] Once humanity's progenitors broke their agreement with their Creator and disobeyed Him by eating from the forbidden tree, they subsequently lost their claim of dominion over the earth, thereby making their tempter—the fallen angel Satan—the "ruler of this world" (John 14:30; see Genesis 2:16-17; Matthew 4:8-10; John 14:30).

The wickedness committed by Adam's descendants became so great that God drowned all but the righteous Noah and his family in the Flood. As the waters receded, God presented a covenant between Himself and all creation. God promised He would never again flood the earth in His wrath (Genesis 7–9). Now called the Noahic covenant, this covenant also instituted governments under human control, and it became God's intended charter for all earthly governments, even to this day (Genesis 9:1-17).[21]

2. *The Abrahamic Covenant*

Disastrously, human governments failed to be guided by the consciences of men. So God chose a man named Abram, later renamed Abraham, to engage in a contract that would involve a new and unconditional covenant (Genesis 12:1-3). This covenant was later confirmed and passed down to Abraham's son Isaac and grandson Jacob, also called Israel (Genesis 26:1-5; 28:10-15).

Abraham and his descendants were to become living witnesses to the Gentile nations of what it's like to live under the blessings from following the one true God, as well as to serve as heirs of the promise of redemption by looking forward to the arrival of God's Messiah-Redeemer.[22] Israel's descendants were also to inherit a very specific tract of land—the land of Canaan—in perpetuity (Genesis 12:2; 15:18-21; 17:7-8). The Gentile nations were then severely warned by God that they would receive blessings and curses depending on how they treated Israel (Genesis 12:3; Matthew 25:31-46). Centuries later, to help the children of Israel understand the differences between right and wrong, God codified His moral law by giving the Mosaic law, as well as His very presence, which dwelled in the tabernacle and then the temples.

3. *The Davidic Covenant*

This now leads the timeline of human government up to 1000 BC and the era of King David, and also to what theologian Arthur Kac called the giving of "The Nathan Prophecy" (2 Samuel 7:5-16; 23:1-4; 1 Chronicles 17:1-27; 28:4-7).[23] David had built a magnificent palace but felt some self-reproach because God still dwelt in a simple tent. So David summoned his prophet, Nathan, to share with him his plan to build a great temple dedicated to Yahweh God. Even though the prophet presumptuously gave this building project his blessing, that very night, God corrected Nathan and instead presented His plan for David's son Solomon to build the temple. In doing so, God would establish yet another covenant—the Davidic covenant.

God established this third covenant between David and Himself. As the prophet Nathan relayed God's message, he rejoiced that God had cut off all of Israel's enemies. This new era of peace resulted in David's name becoming truly great and remembered throughout history (2 Samuel 7:9). Israel's land covenant was confirmed yet again with a promise that the nation would one day dwell securely within its borders and that no nation would ever again oppress the Jewish people (verse 10). On top of these blessings, the Lord would also establish David's house and lineage in perpetuity (verse 11). David's son Solomon would serve as the chosen builder of the temple, and through his bloodline, the Davidic kingdom would be established (verses 12-13).

The duration of the reign of the Davidic line and kingdom is quite stunning, for it "shall be established forever" (verse 16). As Bible scholar Eugene Pond explained, David's "house" would be his dynasty and the continuation of his descendants the uniquely authorized kings over Israel; David's "kingdom" would be his realm, along with the people over whom his descendants' rule would extend; and David's "throne" would provide his divine right to rule and execute judgment in God's stead.[24]

But there appears to be a caveat—a legal requirement—to this promised forever rule. The Davidic kings reigned for an impressive four centuries, claiming the second-longest dynasty in ancient Near Eastern history, but the scepter was lost in 586 BC with the destruction of Jerusalem and the temple and the exile of Judah's final king, Zedekiah.[25] On the surface, the line of David's governmental authority appears to have dissolved a few decades later with Zerubbabel. The children of Israel had been cast out of their land and into exile, not once, but twice, leaving any true descendant of David completely unknown. And yet, the word "forever" was used eight times in 2 Samuel 7, in addition to the many other phrases that bear the same concept.[26]

How, then, could God's promise to David be both irrevocable and eternal?

God's covenant with the Davidic dynasty stands as unconditional in that it must last forever, as per Nathan's prophecy, but the actual continuation of the monarchy entered into periods of conditionality based on the faithfulness or faithlessness of David's line of kings.[27] Unconditionality rests on the fact that, as theologian Walter Kaiser Jr. identified, "The descendants may forfeit their personal share in the promise, but they cannot stop the benefits from flowing to eternity as planned by God (1 Chronicles 28:7; Psalm 132)."[28] Therefore, the conditional caveat of the covenant is dependent on the Davidic kings being faithful to God, and when they were not, God made sure they were either disciplined or removed from power. Though the kingdom may have appeared to cease to exist when the faith conditions set down by Yahweh had not been met, it has always remained unconditional in that God's will has never departed from His kingdom (1 Chronicles 17:13).[29]

So there is a conditional clause to the unconditionality aspect, as each new generation in David's line provided the hope of a faithful king. Unfortunately, such faithful kings were as rare as seeing a peacock strutting among a flock of chickens. God finally acted on the punishment He had promised through Moses—exile—with the rebellious Israel sent to Assyria, and not long after, the faithless Judah to Babylon, so that there were no longer any Davidic kings sitting on Jerusalem's throne (Deuteronomy 28). Once the Medo-Persian Empire allowed the Jews to return to their native land, Israel appeared to have been reinstituted, but the land remained under the rule of foreign satraps, the equivalent of governors, and not Jewish kings. Absent a native king, Israel increasingly turned to the religious caste, such as Joshua the high priest, to serve in the important roles as leaders of a newly rebuilt temple-centered community.[30]

Regardless, the ongoing priesthood couldn't fulfill the necessary line of Davidic kings to meet the unconditionality requirement of the Davidic covenant. So, the student of the Bible must turn to the Prophets and Psalms to find the proper solution.

Let's look at one example. In Isaiah 11, the prophet Isaiah was, as professor John MacKay described, "Drawn forward over the centuries to envisage another figure whose impact on the destiny of God's people will far exceed that of any Assyrian emperor."[31] This figure would be identified as "a Rod from the stem of Jesse, and a Branch shall grow out of his roots" (Isaiah 11:1). By referencing Jesse, David's father, a messianic figure had been identified—the One who will rise from out of the line of Jesse.

This, Isaiah's third prophecy concerning the coming Davidic King, sketched for us the messianic profile: His Spirit-endowed character (verses 1-5), the divine nature of His kingdom (verses 6-9), and the people over whom this prophesied figure will rule (verses 12-16).[32] Many other Old Testament prophets would point to this messianic descendant of Jesse who would inevitably sit on David's throne as the ultimate and eternal King. Unlike the unworthy and lackluster earthy descendants from King David's line, it is this very "Rod" and "Branch" who will serve as the chosen One, and He alone will ultimately fulfill the unconditional requirements of the Davidic covenant.[33]

In the New Testament, we at last learn the name of this long-foretold Davidic King—Jesus Christ. As theologian Andrew Steinmann exclaimed, "If there is one certainty about the identity of the Messiah in the New Testament, it is that He is a royal descendant of David."[34] Steinmann pointed out that those in the Synoptic Gospels who appealed to Jesus as the Christ also often refer to Him as the "Son of David," demonstrating a clear understanding that Jesus was indeed the prophesied Davidic King.[35]

Angels also identified Jesus as the prophesied Davidic King. It's often at Christmastime that we read about God's mighty messenger—the angel Gabriel—proclaiming that Mary's child would be birthed in the City of David, Bethlehem, and that it is He who would occupy the throne of David (Luke 1:32; 2:11). And after a startling encounter with said angel, Zechariah, the father of John the Baptist, prophesied that salvation would come from the house of David and that his son would become the prophesied "Elijah" who would prepare the way for the Messiah (Malachi 4:5-6; Luke 1:69). This One born of the virgin Mary, in fulfillment of Isaiah's prophecy about the divine origins of the ultimate Davidic King, was indeed born in Bethlehem. And from the earliest days of His earthly ministry, Jesus announced the kingdom as being "at hand" (Matthew 4:17).[36]

Even Jesus' opponents had to acknowledge that He was verifiably and legally a son of David (Matthew 22:42-45; Mark 12:35-37; Luke 20:41-44). And some years later, the apostle Paul also emphasized Jesus as being "of the seed of David" and argued that the facts surrounding Jesus leads one to the conclusion that He alone is the Christ (Acts 9:22; Romans 1:3; 2 Timothy 2:8).

Finally, in the book of Revelation, Jesus was identified three times with David as either "He who has the key of David," "the Root of David," and "the Root and the Offspring of David," with "Root" meaning "that which descended from David," rather than "that from which David descended" (Revelation 3:7; 5:5; 22:16). This small but vitally important difference in wording acknowledged the Messiah as having both a human nature and family connections as a descendant of David, while at the same time emphasizing His divine standing among the Trinity as David's forerunner.[37]

4. The New Covenant

A thousand years after David's passing, the Bible presents one final covenant that's crucial to a foundational understanding of the subject of the Davidic kingdom—the new covenant. Jesus may have preached His kingdom as being "near," but both the King and kingdom had been rejected at His first advent.[38] The very people who were to be the subjects of the fulfilled Davidic kingdom instead despised their King and had Him crucified.

Because the would-be citizens had rejected their prophesied Messiah, humanity demonstrated that it still lacked the faith necessary for accepting salvation so as to be made pure and ready to participate in the Davidic kingdom (Matthew 12:1-50; 16:21).[39] Jesus Christ turned this tragedy into triumph with His subsequent death, burial, and resurrection. In beating death, Christ alone became the conduit and only way to salvation for all who place their faith and trust in Him (John 14:6; Acts 4:12). Under this new covenant of grace, the Holy Spirit indwells the hearts of believers, setting the followers of Christ apart as members of that universal body of believers known as the church. Under the new covenant, mankind now lives under the age of grace, expectantly waiting for the return of the King.

THE KINGDOM IS THE CHURCH?

Does the institution of the new covenant mean that the Davidic kingdom found its ultimate fulfillment in the church, as many today claim? Old Testament scholar Merrill Unger disagreed with those who say yes, though conceding that, in a sense, with the birth of the church at Pentecost, the "mystery form" of the kingdom had come into existence because Jesus Christ now rules in the hearts of those who believe in Him (Matthew 13:11).[40] The new covenant, which is based on the redemptive work of Jesus Christ and makes salvation available by grace through faith (Ephesians 2:8-9), has indeed replaced the old Mosaic law. But the true fulfillment of the kingdom of Christ has been postponed until the Messiah's second coming (Revelation 19:11-16). Many scriptures point to the fact that the new covenant applies not just to the church in this age, but also points to the salvation of a restored nation of Israel in an age still yet to come (Jeremiah 31:31-34; Hebrews 8:6-13).[41]

Think of the church age, then, as merely serving as a spiritual down payment, so to speak, leaving Christians longing for the physical, future manifestation of the fourth fold of the kingdom of Christ. The apostle Paul spoke of this when he noted, "In the dispensation of the fullness of the times He might gather together in one all things in Christ, both which are in heaven and which are on earth—in Him" (Ephesians 1:10). At Christ's ascension, the apostles asked Jesus when His kingdom would be instituted, but Jesus said He would not yet reveal the timing of the coming kingdom (Acts 1:6-8).[42] That's a very different message from Jesus' earlier statements that the kingdom was at hand. At Christ's ascension, the Ecclesiastical Kingdom was indeed at hand, instituted a mere ten days later on Pentecost, but Christ still left His followers waiting expectantly for that fourth fold to commence—the Davidic kingdom.

The reason for the apparent disparity is that the rejection of the King and kingdom triggered the need for a time of preparation, whereby the church would serve as a spiritual form of the kingdom for the interim, while anticipating a future, earthly form as its final fulfillment (Matthew 25:34).[43] Because Christ's kingdom message had been initially rejected, the Messiah inaugurated a new ecclesiastical form of God's rule on the earth—the church.[44] Christ currently occupies the place of privilege and prominence in sitting at the right hand of the Father, ruling from heaven as head of the church, and serving His subjects as the intercessor and High Priest according to the order of Melchizedek. Christ's followers, in turn, have been tasked with the Great Commission to represent Jesus as faithful witnesses to all the world while we wait for our Lord's return to usher in the Davidic kingdom (Matthew 28:16-20; Acts 1:8).

In contrast to the first advent of Christ, which saw His rejection and apparent defeat, at Jesus' second advent, the world will witness the Messiah triumphing over His enemies, taking His seat upon the Davidic throne, and establishing His eternal kingdom. Theologian L.S. Chafer stressed the importance of this literal and earthly progression of the Davidic covenant, pointing out that there is no evidence David ever foresaw an earthly throne merging into a spiritual reign, nor a kingdom and throne established only in heaven, but through the Davidic covenant, God has always planned for a literal, earthly kingdom.[45]

A LITERAL OR SPIRITUAL KINGDOM?

When it comes to understanding the Davidic aspect of the kingdom of Christ, who has gotten it right?

Was God promising a literal kingdom, with a literal descendant of David, who would sit on a literal earthly throne that would last literally forever? Or is the Davidic kingdom just rolled up in the initial three folds Cotton Mather defined?

How, then, should the kingdom of Christ be interpreted—literally or spiritually?

Should Christians follow what Semitic languages expert Charles Feinberg posited? "It is either the grammatical, literal, historical interpretation or we are adrift on an uncharted sea with every man the norm for himself."[46] Or are we misunderstanding Christ's teachings, and instead, should we go with a spiritualized interpretation of the Scriptures?

As we continue to unwrap this potential enigma that is the kingdom of Christ, remember, we must rest our understanding on two critical beliefs: Scripture is the very infallible Word of God (2 Timothy 3:16), and God desires mankind to know His great plan for the ages (1 Corinthians 2:10-16). That means we are going to turn to the Bible and the Bible alone as our guiding light.

And, when it comes to interpreting the Bible, we will take care not to fall into the trap of spiritualizing Scripture. Instead, we will chart our course utilizing that steadfast friend of Bible students everywhere—the golden rule of interpretation:

> When the plain sense makes sense, look for no other sense, lest you end up with nonsense.

Stalwart students of the Bible read Scripture simply for its plain-sense meaning. They seek no extrabiblical or mystical form of interpretation. To do otherwise, they know, would lead them down the dark path of misunderstanding and doctrinal confusion.

With the golden rule of interpretation firmly established, we are now equipped to explore the soul and substance of what the Bible specifically teaches about the coming millennial kingdom. I promise you will be amazed and blessed!

CHAPTER 3

THE PROMISED RETURN OF CHRIST

There is no structural organization of society which can bring about the coming of the Kingdom of God on earth, since all systems can be perverted by the selfishness of man.[1]

William Temple, *Archbishop of Canterbury*

The kingdom of Christ was established on the ironclad promise given by none other than Jesus Christ Himself—I WILL RETURN!

THE PROMISE AFFIRMED

Should there be any doubt, Jesus went so far as to wrap up the entirety of the Bible by reinstating His promise not just once, nor twice even, but three times. "Behold, I am coming quickly, and My reward is with Me, to give to every one according to his work" (Revelation 22:12; see also verses 7, 20). Not once, nor twice even, but three whole times, Jesus promised, "I am coming back." To which the apostle John could only exclaim: "Amen. Even so, come, Lord Jesus!" (verse 20).

At First Mention

Because John had learned the Scriptures as a disciple sitting at the feet of the Son of God, he would have recognized Christ's promise to return in the most ancient of the second coming prophecies, one given in a vision attributed to Enoch, a few generations removed from Adam.[2] The Lord's half brother, Jude, preserved the prophecy of Enoch when he stated:

> Now Enoch, the seventh from Adam, prophesied about these men also, saying, "Behold, the Lord comes with ten thousands of His saints, to execute judgment on all, to convict all who are ungodly among them of all their ungodly deeds which they have committed in an ungodly way, and of all the harsh things which ungodly sinners have spoken against Him" (Jude 14-15).

While recording the book of Revelation, John was propelled into the future to witness the fulfillment of this ancient messianic prophecy. God allowed John to foresee the triumphal return of Jesus Christ, accompanied by His purified saints, to pour out God's wrath by executing judgment on a wicked world before establishing His kingdom.

The Golden Thread

Enoch's prophecy foretelling the Lord's majestic return isn't the only kingdom prophecy God revealed in Old Testament times. It's merely one out of an incredible 129 verses scattered throughout these venerable scriptures.[3]

Messianic pronouncements concerning the Lord's glorious return to establish His kingdom on this earth form what commentator Henry Halley called the "Golden Thread"—a theme that extends throughout and binds together the many diverse books of the Old Testament into one amazing unity.[4] As Walter Kaiser so colorfully noted concerning the messianic presence binding as if by a golden thread the Old Testament together, it does not exist to serve "as a side dish to spice up what would otherwise have been a wearisome diet of Jewish history," or "as the result of some heroic smuggling or spiritual importation of Christian values into the Old Testament," rather, Christ's ever-presence serves as the central feature of those books, and certainly by divine design.[5] The Lord wants us to notice the Messiah's presence threaded throughout the entirety of the Old Testament, for it prevails as an essential element contributing to the larger unity and controlling concept of Gentiles also joining in becoming "fellow heirs, of the same body, and partakers of His promise in Christ through the gospel" (Ephesians 3:6).[6]

Now that the presence of this golden thread has been brought to light, its revelation is meant to transform how you and I think about the Old Testament. Climb to the 30,000-foot view so as to behold the Old Testament in its entirety, and you will marvel at the realization that God—throughout all 39 books—was pointing our focus directly at His Son establishing His earthly Davidic kingdom.

The Farewell Discourse

As if Old Testament revelation wasn't enough, Christ's promised return can also be found in the Gospels and the book of Acts. These five books dedicate 75 verses entirely to Christ's coming kingdom.[7]

The quintessential teaching on this subject can be found in the Gospel of John chapters 13–17, known as Christ's Farewell Discourse, and particularly in John 14:1-14. Reading these chapters is like being given our own special seat at the Last Supper. We witness the Lord with great emotion sharing His most deeply personal teachings with

His disciples on the evening before He was crucified. And because this discourse was the Lord's final message pre-crucifixion, God meant for us to take note of its significance as containing a greater degree of importance, and so give it special attention.[8]

In the Farewell Discourse, a solemn Jesus stressed that even though He and His followers would soon be separated for some time, the separation would serve various purposes until that inevitable reunification. First, Christ's crucifixion, resurrection, and ascension would complete His great work of bringing salvation to mankind. The duration of the delay that followed would then provide the proper amount of time to satiate Christ's longsuffering patience in bringing everyone who will come to Him in repentance (2 Peter 3:9). Just think, if Jesus had taken possession of His Davidic throne back in the first century, His kingdom would have had 2,000 years' fewer citizens (as well as leaving you and me out).

Second, the duration of the delay was meant to provide Jesus with the time necessary to build a home for His redeemed children in preparation for that day when we can all finally dwell in the presence of our heavenly Father. As Jesus explained:

> Let not your heart be troubled; you believe in God, believe also in Me. In My Father's house are many mansions; if it were not so, I would have told you. I go to prepare a place for you. And if I go and prepare a place for you, I will come again and receive you to Myself; that where I am, there you may be also (John 14:1-3).

When Thomas responded with, "Lord, we do not know where You are going, and how can we know the way?," Jesus replied, "I am the way, the truth, and the life. No one comes to the Father except through Me" (verses 5-6). As one commentator so beautifully put it, Christ, in essence, became a living Via Dolorosa (The Way of Sorrows), providing the one and only way to the Father, so that all those who are saved can dwell with our Lord in perfect fellowship.[9] And Christ assured us that one day, He will indeed return to "catch up" (rapture) His children to dwell with Him in that home He has prepared for us, and there, we will live forever and ever (1 Thessalonians 4:13-18).

Among the Letters

Besides the books of the Old Testament, the Gospels, and Acts, one can also find Christ's promise to return to set up His kingdom in a prodigious 76 verses of the Pauline epistles and 25 verses of the general epistles.[10] The writer of Hebrews, for example, noted that Christ's reign had not yet been fulfilled by His first coming because there remains a cosmic struggle for domination over the earth. Jesus reclaimed the title deed to this planet from Satan, having earned it by His perfect sacrifice on the cross. But the fact that Jesus does not yet exercise total control over the earth, for we're told that "now we do not yet see all things put under him," shows that Christ must still return to receive what is His—complete dominion over the world, as promised (Hebrews 2:5-8).[11]

Then there's the book of Revelation. Too many people erroneously believe chapter 22 contains the only reference to Christ's promise to return. But look especially at the letters Christ wrote to the seven churches in chapters 2–3. In letter after letter, Jesus exhorted the churches to "hold fast" to what they have till He comes, bearing eternal rewards. With Revelation adding 24 verses to the 129 from the Old Testament, the 75 from the Gospels and Acts, the 76 from the Pauline epistles, and 25 from the general epistles, a grand total of 329 verses can be found across the breadth of the entire Bible reiterating Christ's promise that He will indeed return.[12]

God wants us, as readers of Scripture, to fully understand that when He makes a promise, it will indeed happen. "What I have said, that I will bring about; what I have planned, that I will do" (Isaiah 46:11 NIV).

God's promises are ironclad. The Lord wishes to leave no doubt in our minds that Jesus Christ is indeed coming back to this earth to personally rule and reign over it. Therefore, our hearts are not meant to be troubled over our Savior's temporary absence, but rather, brimming with hope in the anticipation of His soon return. The golden thread proves this promise is trustworthy. Our Lord beckons us with open arms to take this truth to heart, allowing it to guide our lives in the here and now. Truly, without a doubt, the Bible is God's love letter to you and me.

TWO MESSIAHS?

Some people, however, ask, "Just which Messiah is returning?" You may find this a strange thing to ask, but not everyone interprets the prophecies of the coming of our Lord as, say, your everyday Protestant Christian does.

How do the Jewish people interpret the messianic passages?

Jewish studies expert John Metzger explained there are those within conservative, Reformed, and secular Judaism who do not foresee the coming of any personal, human messiah, but rather, are taught that it remains up to each individual Jew to become their own "messiah" in making the world a better place.[13] We cannot count on divine intervention, they conclude, and so each of us is responsible for "saving the world."

Then there's rabbinic Judaism, which Metzger explained disagrees completely with Christianity's interpretation of there being only one Messiah, anticipating instead the coming of two individual messiahs who will make two separate appearances.[14] When rabbinic Jews read the Torah and the Prophets, they interpret the messianic passages as pointing to a "suffering messiah," one who is separate and distinct from a "victorious messiah."[15] The former they identify as Messiah ben-Joseph—a suffering servant and gentle healer who, even though he laid down his life for the sins of Israel, was eventually rejected.[16] The latter they identify as Messiah ben-David—a Davidic warrior-king who will usher in world peace by taking vengeance on God's enemies and then rule with justice and righteousness through the setting up of a divine order.[17] Much like the Jews of the first century, rabbinic Jews take one look at Jesus of Nazareth and shake their heads at how woefully lacking Jesus appeared compared to the prophecies concerning Messiah ben-David. Jews have historically ignored the prophecies surrounding Messiah ben-Joseph because they invariably point to the life of Jesus of Nazareth, whom they have long rejected as their deliverer.

To harmonize these disparate messiahs, the rabbis interpret the messianic prophecies found in the Tanakh as meaning two different messiahs who will arrive in two different eras.[18] As biblical archaeologist Roger Liebi noted, a Jew reading through the Old Testament experiences a profound sense of yearning for the coming of a messiah who will provide the solution to mankind's problems by ushering in everlasting righteousness, a feat only a warrior-king can achieve, and never a suffering servant.[19]

What is the answer to the Jewish conundrum surrounding their expectation of two messiahs? The answer is experience.[20] The prophecies concerning the coming Messiah will eventually play out in a not-so-distant future. Once these seemingly divergent messianic prophecies are at last fulfilled, the Jewish people will finally understand that there are not two messiahs but only one, who will come in two advents. The Messiah first came as a suffering servant to sacrifice Himself for the sins of the world, providing the one and only means for restoring a personal relationship between a holy God and sinful man. And this same suffering servant will later return as the triumphant warrior-king to establish the Davidic kingdom and fulfill all the promises that God had made to the patriarchs and David.

A day is coming, one in the not-too-distant future, when the

Jewish people are going to be shocked by the sudden realization that the two messiahs are in truth one—Yeshua Hamashiach. This day of realization is revealed prophetically in Psalm 118:26. Jesus quoted this verse when He was speaking to the scribes and Pharisees (Matthew 23:39). On that long-anticipated day when the Messiah bursts from the clouds at His second coming, the believing remnant of Jewish people will at last recognize that Messiah ben-Joseph and Messiah ben-David are one and the same. In response, they will weep and wail and cry out in Hebrew, "Baruch haba b'Shem Adonai," meaning "Blessed is He who comes in the name of the LORD!" And what a day that will be!

CHAPTER 4

THE JEWS REGATHERED IN ISRAEL

Today, in Israel, you can still find a culture of empty, it's-all-about-me religiosity. What Jesus said in the first century is still true today. "But all their works they do to be seen by men..." (Matthew 23:5-6). But what God told Daniel through Gabriel is that within the 70-week period, the people of Israel would turn aside from their religiosity and sinful indulgences. Instead, they would desire a true righteousness that is everlasting, and they will receive it.[1]

Amir Tsarfati, *Discovering Daniel*

Jesus Christ's steadfast promise to return to sit upon the throne of David is tied timing-wise to yet another of the most significant Bible prophecies ever made—the regathering of the Jewish people back to the land of Israel.

THE DIASPORA

As we learned in the last chapter, though one and the same, the Jewish people's rejection of the suffering Messiah resulted in the delay of the victorious Messiah. As Moses prophesied in Deuteronomy 28, as long the Jewish people remain in continuous rebellion against God and reject His salvation, God would exile the Jews from their covenantal land and scatter them across the face of the earth. True to prophecy, history records that the Jews in Nebuchadnezzar's time were exiled and scattered. Later, Moses' prophecy concerning rebellion and exile was executed yet again, this time carried out by the Romans in AD 70.[2] But, like the earlier Babylonian exile, this second exile would also not be permanent. The Bible prophesies that just before the second advent of the Messiah, the Jews must return from worldwide dispersion and be regathered back into the land of Israel.[3]

The fact that over the course of 19 centuries the scattered Jewish people have not been absorbed into the nations and cultures into which they had fled and have still retained their own unique heritage and cultural identity led the eighteenth-century English cleric Thomas Newton to conclude, "The preservation of the Jews is really one of the most single and illustrious acts of divine providence."[4]

Jonathan Bernis, the president of Jewish Voice Ministries, echoed Newton's sentiment when he observed, "By man's logic, Israel should not exist...despite being continually overrun by foreign oppressors and scattered throughout the world, they have survived."[5] Bernis added that of the 50 nations he visited in his travels across what the scattered Jews call the Diaspora, all the Jewish communities have retained their "Jewishness."[6] This led him to conclude: "These people are not lost. God knows where every last one of them is, and He is going to restore them."[7]

How have the Jewish people been able to maintain their identity when every other dislocated culture over time has been absorbed into a larger cultural collective?

It seems impossible, after two millennia, that we can still recognize a Jew to be a Jew. Dismissing the obvious divine protections, Jewish studies expert Étan Levine noted his belief that the answer lies in a few factors.[8] For one, being dispersed to so many different geographic locations has kept the overall Jewish culture from being consumed by a few predominant cultures. And two, Jewish communities tend to remain small and close-knit, as opposed to when their community had grown into a massive population center as it did back during the 400 years of Egyptian slavery. These smaller enclaves make the Jewish settlers appear less threatening to their host nation.

While not appearing significantly threatening, the fact remains that living as a minority in every culture in which the Jewish communities have attempted to embed themselves has inevitably left them open to ongoing persecution by the majority. Persecution would appear to counter the need for demographic diffusion as a survival mechanism. And yet, as these communities circle the wagons, so to speak, to provide and protect themselves from persecution, they grasp more strongly onto their "Jewishness" and use their shared culture to successfully enlighten, guide, inspire, and elicit loyalty in their progeny.[9] In noting the Diaspora chutzpah to survive and the stalwart character adversity creates, Levine remarked, "If Judaism has nothing vital to say to the hearts and minds of men in the Diaspora, it will say equally trivial things in Israel, albeit in Hebrew."[10] So, dispersion across a multitude of nations and the need to unite against persecution have kept the Jews Jewish.

GOD'S PURPOSE FOR THE RETURN

Why has God kept a remnant of Israel intact throughout the centuries of dispersion?

Having endured homelessness, persecution, pogroms, and even the Holocaust, why is the survival of the Jewish people, as one evangelistic ministry to the Jews has claimed, the greatest miracle in history?[11] The answer is firmly because God is faithful.

The Bible tells us that God does not change His mind (Numbers 23:19). He always keeps His promises (Deuteronomy 7:7-9). He never breaks His covenants (Judges 2:1). His promises never fail (1 Kings 8:56), and that includes His Davidic promise (Psalm 89:1-4). God is always faithful to His people (Psalm 117:2). And the Almighty has proclaimed that the descendants of Israel will never cease to be a nation (Jeremiah 31:35-37). He already promised that His law will one day be written on their hearts (Jeremiah 31:31-34; Romans 2:15; 11:28-32). And, as stated, Jesus foretold that the advent of His return will happen only when Israel is finally ready to cry out in a combination of weeping and joy, "Blessed is He who comes in the name of the Lord!" (Matthew 23:37-39; see also Zechariah 12:10-11).

THE RIGHT TO THE LAND

Do the Jewish people even have a right to return to their ancient land, the geographic location many today would call Palestine? Or have they lost the title deed due to their past disobedience and rejection of the Messiah?

To answer this vital question, let's briefly review the aforementioned covenants. After all, many in the church today would benefit from making sure they align with what the Bible has to teach concerning the specific and unconditional promises God has made to the Jewish people.

We first must look back to the Abrahamic covenant. God promised Abraham that his descendants would grow into a great nation, and that nation would become a tremendous blessing to the entire world (Genesis 12:2-3). The Lord later confirmed the Abrahamic covenant with Isaac, and then Jacob (known as Israel), which narrowed God's foundational promise to the Jewish people alone and not the descendants of Ishmael and Esau (Genesis 17:19, 21; 25:23; 35:9-15). The Abrahamic covenant was guaranteed by God as an eternal covenant (Genesis 17:19). Not long after, the Land (or sometimes called the Palestinian) covenant was added, granting a specified territory be given as a homeland to the Jewish people, and in perpetuity (Genesis 17:8).[12] Joshua obeyed God and took possession of the land of the Canaanites—the Promised Land (Joshua 1–24).

Though the promise of ownership of the land stands forever as unconditional, God still set one condition for the use of the land. Should the Jewish people become continuously disobedient and remain unrepentant, the nation's punishment would be exile (Leviticus 26:14-39; Deuteronomy 28:15-68). But their exile would only be temporary, for God also promised that He would inevitably regather His wayward people back into their covenantal land, rebuild their waste cities, and restore them into a right relationship with Him (Isaiah 11:11-12; Ezekiel 36:33-36; Amos 9:14-15).

Think of the Abrahamic covenant this way. When my son got his driver's license, we bought a car that he could drive. His name was on the title. But, like the Land covenant, he could only drive it on the conditions his mother and I had set: drive cautiously, be home by curfew, pay for the gas, and so on. Should he disobey our requirements, we would take his car keys and lock the vehicle in the garage. But only for a set time. The car would always remain his, but the right for him to use it depended on his obedience to our rules. Likewise, the Jewish people will always own the land of Israel, but they must meet God's conditions of righteousness to enjoy their ownership of the land.

Like me deciding when my son's time of punishment was over and he'd be allowed to drive his car again, it's always been up to the Father to decide when the Jewish people's time of exile was over and they could use their land again. Once God had made that decision, the prophets foretold of a future period of spiritual cleansing when the Jewish people would, at last, give up their rebellion and recognize their Messiah (Zechariah 12:7-14; 13:9). As God comforted the prophet Jeremiah:

> "For I am with you," says the LORD, "to save you; though I make a full end of all nations where I have scattered you, yet I will not make a complete end of you. But I will correct you in justice, and will not let you go altogether unpunished" (Jeremiah 30:11).

Once the determined sentence of punishment had concluded, then and only then would the Messiah inaugurate a new covenant with Israel, cleanse the Jewish people of their sins, and reconcile them as a nation with the God of their fathers (Zechariah 13:1).[13] And so the messianic administration hinges on both the unconditional right of the Jewish people to own their land forever, as well as God's decision when to at last allow wayward Israel back into their land. This has been God's perfect plan since the exodus (and possibly even before creation) to regather, restore, and bless the Jewish people once they have returned to their covenantal lands (Deuteronomy 30:1-10).[14]

Many who hold an amillennialistic viewpoint (more on that in a later chapter) claim that Christ's new covenant makes null and void the Land covenant. David Stern, a Jewish translator, objected to this outlandish claim by pointing to the apostle Paul's teaching in Galatians 3:15-17. Stern believes this passage provides the biblical proof that "a later covenant does not alter an earlier one," and so God's land promise made to the patriarchs is "altered neither by the coming of the New Covenant nor by the supposed abrogation of the Mosaic one."[15] As proof, look at Christ's prophecy in Matthew 24:30, where Matthew revealed that when the Messiah returns "coming on the clouds of heaven with power and great glory," the 12 tribes of Israel are foretold to already be living in the land of Israel, and it is there where they will see Him.[16] Prophecy confirms the future presence of the Jews in their Promised Land, whether one wishes to believe the Land covenant remains current or not.

A SECOND REGATHERING

What about the claim that the return of the Jews to Israel from Babylonian exile in the fifth and sixth centuries BC already fulfilled Moses' prophecy of blessings and curses?

We turn to the prophet Isaiah for the answer.[17]

> The Lord shall set His hand again *the second time* to recover the remnant of His people who are left...He will...gather together the dispersed of Judah from *the four corners of the earth*" (Isaiah 11:11-12, emphasis added).

Isaiah, in pointing to a second time, prophesied two regatherings. The first was only a migration from Babylon to Judea, while the second was an international regathering from out of "the four corners of the earth."[18]

Ezekiel likewise made a similar prophecy concerning two gatherings. "Now I will bring back the captives of Jacob, and have mercy on the *whole house* of Israel" (Ezekiel 39:25, emphasis added).[19] Whereas the first regathering from Babylon focused specifically on the tribe of Judah, the second regathering will assemble all of Israel's 12 tribes that had been dispersed by the Assyrians, Babylonians, and Romans so that Judah and Ephraim are no longer in conflict but reunited as one people once more.[20]

A REGATHERING IN UNBELIEF

What about the claim that the modern-day regathering of the Jewish people back to the land of Israel must be a counterfeit regathering because they have yet to acknowledge Jesus as their Messiah?

After all, some 60 to 70 percent of Jewish Israelis today fall into the nones faith category. Well, three key passages from Ezekiel demonstrate that the worldwide regathering of the Jewish people must first take place while the people are just that—in a state of unbelief.[21]

The first passage is Ezekiel 20:33-38. Read it and you will wonder why the Lord God told the prophet that He will regather His scattered people out of one wrath for the purpose of having them confront yet another wrath. This sounds rather confusing, doesn't it? But Arnold Fruchtenbaum pointed out the wrath of the Holocaust, during which six million Jews died, was the event that finally allowed the Jewish people to be granted the right by the United Nations to create the nation of Israel, officially declared on May 14, 1948, in preparation for a much more severe holocaust prophesied to come.[22] This twentieth-century regathering was not made in faith, but in unbelief, as seen by the fact that God did it "with a mighty hand, with an outstretched arm, and with fury poured out" (verse 33). In regathering the Jewish people from one wrath to confront yet another, God makes His purpose clear: to plead His case, purge those who remain in rebellion, and produce a purified nation. The Messiah will then rule through a people purified, and they will serve Him in priestly roles administering His messianic kingship over the entire world.

The second passage, Ezekiel 22:17-22, also foretold God's plans for an unprecedented Jewish regathering in unbelief before Israel goes through a time of refining. This regathering can only be in unbelief because Ezekiel compared the Jewish people's sins to the impurities found in metals.[23] Once the wrath of God had created a furnace of affliction, only then will the nation of Israel become purified of its sins, like dross removed from metals over a smelter. Once safely through the wrath to come, only then will Israel be deemed ready to serve the Lord.

The third of Ezekiel's passages, Ezekiel 36:22-24, like his preceding passages, makes it clear that this second regathering of the Jewish people in unbelief must take place before national regeneration can occur.

> I will sanctify My great name, which has been profaned among the nations, which you have profaned in their midst; and the nations shall know that I am the LORD (Ezekiel 36:23).

Not only will the Jewish people repent of their sins, but in doing so, the Gentile nations will come to know the Lord as well.

Still other Old Testament prophets prophesied the regathering of Israel in unbelief. The prophet Zephaniah, for instance, pointed out how God labeled Israel as an "undesirable nation" that will be gathered together to face the fierce anger of the Lord (Zephaniah 2:1-2). Likewise, the prophet Zechariah affirmed God's purpose for this regathering to wrath:

> I will bring them back, and they shall dwell in the midst of Jerusalem. They shall be My people and I will be their God, in truth and righteousness (Zechariah 8:8).

God's ultimate purpose extends well beyond the refining of the Jewish people, though, for He performs this amazingly gracious act ultimately for "My holy name's sake" (Ezekiel 36:22). The salvation of the Jewish people is a feat that will glorify the name of God before the peoples of the world.

What Ezekiel and the other prophets foretold concerning the return of the Jewish people to the Promised Land in unbelief is being played out as a reality before our very eyes. Donna Divine pointed out that the modern-day nation of Israel was founded on secular humanism, initially with a bent toward utopian socialism, though later transformed by an entrepreneurial spirit due to being a start-up nation.[24] In her understanding, the Zionist movement to reclaim Israel had rejected the pious religious culture their dispersion had nurtured, not to be rekindled until the Six-Day War in 1967 put Jerusalem back into the control of the Israeli government.[25] Sadly, the newly sparked religious commitment to redeem the land of Israel that had been birthed by the war did not last long over the successive decades once confronted by a hostile political reality. With Israel now facing a crisis of national faith, Divine exhorted, "Zionism's compelling legacy: that Israel must stand for something if it is to continue to stand."[26]

As we've just learned, though war sparks short-lived revivals, Israel's currently anemic spiritual condition is exactly what the prophets had predicted! For, as God purposed, "I do not do this for your sake, O house of Israel, but for My holy name's sake" (Ezekiel 36:22). The restoration of the faith of the Jewish people in God is meant to affirm the Almighty's name as being faithful to His covenants.

MAKING ALIYA

I cannot emphasize enough what a miracle we are witnessing in seeing the Jewish people return to their promised land after nearly 1,900 years of exile. Ancient Bible prophecies are coming true, right before our eyes!

Whether for Zionism, Utopianism, messianic fervor, or to escape the vile hand of antisemitism, the Jewish people have been returning to their covenantal land in great waves since the early 1880s. Jewish historian Hizky Shoham labeled this siren call to return with the Hebrew word *aliya*, meaning "going up," as when a Jewish person feels a tugging in his or her heart to immigrate to Israel and nowhere else.[27]

Following the two ancient biblical immigrations from Babylonia, six modern and distinct immigration waves, called *aliyot*, have occurred.[28] The First Aliya (1881–1904) was mainly composed of the lower- and middle-class poor who fled from Russia, Romania, and Yemen as the political and economic conditions for the Jews deteriorated in those countries.[29] The following Second Aliya (1904–1914) consisted of ideologically motivated immigrants called *halutzim* ("pioneers"). The Third Aliya (1918–1924) gained speed just after the Balfour Declaration announced the British government's support of the establishment of a national home for the Jewish people in Palestine.[30] The Fourth Aliya (1924–1933) saw a great influx of Polish immigrants escaping economic recession. The immigrants of the Fifth Aliya (1933–1939) were called "Hitler refugees" who fled Europe due to the increasing power of the Nazi party.[31]

Though many Ashkenazi Jews continued to make Israel their new home after it became a nation again in May 1948, the large sixth wave of immigration didn't occur until the 1990s, when Israel welcomed more than one million immigrants from the former Soviet Union.[32] Soon after, close to 100,000 Ethiopian, or *Mizrahim*, Jews—known as Beta Israel—brought a new dimension to the racial makeup of the rebirthed nation.[33] The Israeli government has also allowed a sizeable influx of migrant workers to enter the country via work permits.[34]

Increase Mather, when he wrote *The Mystery of Christ* in 1686, believed that when the prophecies concerning the return of the Jewish people became realized, their numbers would become so great that Israel would have to take possession of adjoining nations.[35] Little did Mather know how much the regathering of the Jewish people "out of wrath for the purpose of gathering them to wrath" would deplete their numbers—so much so that as of 2020, the total population of Jews worldwide remains at a shockingly low 14.7 million.[36] Still, Mather took the Bible for its literal, plain-sense meaning, and so took by faith the eventual and inevitable second regathering of the Jewish people back to the land of Israel, which has been happening in our day.

When asked why he believed God would still wish to save Israel, Increase Mather replied: "Doubtless there are diverse reasons for it; one is, because the Lord would not, by any means, have His people ignorant of this great truth."[37] And his second reason: "Because it is that which men are most unapt to believe."[38] When Mather was pressed to explain why he thought people couldn't believe that the Jews would return to Israel as prophesied, he answered, "Because of the strangeness and wonder that is in it; it is a thing beyond human sense and reason."[39] Certainly, for centuries, the church has taken this amazing prophecy to be strange and beyond reason, and yet it is being fulfilled right before our very eyes!

A DIVINE MIRACLE

Let's summarize what we've learned so far concerning this divinely orchestrated second regathering of the Jewish people back to the Promised Land. God has enacted His plan to regather the Jewish people—while in unbelief—back to their land in Israel. He will then refine them through a great trial so that a remnant will become saved. When this happens, God's name will be glorified by the people, and that event will coincide with Christ's timing to put an end to failed earthly human governments. After so many centuries, in what could only be called a divine miracle of God, the Jewish people are indeed being brought back in droves to dwell once more in the land God had promised the patriarchs.

More than seven million Jews call Israel their home today. They now have control over their historic capital, Jerusalem. They salute their national flag, one emblazoned with the Star of David. And why? Because God has been bringing these long-lost people back to fulfill His promise to the Jews. A believing remnant will become His people once more, though a people refined to love His truth and righteousness, and finally be committed to Messiah Yeshua.

Truly, we are living in prophetic times!

CHAPTER 5

THE DAY OF THE LORD

Global war, billions of deaths, massive earthquakes, the pollution of rivers and oceans, devastation from meteors and asteroids, one-third of the trees and all green grass will be burned, pollution from war perhaps nuclear, volcanic eruptions: all this will make the earth an undesirable place to live. "Climate change" is indeed coming, compliments of Jesus Christ and His wrath.[1]

Jeff Kinley, *God's Grand Finale*

God has plans to save the regathered Jewish remnant. How exactly will this unfold, and what does the salvation of the Jews have to do with God's purpose to end failed human government?

THE DAY OF THE LORD DEFINED

The Lord will bring salvation to the Jewish people though the Day of the Lord. Of the 19 teachings concerning this subject made by eight Old Testament prophets, Zephaniah may have given the most colorful yet comprehensive description:[2]

> The great day of the LORD is near; it is near and hastens quickly. The noise of the day of the LORD is bitter; there the mighty men shall cry out. That day is a day of wrath, a day of trouble and distress, a day of devastation and desolation, a day of darkness and gloominess, a day of clouds and thick darkness, a day of trumpet and alarm against the fortified cities and against the high towers (Zephaniah 1:14-16).

How will mankind react to this apocalyptic "day"? In the opening of verse 17, God added, "I will bring distress upon men, and they shall walk like blind men." Like a little child woken late at night, alarmed as the pitch blackness is shattered by lightning bolts and terrified as the walls shake due to titanic thunderclaps, so the people during that time will find themselves stumbling about and wailing in terror at God's great day of judgment.

And why exactly did Zephaniah say God will bring such devastation upon the earth? Because, as the next part of verse 17 states, men "have sinned against the LORD." The sins of the world will have become so egregious—off-the-chart levels of evil, just as in the days of Noah and Lot—that God's perfect sense of justice will compel Him to wage a full-scale apocalypse on the earth.

> On the day that Lot went out of Sodom it rained fire and brimstone from heaven and destroyed them all. Even so will it be in the day when the Son of Man is revealed (Luke 17:29-30; see also Matthew 24:37-39).

What sentence will be passed down to a world reveling in their wickedness? Death! For, as verse 17 concludes, "their blood shall be poured out like dust, and their flesh like refuse." And there will be nowhere on, above, or under the planet where those enduring God's punishment can escape from the Almighty's wrath. Zephaniah went on and described the hopelessness of the guilty in verse 18:

> Neither their silver nor their gold shall be able to deliver them in the day of the LORD's wrath; but the whole land shall be devoured by the fire of His jealousy, for He will make speedy riddance of all those who dwell in the land.

God's Intervention in Human History

Through the book of Zephaniah and other key prophecies concerning the Day of the Lord (read them in Ezekiel 28:26; Obadiah 15; Habakkuk 3:3-13; Zephaniah 1:1-5, 14-18; Haggai 2:22; Zechariah 14:1-5), the Almighty proclaimed His desire to directly intervene in human history. Mankind's moral degeneration, having plummeted to the abominable and disgustingly low levels of Sodom, will enflame the Almighty's wrath, and He will dole out divine judgment with mind-numbing levels of violence. In the dispensing of His perfect justice, God will make righteous a remnant who will turn from their wickedness and believe in Jesus Christ as Savior.

Prophetic literature often ascribes the coming day of God's wrath in an abbreviated form, such as "the day" or "in that day," which are condensed expressions used more than 200 times in the Bible.[3] These oracles portray God as a divine warrior acting as the decisive force for victory in the battle against Israel's target enemies—for example, such as in "the day of Midian" (Isaiah 9:4). Sixty of the biblical references to the Day of the Lord reveal that once God has achieved victory over His enemies, some form of restoration of Israel's inheritance, which had either been taken by their enemies or lost due to their sinful condition, will soon follow.[4]

What's fascinating about the Old Testament prophecies concerning the Day of the Lord is that they often hold dual fulfillments, containing both near historical realizations while at the same time foretelling some far-off prophetic event.[5] So while God's smaller victories over Israel's enemies are also called the Day of the Lord, many of the Day-of-the-Lord passages (such as those in Obadiah, Joel, Isaiah, and Zephaniah) reveal a full-on bigger picture. They are also relating specifically to God's future judgment that will be poured out on a global scale. God used the near judgments on these objects of His wrath, such as against Egypt, Israel, and so forth, as mere illustrations. They are meant to point to that future day when God will inflict His great wrath upon all the nations of the world through the 21 terrible judgments described in Revelation chapters 6–19.

This prophesied future time of God's wrath is none other than the pivotal apocalyptic era of judgment most commonly known as "the tribulation."[6] There and then, God will judge the entire world of its prodigious sin with the same earth-shattering level of carnage that He used in the Flood. Going forward, then, I am going to refer to the ultimate prophetic fulfillment of the Day of the Lord by the label "the tribulation." Don't confuse this apocalyptic event with the everyday tribulations that we all must endure due to living in a fallen world. Rather, the Day of the Lord is specifically a time period known as the tribulation (think capital *T* levels of trouble), when God's wrath will be poured out on the earth. And, like the Flood, once the carnage has subsided, life on this planet will never be the same again.

The Dual Purpose of the Tribulation

Embedded within the Day of the Lord prophecies' dual aspect of time—a smaller scale near fulfillment as well as a grander scale future fulfillment in the tribulation—also rests the dual aspect of purpose. So, while one purpose for the tribulation is to dispense righteous judgment on an evil people for their sins, the other purpose presents God's gracious nature, which causes Him to show mercy in the face of true repentance. Mercy is then swiftly followed by a loving outpouring of God's blessings on the penitent.

Commentator A.T. Pierson explained God's dual motive this way:

> God's anger was seen to be not a passion, but a principle—the eternal hatred of wrong, which corresponds with the eternal love of right, and which is only another aspect of love.[7]

Pierson called God's principle the "magnetic needle" that "swings on its delicate axis; it attracts at one end; it repels at the other."[8] In other words, for those who stand defiant in their rebellion, God's wrath continues to burn hotly against them. But for those who surrender before that same wrath, bending a knee in repentance, God, in His gracious and merciful nature, relents, forgives, and blesses.

For those insurgent souls confronted by such a divine and awful wrath, during what theologian Arthur Kac identified as "an age of anxiety, an age in which mankind is adrift, not knowing what tomorrow will bring," how could they possibly stand?[9] Don't feel sympathy for the degenerate lost, my friends. If only they would acknowledge that God's judgment is used to express His desire to reconcile with them. If only they would submit to the triumph of justice that stands as God's ultimate act of love to His faithful. Should the wicked relent, our Lord would most definitely redirect them to the proper course of action—repentance. Even in His wrath, "the Son of Man has come to seek and to save that which was lost" (Luke 19:10), just as He did with you and me during this church age.

THE DAY OF THE LORD DEPICTED

The Day of the Lord in the Psalms

The concept of the Day of the Lord is no stranger to the book of Psalms. As our foreword's author, David Reagan, has noted, while King David and the other psalmists composed their songs, they kept one eye locked on what he called Moses' Moab Discourse.[10] In his discourse, Moses prophesied that the Jewish people during the "latter days" would experience a period of "distress" (i.e., the tribulation), which would finally motivate them to "turn to the LORD your God and obey His voice" (Deuteronomy 4:30-31). Once God's chosen people had reached the end of themselves and repented, the Lord would respond by blessing Israel through the fulfillment of His covenantal promises to Abraham.

The writers of the Psalms knew all too well the suffering of their fellow Jews through their various tribulations, having penned 59 prayers of deliverance in general and 12 entire psalms pleading for deliverance from intense suffering (Psalms 80; 82; 88; 90; 120; 126; 129; 137; 141–144).[11] Two particular psalms prophesy future events that will bring about great upheaval to society (Psalms 80; 83), with three more so horrific in scope that they can only be reserved for the apocalyptic tribulation (Psalms 14; 60; 94).

The Day of the Lord in Isaiah

THE NEGATIVES

The prophet Isaiah wrote so prolifically about this coming apocalypse, particularly those aspects that national Israel will one day face, that Arnold Fruchtenbaum labeled Isaiah 24:1 through 27:13 as "The Little Apocalypse of Isaiah."[12] These passages convey the utter destruction of the earth as a judgment due to mankind's sin (Isaiah 24:1-13, 19-20). Isaiah reiterated this essential element found throughout apocalyptic literature: through trials, the inhabitants of the earth learn righteousness (Isaiah 26:8-10). And, through all the suffering, God, in His mercy, will provide some level of protection for His righteous remnant (Isaiah 26:20-21).

You'll find many other descriptive teachings concerning the tribulation peppered throughout the book of Isaiah—some 35 times, mostly in the first 27 chapters.[13] For example, Isaiah identified the source of the coming distress: "Wail, for the day of the Lord is at hand! It will come as destruction from the Almighty" (Isaiah 13:6). And again, Isaiah shouted a prophetic warning to the future rebels of the tribulation by describing the epic scope of God's judgment: "Behold, the day of the Lord comes, cruel, with both wrath and fierce anger, to lay the land desolate; and He will destroy its sinners from it" (Isaiah 13:9).

In Isaiah 37:3, King Hezekiah explained that the tribulation will be a "day of trouble and rebuke and blasphemy." He went on to compare the decrepitude of the living during those days to a miscarriage: "For the children have come to birth, but there is no strength to bring them forth."

It will be "a day of trouble and treading down and perplexity" (Isaiah 22:5). The prophet associated the tumult and confusion of that day with a city under siege. Isaiah also reiterated the fact that when it comes to the Day of the Lord and the great outpouring of God's wrath, as punishment for the world's sin is finally meted out, by the final moments of the tribulation, all sinners will be destroyed (Isaiah 13:9).

Pride is celebrated nationally in our day, but during the tribulation, the haughty and proud will lose all their strength: "I have trodden down the peoples in My anger, made them drunk in My fury, and brought down their strength to the earth" (Isaiah 63:6). The Almighty equated the tribulation to a day of vengeance and a year of retribution (Isaiah 34:8; 61:2; 63:4). God most certainly will answer the tear-stained prayers of the righteous by bringing forth justice.

Among the many instruments God will wield in pouring out His divine judgment will be natural disasters. He will inflict judgment by fire (Isaiah 1:31; 66:24). A tremendous shaking of heaven and earth will accompany the Day of the Lord. And terrifying wonders will be revealed in the heavens and on the land by mountain-crumbling earthquakes and violent storms (Isaiah 13:10; 24:18; 34:4, 13).

God's judgment will come not only to mankind, for Isaiah revealed that there's long been a spiritual war lurking behind mankind's fallen human kingdoms. Isaiah pointed particularly to the final destruction of "Babylon" and "Edom" as the object of God's wrath, using Israel's ancient enemies as the personification of Satan's behind-the-scenes empire (Isaiah 13 and 34). Great desolation will occur as the Lord lays waste to Satan's claim as ruler over the planet (Isaiah 13:19; 24:1; 34:9-10). The Almighty will also wage war in the spiritual realm, inflicting judgment on the powers of heaven as His angelic forces battle against the fallen demons (Isaiah 24:21).

The Positives

When I read Isaiah's teachings concerning the Day of the Lord, I come away struck by the feeling that they're overtly negative; and in truth, for the most part, they are. But Isaiah didn't want us to get caught up in the horrors of it all, though. Rather, God wants us to be captivated by the blessings that will come about as a result of the tribulation. (I'm anxious to get to exploring those blessings in greater detail in the chapters ahead.)

Isaiah emphasized the positive connotations as well, as if this gloomy subject provides what theologian Herbert Wolf described as "two sides of the same coin."[14] What we perceive to be the negative side of the coin includes the elements surrounding God unleashing His wrath upon the evil nations, doling out divine judgment upon His enemies, shaking the heavens and the earth with His rage, and mankind responding with doleful and distressed wailings. And yet, flip the coin over, and you will behold the positive that outshines all the negative. This side portrays the tribulation as God's inevitable victory over evil. It's what the righteous across the ages have earnestly been praying for, and to which, when received, we'll all cry out in unison, "Amen!"

Along with God's great victory over evil, the tribulation will also provide God's gracious redemption to the righteous remnant of Jews. They will be rescued from Satan's clutches and returned to dwell securely in their homeland. Likewise, the Gentile nations will also experience salvation, for another righteous remnant will survive the tribulation to become followers of the coming King of Zion. Wolf summarized this both negative and positive duality of God's purpose as follows: "When God intervenes directly in human affairs, it is to punish the wicked and to rescue the righteous."[15]

If you're looking to read some positives concerning the Day of the Lord, turn to Isaiah 2 in particular. Here, we find some remarkably positive verses. They foretell how, as a result of the tribulation, a worldwide peace accompanied by a profound godliness will at last settle upon the righteous remnant. As horrific as the tribulation will be, we're meant to understand that God's wrath will refine the world into something ultimately better than it has been since mankind's fall. In the chapters ahead, please take this to heart as we explore the joys of life during the millennium.

The Day of the Lord in Daniel

Whereas Isaiah provided us with a vivid description of the tribulation, the prophet Daniel provided us with details about its length and timing. Let's look at Daniel 9:20-27, better known as Daniel's seventieth-week prophecy.[16]

The angel Gabriel prophesied to Daniel, "Seventy weeks are determined for your people and for your holy city" (Daniel 9:24). The Hebrew word for "weeks" is *shavua*, meaning a "unit of seven years."[17] Seventy "weeks" times seven equals 490 years. Note that prophetic years in the Bible are counted as 360-day years and not as 365-day years.[18]

Gabriel also revealed the starting date for when these 490 years would begin—from the day that a "command to restore and build Jerusalem" was given. The "weeks" would keep counting down until the Messiah was "cut off" (Daniel 9:25-26). Much debate has swirled around which Persian king had made this particular prophetic decree, but the majority of scholars tend to point to Artaxerxes' decree to rebuild Jerusalem, which he made in 445 BC, nearly 100 years after Daniel had received this prophecy.[19] We also know from the Gospels that the time when the Messiah was "cut off" was the very day when Jesus Christ made His triumphal entry into Jerusalem, only to subsequently be rejected and killed by His people. Interestingly, Palm Sunday brings us to only 483 of the 490 prophetic years, leaving one remaining seven-year period equaling 2,520 days. This final "week" is commonly called Daniel's seventieth week.

We are left with a gap in time between the sixty-ninth and seventieth weeks. Daniel skipped over this unspecified interlude, which we now know is the church age—the era we are living in today. Once God determines the church age to be over, He will restart the countdown once more to finish out Daniel's seventieth week.

We're also given the exact day when Daniel's seventieth week will commence, as well as its midpoint three-and-a-half years later. It will begin on the day when the "prince who is to come" "shall confirm a covenant with many for one week," and then midway through the seven final years, he will bring "an end to sacrifice and offering" (Daniel 9:26-27). This prophesied prince's confirmation of a peace covenant with Israel and "the many" will serve as the event that triggers the beginning of Daniel's seventieth week. Daniel's week and the tribulation week are one and the same. Therefore, the angel Gabriel let us know that the Day of the Lord will last for a grueling seven prophetic years.

The apostle John later revealed the identity of this prince—the Antichrist (1 John 2:18, 22; 4:3; 2 John 1:7). The terms involved in this treaty between the Antichrist and Israel have also been widely debated. Some scholars believe the Antichrist will not renew an existing covenant; rather, he will draft an original one containing many strong guarantees that will provide for Israel's security, as well as permissions to begin construction of the third Jewish temple.[20]

My own theory about what's involved in this covenant takes into account God's miraculous victory in the Gog-Magog War (Ezekiel 38–39). The timing clues point to this prophetic war as happening after the rapture of the church but just before the tribulation begins (and that's a topic for a whole other book). By His defeat of the Russian and Islamic invaders, the Lord will strike such fear into the hearts of the world's leaders that they will seek protection from the God of Israel. The Antichrist, who is seen in the first seal judgment (Revelation 6:1-2), will hide behind these protections while he goes out to conquer the world, as described in the second seal judgment (Revelation 6:3-4).

So we now know that the first day of the seven-year tribulation will begin the very day the Antichrist signs a peace covenant with Israel, as well as its length, which will be seven years equaling 2,520 days. But whenever you make a deal with the devil, expect to get a raw deal, for this covenant will bring anything but peace. As Arnold Fruchtenbaum pointed out:

> God declares that this is not a covenant of life, but a covenant of death. It is not a covenant of heaven, but a covenant of hell. Rather than gaining security, Israel will receive a strong measure of insecurity.[21]

Gabriel also told Daniel that this poisonous prince will break his treaty, and he will do so by ending the sacrifices offered up to God in the only place where the Jews are allowed to hold these ceremonies—on the Temple Mount. The angel revealed, "He shall bring an end to sacrifice and offering. And on the wing of abominations shall be one who makes desolate" (Daniel 9:27). As of the time of this writing, there is no temple currently standing on the Temple Mount—just the Islamic Dome of the Rock and Al-Aqsa Mosque. But the preparations have already been made by the Temple Institute, and the third temple is being readied as you read this!

Was the Daniel 9:27 prophecy about the abomination of desolation fulfilled by Antiochus Epiphanes when he desecrated the Temple in 167 BC?

Maybe in the near sense of fulfillment, as we learned earlier. But no, the tribulation-era desecration exceeds in scope the historical desecration of the temple committed by Antiochus "the Madman" Epiphanes, as Antiochus's desecration did not include the destruction of either the temple or Jerusalem.[22] This arch-villain, Antiochus, merely served as a type pointing to the ultimate arch-villain, the Antichrist. Nor was Daniel giving an after-the-event description of the desecration by Antiochus, as claimed by some critical scholars who incorrectly late-date the book of Daniel.[23] We are meant to look at Antiochus's bloody sacrifice of an unkosher pig on the temple's altar, as well as the raising up of a statue of himself, for he claimed to be Zeus reincarnated, and the ordering of the Jewish people to worship his statue, as a template for the tribulation-era people to use in identifying the "prince who is to come" (Daniel 9:26).

The Day of the Lord in the Minor Prophets

References to the tribulation are resplendent throughout the writings of the minor prophets. For instance, in Zechariah 14, God revealed that "the day of the LORD is coming" when the Antichrist's forces will amass and besiege Jerusalem (verses 1-2). Facing their extinction, the Jewish people will be confronted by their darkest hour. At the final moment, when all hope seems lost, Zechariah declared that's when the Messiah will at last return in all His glory, and He will personally fight against the invading nations of the world. The Righteous King will land upon the Mount of Olives with such seismic force that the hill will crack in two, thereby creating a whole new valley running across the Kidron, and through which the beleaguered Jewish remnant can escape from the Antichrist's homicidal clutches (Zechariah 14:4).

Likewise, we find four times where Malachi had swept forward to this climatic messianic return during "the coming of the great and dreadful day of the Lord" (Malachi 4:5; see 1:11; 3:1-6, 16-18; 4:1-6). As commentator Henry Halley noted, "The plight of mankind would be hopeless should the Lord fail to come."[24] It's well understood that if Jesus didn't return during that cursed day, no Jew in Jerusalem would be spared the Antichrist's sword.

Haggai identified this critical point in the tribulation narrative when he proclaimed the Messiah's intention upon His arrival to at last end failed human governments. "I will overthrow the throne of kingdoms; I will destroy the strength of the Gentile kingdoms" (2:22).

Additionally, the minor prophets revealed the exact day when human governments will have finally reached their end. They will end on the terminal day of the tribulation. As the fall of the Gentile powers is tied to the completion of Daniel's seventieth-week prophecy, we now know that human governments will end exactly 2,520 days after the Antichrist signs his peace covenant with Israel, which is 2,520 days before the Messiah arrives in great victory.

The Day of the Lord in the New Testament

The biblical concept of the Day of the Lord is not limited to the Old Testament; the New Testament writers also provided voluminous teachings on this subject. They showed that their understanding rested upon certain Old Testament teachings (read Acts 2:20; 1 Thessalonians 5:2; 2 Thessalonians 2:2; and 2 Peter 3:10). In the New Testament, the concept (Matthew 24:21; 2 Peter 2:9; Revelation 3:10) and nature (Matthew 24:22; Mark 13:19-20; Luke 21:22; Romans 5:9; 1 Thessalonians 1:10; Revelation 15:1) of the tribulation are further fleshed out.

The book of Revelation confirmed Daniel's understanding of the length of the tribulation to be "one week," meaning seven years long. The length of Daniel's seventieth-week prophecy can be described in a variety of ways—as one seven-year block (Daniel 9:27), "time and times and half a time" (Revelation 12:14's reference to the second three-and-a-half years), consisting of two 1,260-day periods (Revelation 11:3), or two 42-month periods (Revelation 11:2; 13:5).

Just as the Old Testament writers imbued within the Day of the Lord both a near and far fulfillment, so too did the New Testament writers. They likewise interpreted prophetic events with a near historical fulfillment, but always under a future eschatological light, especially as they pertained to the coming outpouring of God's wrath.[25] The New Testament writers picked up on the far use in their application of the tribulation as both a near judgment that would climax during the tribulation period, but then went so much farther than the Old Testament writers, prophesying a yet farther-reaching judgment that will usher in the new earth.[26] (We will explore those amazing prophecies concerning the eternal state in a later chapter.)

When it came to Jesus', Peter's, Paul's, and John's teachings concerning the Day of the Lord, we discover how Jewish-centered they are, for the tribulation is also known as "the time of Jacob's trouble" (Jeremiah 30:7). Likewise, the Jewish remnant's rescue by the coming Messiah, as revealed throughout the Old Testament (such as in Deuteronomy 4:30; Jeremiah 30:7; Daniel 12:1), was later echoed by these New Testament authors (such as Matthew 24:29; 2 Thessalonians 2:8). Christ especially noted the harsh persecution Israel will face by the prince who will desecrate the temple—the Antichrist—during the second half of the seven-year tribulation, a time He solemnly labeled as the Great Tribulation of the Jewish people.

> Then there will be great tribulation, such as has not been since the beginning of the world until this time, no, nor ever shall be (Matthew 24:21; full passage verses 15-28).

Jesus built upon the Old Testament teachings that the Messiah will return to rescue Israel, but only when the people finally confess their national sin and plead for Him to rescue them (read Leviticus

26:40-42; Jeremiah 3:11-18; Hosea 5:15; Zechariah 12:10; summarized in Matthew 23:37-39).

The New Testament added many more details concerning the timing of the Day of the Lord (such as in Matthew 24:33; Mark 13:29; Luke 21:31; Acts 17:31). For instance, we learn that the tribulation can commence only after the nation of Israel exists again. And it does exist now! Jesus likened Israel's rebirth to the blossoming of a fig tree, which did indeed "bloom" once more upon Israel's declaration of statehood on May 14, 1948 (see Matthew 24:32-35; Mark 13:28-31; Luke 21:29-32). The generation (Greek *genea*, meaning "era") that witnessed Israel's reestablishment as a nation would be the very generation that would also witness Christ's return (prophesied in Matthew 24:34; Mark 13:30; Luke 21:32).

Other New Testament prophecies have been fulfilled in the final days of what Cotton Mather called the Ecclesiastical Kingdom. For example, it was prophesied that the Jews would once more control Jerusalem, which they achieved in part in June 1967, and will purge all Gentile influence upon the Messiah's return (Luke 21:24). And we know this church age will end once the full number of Gentiles have been saved (Romans 11:25-26). The characteristic of the final days of the Ecclesiastical Kingdom will be a time of great apostasy when little faith in God is left in the world (Luke 18:8), which we have witnessed, as only 6 percent of self-professing Christians even hold to a biblical worldview.[27]

Prophecies concerning the tribulation are often reiterated in the New Testament. For example, the clock will begin ticking, counting down the 2,520 days the tribulation will last with the revealing of the Antichrist (2 Thessalonians 2:2-3). And Jesus Christ will return at the end of the tribulation in what is specifically called the "last hour," in concert with a celestial show of cataclysmic proportions (1 John 2:18; see also Matthew 24:29; Mark 13:24).

God's purposes for the Day of the Lord are likewise restated in the New Testament.[28] Jesus the Messiah will use the tribulation as His appointed time to make war against His enemies (Revelation 19:11). Christ will execute His vengeance against them (see Romans 12:19; 2 Thessalonians 1:7-8; Hebrews 10:30-31; Jude 14-15; Revelation 6:9-11) by the pouring out of His wrath (see John 3:36; Romans 2:5; 5:9; Colossians 3:6; 1 Thessalonians 1:10; Revelation 6:16-17; 11:18; 14:19-20; 19:15).

Once God's tribulation judgments (see John 5:27; Acts 10:42; 17:31; Romans 2:5; 1 Corinthians 4:5; 2 Timothy 4:1; Hebrews 10:30; James 5:9; Jude 14-15; Revelation 11:18; 14:14-20; 19:11) are all executed, that is when His Son will take dominion over the earth (Revelation 5:8-14; 10:1-7). Jesus Christ will reign over a purified people as the King of kings (1 Timothy 6:15; Revelation 17:14; 19:12, 16).

As we've just learned, the New Testament provides us with a dizzying array of details that help us further our understanding of the *hows* and *whens* concerning the demise of fallen human governments. We will now go on into the next chapter marveling at Jesus Christ achieving His great victory in conquering both failed human governments and the satanic forces that rule behind them. Know that by the end of the tribulation, good will prevail over evil. God will confirm our cries for justice. The prayers we so desperately plead for today will soon be answered. Christ alone will manifest His glory over the entire earth through the setting up of His Davidic kingdom. So let's now read on and discover how Christ's victory turns out in the aftermath of the most terrible seven years in all of human history.

CHAPTER 6

THE AFTERMATH

What thrilled these expectant believers was not that God would rule in Heaven—He already did. What fueled their hope in the hardest of times was that one day God would rule on Earth; that He would forever remove sin, death, suffering, poverty, and heartache. They believed the Messiah would come to Earth, and in doing so bring Heaven to Earth. The Messiah would make God's will be done on Earth as it is in Heaven.[1]

Randy Alcorn, *50 Days of Heaven*

Let's recap where we're at on the prophetic timeline. The Day of the Lord will have reached its climactic conclusion on day 2,520 of the tribulation, or the final day—designated as the Day of Christ.[2] The remaining third of the Jews whom the Antichrist has not yet slaughtered will either be safely tucked away in protective hiding in the wilderness (Revelation 12:14), or will be embattled in Jerusalem and under assault by the armies hailing from all the nations of the world (Isaiah 29:5-8; 31:4-5; Zechariah 14:1-2). The Jewish people will be facing their darkest hour, for the total extermination of

Jerusalem's Jewish population will appear imminent. As the cries from the siege clash all about them, Satan and his Antichrist will start to believe they can halt the return of the King, because soon there will be no more Jews in Jerusalem left alive to cry out, "Blessed is He who comes in the name of the LORD!" (Psalm 118:26; Matthew 23:39).

THE GLORIOUS RETURN OF THE KING

The enemy's smugness over his perceived triumph will be short-lived, though, for the Lord has promised to return to Israel and claim His victory—"He who is coming will come and will not tarry" (Hebrews 10:37). The Day of Christ will be a day like no other. Shaking apart the earth with great claps of thunder and earthquakes, storms and tempests, and the scorching flames of a devouring fire, the King of kings will visibly break from out of the clouds accompanied by His redeemed holy ones (read Isaiah 29:5-8; 30:19-20; 35:2; 60:2; Zechariah 12:10; 14:5). The Messiah will return emitting pure and radiant glory, awing all who shade their eyes at His staggering magnificence (Isaiah 63:1; Habakkuk 3:3-4). The suffering Lamb will return as the roaring Lion!

This is no feeble "spiritual earthquake," as those who spiritualize this event claim.[3] Like a meteorite streaking out of the sky, Jesus will land on top of the Mount of Olives with such earthshattering force that the hill splits in two. With epic fury, the long-foretold deliverer—the Lord of Hosts—will charge into battle and fight for Mount Zion in His role as defender and preserver of His city, Jerusalem (Isaiah 31:4-5). Jesus Christ will reveal Himself no longer as an impoverished itinerate rabbi ready to turn the other cheek. No! Christ will arrive in all His glory as the long-awaited deliverer—the King of kings (see Isaiah 33:22; 45:23; Daniel 7:13-14; Micah 4:7; Zechariah 6:13; 14:9). When Jesus comes to claim His dramatic victory by defeating His enemies, He will judge the inhabitants of the earth, and not by blade nor gun, but simply by using the awesome power of His spoken words (see 1 Samuel 2:10; 1 Chronicles 16:33; Nahum 1:5; 2 Thessalonians 2:8).

What a scene! In expounding on Psalm 2, famed pastor and theologian Charles Spurgeon explained:

> While the heathen and their princes are plotting and planning how to break His bands asunder, and cast His cords from them, He has already defeated their devices, and He says to them, "Yet have I set my king upon my holy hill of Zion."[4]

Upon being rescued by their Messiah, the Jewish survivors will, as prophesied, weep and mourn over the One "whom they pierced" (Zechariah 12:10). Having been rescued through the fires of judgment, Israel's survivors will turn their hearts to Yeshua Hamashiach by lifting the banner of the "Root of Jesse" and proclaiming Jesus as King, a prophecy at long last realized (Isaiah 11:10).[5]

THE ANTICHRIST DEFEATED

As Christ's second coming victory continues to unfold, there will remain the Antichrist and his demonic forces with which to contend. The apostle Paul, in 2 Thessalonians 2, designated this villainous world ruler with four different titles: "the man of sin," "the son of perdition," "the lawless one," and a title most pertinent to the story of the return of the King—"the son of destruction."[6] The defeat of Satan and the Antichrist has long been foretold, and so is well assured.[7] We can have confidence that Satan's inevitable demise is indeed coming.

Jesus Christ will "strike the earth with the rod of His mouth, and with the breath of His lips He shall slay the wicked" (Isaiah 11:4). With just a few mere words spoken from out of the mouth of the

Almighty, the Antichrist's evil armies will melt like wax before Him. Their blood will fill the Valley of Jezreel (Armageddon) as high as a "horses' bridle" for 184 miles, and the carrion birds will rip apart their flesh (Revelation 14:20; 19:21). Millions to one, and Jesus merely speaks, and His vile enemies will melt before him!

The apostle John explained that at this point in the battle of Armageddon, the Antichrist will be captured, along with his false prophet, who worked lying signs in his presence. Having the blood of millions of martyrs on their hands, they will be justly cast alive into the lake of fire to burn for their grievous sins forever and ever and ever (Revelation 19:20). Thus, as Paul described, "Then the lawless one will be revealed, whom the Lord will consume with the breath of His mouth and destroy with the brightness of His coming" (2 Thessalonians 2:8). The final judgment of the ultimate, terminal ruler over human government, along with all who will slavishly revel in his debauchery and gleefully engage in persecuting Christ's followers, will confirm the tribulation saints' belief that their faith has at last been vindicated. The demonstration of God's justice through the punishment of our accursed enemies also provides Christians today with comfort and surety of our salvation.[8]

THE DEMONIC FORCES DEFEATED

Next, King Jesus will deal swiftly with Satan and his demonic forces. John saw an angel come down out of heaven, holding the key to the bottomless pit and a great chain in his hand. The angel laid "hold of the dragon, that serpent of old, who is the Devil and Satan," bound him securely within the chain's unbreakable links, and then cast Satan into the bottomless pit to fall raging for 1,000 years (Isaiah 24:21-22; Revelation 20:1-3). (The reason Satan will be banished for only 1,000 years and the matter of Satan's final fate will be addressed in detail in a later chapter.)

What about the fate of Satan's demonic minions? There's much debate surrounding that topic, for the Bible is silent about when the demons will receive their due punishment. But I believe from the idyllic description of the coming millennial kingdom that I'm about to give you shows the demons can have no place in it. And so, logically, the demons, too, must find themselves consigned to the lake of fire, cast into it immediately after the Antichrist and false prophet.

THE SHEEP-GOAT JUDGMENT

With Christ's enemies—Satan and his demonic forces, as well as the Antichrist and his marauding armies—defeated, the newly returned King of kings will turn His scepter of judgment toward the Gentile nations. Jesus had warned the world long ago that His judgment of the fallen human governments and their subjects must inevitably come. We can read all about this in Matthew 25:31-46, which is part of Jesus' Olivet Discourse. This event is called the sheep-goat judgment.

The Son of Man: The Judge

Eugene Pond observed that Jesus, in this climactic portion of the Olivet Discourse, "presents in a solemn tone the eternal judgment of men and women by the Son of Man."[9] Christ's claim to the title "Son of Man" is crucial to identifying Himself as Judge. "When the Son of Man comes in His glory, and all the holy angels with Him, then He will sit on the throne of His glory" (Matthew 25:31). And Jesus' frequent use of the personal reference "Son of Man," occurring some 30 times in Matthew's Gospel alone, was also Christ pointing to Daniel 7:13-14 so that He could identify Himself as the future Davidic King prophesied to rule over the entire earth.[10]

In fact, every time Jesus applied the title "Son of Man" to Himself, He was letting it be known that He was the prophesied King who would fulfill Daniel's kingdom prophecy. Jesus was proclaiming Himself to be that very stone from Nebuchadnezzar's dream, the one not cut out by human hands, that will smash the empires of the world and "break in pieces and consume all these kingdoms," and His kingdom "shall stand forever" (Daniel 2:44). The One who bears the title Son of Man is destined to be the very One who is divinely authorized to both judge and reign from Israel over the entire world, and in doing so, fulfill the Davidic covenant.[11]

The Gap Period: The Court Date

Matthew 25:31 also tells us when this judgment will take place—immediately following the glorious return of Jesus Christ. The King will arrive in full regalia accompanied by His mighty angels, who note His divine authority. Needing no coronation, King Jesus will then seat Himself upon His throne of glory. Theologian John Walvoord pointed out that this throne must be the earthly throne of David, for the judgment that He is about to mete out may yet be considered a partial fulfillment of the following prophecy by Jeremiah:[12]

> "Behold, the days are coming," says the LORD, "that I will raise to David a Branch of righteousness, a King shall reign and prosper, and execute judgment and righteousness in the earth" (Jeremiah 23:5).

Remember how Revelation noted 1,260 days from the midpoint to the end of the Tribulation? Well, Daniel also offered a blessing to those who wait until the 1,290th day, and then the 1,335th day. This isn't a scribal error. Rather, these extra days indicate there will be 75 (30 + 45) extra days past the two 1,260-day periods that comprise the tribulation (Daniel 12:11-12). These 75 days will likely serve as a gap period between the tribulation and the millennial kingdom. Jesus will use those days to judge the nations in the sheep-goat judgment.

He will also use the gap time to rebuild a planet devastated by God's wrath and mankind's proclivity to destroy ourselves.

The Survivors: The Defendants

The identity of those who will be put on trial is detailed in Matthew 25:32: "All the nations will be gathered before Him." Those who are to be gathered are the remainder of the world's inhabitants. They are the ones who will, remarkably, manage to have survived all seven of those apocalyptic nightmare years. And yet, considering the severity of God's wrath during the tribulation, which will leave the world teetering on the brink of extinction, the remaining world population could be quite meager. I would be very much surprised if even a few hundred thousand survive to face the sheep-goat judgment.

Anyone who wasn't conscripted into the Antichrist's world army—maybe due to being too feeble or damaged to be of any use to him—will be spread out in caves and spider holes all across the damaged planet. They must be gathered. The identity of the gatherers can be found in the parable of the weeds—God's angels (Matthew 13:36-43, 49-50). Luke describes how these angelic gatherers will perform a type of rapture of those being brought to judgment—they will find themselves suddenly swept up by mighty hands and carried off to court (Luke 17:20-37).

The Valley of Jehoshaphat: The Courtroom

The prophet Joel gave the location of this gathering, stating that the nations would be collected in the "Valley of Jehoshaphat" (Joel 3:2, 12). Various scholars have speculated as to whether this may be the Kidron Valley located next to Jerusalem, or the valley where God brought deliverance to King Jehoshaphat (2 Chronicles 20). Considering that *Jehoshaphat* means "Jehovah judges," more than likely, Joel's reference is a play on words for a currently unknown site that will be located, in the future, in or around Jerusalem. One must bear in mind that Jerusalem's topography will have been greatly altered by the forceful impact of Christ's second coming, so the Jerusalem of that day will likely look quite different on a map than it appears in our day (Zechariah 14:4).

Good Works: The Witnesses

What will happen at this global trial is detailed in Matthew 25:32-33. Once the nations have been gathered, a process of separating will occur. "He will set the sheep on His right hand, but the goats on the left."

Christ will test each person based on their heart's reaction to the conditions that existed during the tribulation.[13] Those on Christ's right—the sheep—will be commended for taking care of Him during His hour of need, even if they had not remembered doing so (Matthew 25:34-36). And those on Christ's left—the goats—will be condemned for not taking care of Him during His hour of need, which they also will not remember doing (Matthew 25:41-45). Jesus will explain that in showing love and mercy to the "least of these," the sheep were doing merciful acts as if they had been personally done for Him.

Bear in mind that Christ isn't presenting a works-based salvation here. Rather, this tells us that good works are evidence of a person's salvation (James 2:26).[14] The test of the sheep-goat judgment will still be a matter of works, but works done as fruit of the Holy Spirit—meaning those who perform them will have already accepted Christ as Savior. Those who didn't do these works were not exhibiting the fruit of the Spirit, for they remained in rebellion against God by willingly taking the mark of the beast and declaring their loyalty to Satan, and so they will be deserving of hell (Revelation 14:9-11; 20:4).

Hades: The Sentence

Matthew also mentioned the destination of those who will be judged in the sheep-goat judgment: "These will go away into everlasting punishment, but the righteous into eternal life" (Matthew 25:46). As Jesus also taught in the parable of the wheat and the tares, only those who are genuinely saved, whether they be Jew or Gentile, will be permitted to enter the kingdom of Christ (see Matthew 13:24-30, 36-43, 47-50; Revelation 14:11; 19:15).[15] So while the sheep are invited with open arms to inherit God's earthly kingdom, the goats will be killed, their souls cast down into Hades, and there, they will endure a millennium of torment before being resurrected to at last face their final judgment (see Luke 16:19-31).[16]

THE RESURRECTION OF THE REDEEMED

The sheep who enter into the kingdom of Christ will not be its only citizens. Let's look at those who are going to be resurrected to also become citizens of the millennial kingdom.

The Bible tells us about several resurrections of those who, in life, were faithful to God. The following resurrections comprise phases within what's called the first resurrection, also known as the resurrection of the redeemed. Jesus, by resurrecting Himself from the dead, became "the firstfruits of those who have fallen asleep" (1 Corinthians 15:20). Christ will be followed by the church-age saints, both dead and alive, in the rapture, which will occur some time before the tribulation (1 Corinthians 15:23). The third phase of the first resurrection will happen during the interlude between the tribulation and the millennial kingdom. This phase will be comprised of those faithful who had been martyred during the tribulation, along with the resurrection of the Old Testament saints (Revelation 20:4; Daniel 12:1-2).

The citizens of Christ's kingdom will therefore consist of four groups of humans: (1) the "sheep" survivors of the tribulation, who will remain in their earthly bodies; then the resurrected (2) redeemed of the church age, (3) tribulation martyrs, and (4) faithful from the

Old Testament. The latter three groups will all be resurrected into their glorified bodies to join the sheep in living and serving as citizens of the millennial kingdom. Thus, the Davidic kingdom will initially be populated solely by those who are saved.

CONTRASTING DIVINE JUDGMENTS

Is Christ's account of the sheep-goat judgment merely meant to be taken as a parable, thus fictional in nature, as those who spiritualize their interpretation of the Bible claim?

While Matthew 25 does contain some of the literary features found in parables, it rather lacks the elements of a typical parabolic story.[17] Commentator A.H. McNeile affirmed this, noting:

> This is not a parable, but a prophetic picture of the Judgment, the only parabolic features being the simile of the sheep and goats in verse 32, and its metaphorical use in verse 33.[18]

Clearly, then, Matthew 25:31-46 serves as a narrative for Jesus in stating His claim to the throne of David, to present the details as to how exactly He will take it, and to reveal who will become His kingdom's citizens.

Could the sheep-goat judgment described in Matthew 25:31-46 be the same judgment described in Revelation 20:11-15, known as the great white throne judgment?

The differences between these two passages becomes quite apparent once a proper comparative exploration is made. First, there's the matter of who will be judged. The sheep-goat judgment will include both the redeemed and unredeemed from those living, so it cannot be the final great white throne judgment, which will include only the resurrected and unredeemed dead.[19]

Second, there's the matter of where one will be judged. When contrasting their locations, we find the sheep-goat judgment will be held on the earth, whereas the great white throne judgment will be held in a mysterious place where "the earth and the heaven fled away" (Revelation 20:11).

Third, there's the matter of how one will be judged. In Matthew 25, Jesus' criterion for judgment will involve whether a person demonstrated the spiritual fruit of salvation. But in Revelation's account, the basis for judgment will rest on whether or not the person's name was found written in the Lamb's book of life.

Fourth, there's the matter of where one will be sentenced. Those who are tried in the sheep-goat judgment will either be sent to Hades (the goats) or live on into Christ's kingdom on earth (the sheep). With the great white throne judgment, the fate of the condemned will be banishment to the lake of fire.

Therefore, we can only conclude that the evidence overwhelmingly supports the sheep-goat judgment as occurring before Christ's earthly kingdom is initiated. In contrast, the great white throne judgment will occur after the millennial kingdom has ended.[20] (We will further explore the great white throne judgment in an upcoming chapter.)

THE IMPORTANT TAKEAWAY

The most important takeaway from our look at the sheep-goat judgment is the amazing realization that every single person entering the millennial kingdom is going to be saved. With this truth held firmly in our minds, let's move on to our next chapter, which will explore what Louis Armstrong sang so cheerfully about in "What a Wonderful World."

There, we are going to get a glimpse into how joyous life will be when there are no more fallen and failed human governments bringing about so much misery and suffering to the world. Instead, we're going to explore what everyday life will be like living under the rule of our divine King and serving together as a purified citizenry. If you know Jesus as your Savior, then what you are about to read is a look into your future life. So let's go and explore your future!

CHAPTER 7

THE MESSIAH'S GOVERNMENT: THE CHARACTER OF HIS REIGN

To me it is evident beyond all contradiction that according to the whole run of Scripture the kingdom of Christ is to extend over all parts of the earth, and over all races and conditions of men.[1]

Charles H. Spurgeon, *Christ in the Old Testament*

We've reached the point on the biblical timeline when God's wrath poured out during the tribulation will at last have been exhausted. Jesus Christ has returned in all His glory. Evil has been defeated and God's enemies banished. The remnants have been judged so that only the righteous remain. And every one of the long-slumbering saints have been resurrected from the dead and given their eternal, glorified bodies. Most impressively, the Messiah accomplished all this in just 75 days!

The returned King's title of *Messiah*, which in the Hebrew of the

Jewish Tanakh is *Mashiach* (משיח, pronounced *maw-shee'-akh*) and in Greek is *Christos* (transliterated as "Christ"), means "the Anointed One."[2] This title is both unique and extremely rare in ancient literature. It was used exclusively for a king who also served in other official roles, such as an anointed priest, an ordained prophet, and who alone could speak on God's behalf. Only the Messiah is worthy to fulfill such a multifaceted role (Revelation 5:9). Jesus the Messiah stands alone as the only One worthy of executing these three divinely appointed offices.

Alas, the prophetic timeline shows us that it is now time for the King of kings to begin reigning over the entire earth. *What exactly, then, are the attributes that will define the Messiah's reign?*

THE POSTAPOCALYPTIC CONDITION OF THE EARTH

Let's take a moment to consider the horrific condition the world will be in when the King inherits His kingdom. I wouldn't be engaging in hyperbole by claiming the earth will have become the nightmare fuel no postapocalyptic movie could ever match.

In our last chapter, we left the Messiah standing in all His victory atop the embattled, smoking wreckage of Jerusalem. With merely a spoken word, Jesus Christ—in righteous justice—had slayed His nefarious enemies. Their corpses lie rotting by the millions across the polluted, irradiated landscape. Among the animals that managed to evade extinction due to the carnage of the tribulation are the carrion birds who feast greedily upon the decaying flesh of the vanquished.

For seven years, a degenerate humanity, unbound by God's restraining influence, will unleash the horrors of their depraved hearts and prey upon each other. The result is the earth will have been laid waste, and by all accounts, likewise resemble a decaying corpse. Nuclear fallout, coupled with the 21 cataclysmic judgments poured out from heaven, will have left our dear home planet teetering on the brink of extermination and barely able to sustain life. For "unless the Lord had shortened those days, no flesh would be saved; but for the elect's sake, whom He chose, He shortened the days" by graciously bringing His wrath to an end (Mark 13:20).

Both the demonic and human governments that failed so miserably will, at last, be no more. Not a single solitary governmental organization will be left to plan any reconstruction efforts. And rebuild with what? There won't be any money or resources available. Nebuchadnezzar's statue will indeed have been obliterated by the stone not cut out by human hands (Daniel 2:34), the winds will have blown the dust away (verse 35), and the entire world will lay in seemingly hopeless ruins. Earth, to some extent, will almost resemble Mars—an uninhabitable, nearly dead world hurtling around the sun.

But, like a painter who has been presented with a blank canvas, the time will come for that stone to fill the entire earth and rebuild it as the kingdom of Christ. Only the Anointed One possesses the divine power to restore the earth to its pristine condition. Only the Great Architect of the cosmos can transform a dying world into a thriving ecosystem. In addition to the characteristics that accompany the Messiah's super-unique roles as prophet, priest, and king, our Lord possesses the awesome power needed to bring life back to a nearly dead planet.

THE ASSURANCE OF HIS RULERSHIP

In Scripture, Jesus also assures us of His inevitable rulership over that resurrected world. We can know with surety that a primary characteristic of the Messiah's reign is its inevitability.

Assured in the Psalms

To better understand this characteristic of inevitability, let's look to the Psalms.

Charles Spurgeon noted that when one reads Psalm 2, the reader has at last come into the "clear light of prophecy" concerning the "kingdom of our blessed Master."[3] We have the Father's assurance that, as Spurgeon explained, "the kingdoms of the earth, and the earth itself, are Christ's inheritance…and the utmost bounds of the world are to be His possession" (Psalm 2:7-9).[4]

Concerning Christ's inheritance, we learn that the sacrificial death and resurrection of the Son of God earned Him the authority to rule the earth, though Jesus didn't claim His inheritance during His first coming.[5] In commenting on such a steep payment, theologian Mark Heinemann noted, "Instead of sparing Jesus' single life, God purchased through Jesus' death a glorious resurrection to new life for all who trust in Him."[6] When Christ returns in victory, He will at last claim His possession—both land and people.

Now let's look at Psalm 22. The theme of this psalm is the self-sacrifice of the Intermediator who is assured a kingdom for both He and His faithful subjects. This psalm is a favorite among Jews everywhere due to the classical rabbinic commentary, the *Midrash Tehillim*, which is read as Esther's Prayer during the Jewish rituals celebrating Purim.[7] Christianity also highly regards Psalm 22 as the very prayer Jesus Christ recited as He suffered on the cross.

Psalm 22 is extraordinary in its revelation of the messianic character. God had inspired its author, David, to write in such a way that certain aspects of the crucifixion were clearly prefigured.[8] David didn't write only about his human sufferings; rather, he served as a vessel uttering the very words Jesus Christ would speak on the cross an incredible thousand years later.

Psalm 22 also recognizes that after suffering comes victory. As promised, the Father delivered the Afflicted One, and someday, the nations of the world will come to worship the Messiah because "the kingdom is the LORD's, and He rules over the nations" (Psalm 22:27-28). In celebrating this trial swallowed up by triumph, we receive this emphatic declaration in verse 31: "He has done this."[9] Psalm 22 ends with a glorious crescendo, assuring that Christ's great deliverance will be universal to all the generations yet to come who will hear of our Lord's victory and rejoice in the inevitability of the Messiah's kingship.[10]

Assured in the Major Prophets

The assurance of Christ physically ruling and reigning over this earth was reinforced not only by the psalmists, but also by the Old Testament major prophets.[11] For example, Isaiah prophesied that the "house of the God of Jacob" would be established "on the top of the mountains," and there the Messiah would sit "upon the throne of David and over His kingdom," for "the LORD of hosts will reign" (Isaiah 2:1-4; 9:6-7; 24:21-23; see also 11:3-9).

Likewise, Jeremiah foretold of the day when "a King shall reign and prosper" (23:5). It is He who will serve in the trinity of divinely appointed offices.

> Thus says the LORD: "David shall never lack a man to sit on the throne of the house of Israel; nor shall the priests the Levites, lack a man to offer burnt offerings before Me" (Jeremiah 33:17-18; see also Jeremiah 33:6-16).

Ezekiel, too, foresaw the day when Yahweh would regather the Jewish remnant from the wilderness to refine and rule over them. In doing so, the Gentile nations would also learn that there is a God.

> David My servant shall be king over them, and they shall all have one shepherd; they shall also walk in My judgments and observe My statutes, and do them (Ezekiel 37:24; see also Ezekiel 20:33-44; 37:25-28; 39:21-29; 43:7).

Daniel also foresaw the Son of Man, whom he equated with the Ancient of Days, being given dominion and glory and an everlasting kingdom. It's a kingdom where, most assuredly, "all dominions shall obey and serve Him" (Daniel 7:27; see also verses 13-14, 18).

Assured in the Minor Prophets

The Old Testament minor prophets also assured us of the coming era when God's faithful would "seek the LORD their God and David their king" (Hosea 3:4-5). Many of the minor prophets foresaw a reality where the Lord dwells personally from Zion after He has overthrown the Gentile kingdoms (Joel 3:14-17, 21; Micah 4:1-7; Zephaniah 3:14-20; Haggai 2:20-23). Zechariah wrote with great certainty that "the LORD shall be King over all the earth" (Zechariah 14:9; see also Zechariah 2:10-13; 6:12-13; 8:2-3; 9:10; 14:1-8).

Assured in the Gospels

Not only was the assurance of a physical rule by the Davidic King over the entire earth made in the Old Testament, but in the New Testament, Jesus Himself also proclaimed His inevitable earthly reign. Theologian K.R. Harriman identified this kingdom connection that bridges the Old and New Testaments: "As Jesus sits on the Mount of Olives to teach, He also sits before a great mountain range of prophetic tradition."[12]

Jesus spoke quite often about His coming kingdom. From the beginning of Christ's ministry to its end at the ascension, kingdom language was threaded throughout His teachings.[13] Jesus often promised, "To him who overcomes I will grant to sit with Me on My throne, as I also overcame and sat down with My Father on His throne" (Revelation 3:21; see also Matthew 19:28; 25:31; Acts 1:3-6; and Revelation 2:26-27). Jesus also taught in many parables and by direct word that we are to "seek first the kingdom of God" (Matthew 6:33; see also Matthew 5:3, 10), that the Father's pleasure is "to give you the kingdom" (Luke 12:32), and that as His followers we are to expectantly pray, "Your kingdom come" (Matthew 6:10).

Jesus even gave to some of His apostles, such as John, a firsthand glimpse of that earthly kingdom (Revelation 21:1-3). Christ assured the apostles at His ascension that the season would come when the Father would put into place the Son's authority over all the world (Acts 1:6-8). Jesus even proclaimed the coming kingdom before the local Roman authority who ruled at that time—Pontius Pilate (Matthew 27:11; Mark 15:2; Luke 23:3; John 18:37).

Assured by the Apostles

Kingdom teaching was not just an essential part of the preaching message of Jesus, but of His apostles as well.[14] In his sermon on the portico of Solomon, Peter revealed that Jesus would remain in heaven "until the times of restoration of all things" (Acts 3:20-21). Likewise, Paul looked expectantly for "that Day" when the Lord would return to take up His throne and allow the faithful to reign with Him (2 Thessalonians 1:7-10: see also 2 Timothy 2:12). John added to the chorus of Christ's disciples who foresaw a day when a "Child" on whose thigh was emblazoned "King of kings and Lord of lords" would return in great glory to "rule [all nations] with a rod of iron" (Revelation 12:5; 19:15-16; see also Revelation 20:4, 6).

Assured by the Angels

In the New Testament, we read how the assurance of the inevitability of the kingdom of Christ was also reinforced by the angels. For example, when the angel Gabriel delivered his message to the virgin Mary, he made eight promises concerning her son. So far, five have been fulfilled in history, while these three remain to be fulfilled: (1) Jesus will be given the throne of His father David, (2) He will reign over the house of Jacob forever, and (3) His earthly kingdom will be made manifest (Luke 1:26-38).[15]

In heaven, the four living creatures and the 24 elders sing again and again about the day when the Worthy Lamb will take up His kingdom and allow His saints to rule and reign with Him (Revelation 5:9-10). The other angels chime in with, "The kingdoms of this world have become the kingdoms of our Lord and of His Christ, and He shall reign forever and ever!" (Revelation 11:15).

Assured by the Future Saints

Even the tribulation martyrs assured us of the inevitability of the kingdom. They are recorded as praising the worthy Son and proclaiming the day when "all nations shall come and worship before You" (Revelation 15:3-4).

The Bible is replete with the Davidic King's assurances of His inevitable rulership. On this promise rests solidly all the other characteristics of the millennial kingdom that we will now learn about.

A KINGDOM THAT CAN NEVER BE DESTROYED

Another of the prevailing characteristics of the kingdom of Christ is that once it is established, it can never—ever, ever—be destroyed.

Looking again at Nebuchadnezzar's dream in Daniel 2, Daniel clearly prophesied that when the God of heaven sets up His kingdom, it will never be destroyed, neither will it be left to other people, and it will stand forever. Biblical linguist Kenneth Barker even noted that this passage concerning "the kingdom of our Lord and of His Christ" stands out as the central focus of all biblical theology, for the messianic stone will be established on the ashes of failed human governments as an unconquerable empire.[16]

Again, in another of Daniel's prophecies, God's messenger saw "One like the Son of Man, coming with the clouds of heaven," and to Him was given "an everlasting dominion, which shall not pass away, and His kingdom the one which shall not be destroyed" (Daniel 7:13-14). This Son of God is also the great Son of David, and in being

David's heir, He has the right to claim His inheritance consisting of a universal and everlasting dominion that can never be destroyed.[17]

Now turn to Daniel chapter 9. Let's look at the last three of the six messianic promises contained within Daniel's seventieth-week prophecy that pertain to the millennial kingdom: (1) to bring in everlasting righteousness, (2) to seal up vision and prophecy, and (3) to anoint the Most Holy place.[18] While Christ first came to the earth to make it possible for the souls of the lost to be redeemed, we learn from this prophet of old that once the Davidic King returns, He will fulfill the remaining prophecies concerning the establishment of His unassailable and everlasting reign.

THE RIGHTEOUS CHARACTER OF THE KING

If a kingdom bears the reflection of the one or ones who rule over it, then the kingdom of Christ certainly emulates the divinity of its Davidic King. The book of Isaiah especially does great justice in describing the righteous character of its monarch:

> Unto us a Child is born, unto us a Son is given; and the government will be upon His shoulder. And His name will be called Wonderful, Counselor, Mighty God, Everlasting Father, Prince of Peace. Of the increase of His government and peace there will be no end, upon the throne of David and over His kingdom, to order it and establish it with judgment and justice from that time forward, even forever. The zeal of the LORD of hosts will perform this (Isaiah 9:6-7).

In this passage, the Son of God is identified as the ultimate head over all government during His kingdom reign. He will utter wonderful and consoling words to His subjects. As the Son rules righteously from the throne of David, His awesome power will ensure a peaceful regime. Such universal world peace presupposes a universal recognition of God and willful subjection to His judgment.[19] But for those who choose to disobey His moral law, Christ will bring about swift judgment, but all in perfect justice, for He will rule with great zeal and attention over His hosts.

In commenting on Isaiah 9, Martin Luther concluded that when righteousness defines such a kingdom it will naturally conquer what he calls the three tyrants: (1) sin, (2) death, and (3) the devil.[20] Luther elaborated: "The rule of sin is broken. The yoke of death is destroyed. The law which condemns has been subdued."[21]

We learn a whole lot about the righteous character of the King and kingdom from reading Isaiah 11:

> There shall come forth a Rod from the stem of Jesse, and a Branch shall grow out of his roots. The Spirit of the Lord shall rest upon Him, the Spirit of wisdom and understanding, the Spirit of counsel and might, the Spirit of knowledge and of the fear of the Lord. His delight is in the fear of the Lord, and He shall not judge by the sight of His eyes, nor decide by the hearing of His ears; but with righteousness He shall judge the poor, and decide with equity for the meek of the earth; He shall strike the earth with the rod of His mouth, and with the breath of His lips He shall slay the wicked. Righteousness shall be the belt of His loins, and faithfulness the belt of His waist...And in that day there shall be a Root of Jesse, who shall stand as a banner to the people; for the Gentiles shall seek Him, and His resting place shall be glorious (verses 1-5, 10).

In this passage, the righteous ruler is described puzzlingly as both "a Rod from the stem of Jesse" as well as "a Root of Jesse." How can the King be at the same time both a progenitor and a descendant? Orthodox Judaism has traditionally interpreted this twofold designation as indicating the postexilic Jewish community. But this interpretation misses the messianic significance embedded within Isaiah's description. The passage, not only in purposefully identifying an individual king of human descent born out of the line of David's father, Jesse, but by virtue of its context, notes that the king would also be the progenitor of Jesse. In giving us this supposed conundrum, Isaiah wanted us to understand that this righteous ruler can only be the prophesied Davidic King, for while a man, He also hails from divine and ancient origins.[22]

In reading about the righteous character of the King in Isaiah 11, expositor Richard Brand beautifully likened Isaiah's portrayal of the coming of the Holiness of God as if He was "floating airily into one's room on a springtime breeze to the sounds of the lovely stringed music of Vivaldi."[23] The "Branch" will possess three specific pairs of these beautiful gifts, which are identified as (1) wisdom and understanding, (2) the Spirit of counsel and might, and (3) the Spirit of knowledge and the fear of the Lord.[24] Brand explained that according to the first pair, the King will possess the practical acumen required to arbitrate political and judicial affairs; according to the second pair, He will possess the qualities for advancing diplomatic negotiations and consolidating military authority; and according to the third pair, He will validate the piety of the ideal king, thereby confirming His status as God's instrument.[25]

Godly wisdom, divine counsel, and perfect righteousness—does that sound like the leaders of our governments today? No wonder commentators have described Isaiah's messianic passage as "brimming with imagery that has shaped the imaginations of Jews and Christians for centuries."[26] For, as Brand so aptly exclaimed, "All of us will be living together in a harmonious whole. This will be the place where all creation lives in peace."[27]

A REIGN DEFINED BY JUSTICE AND TRUTH

Other defining characteristics of the Davidic King's reign include perfect justice and absolute truth. Let's look again at the writings of Isaiah and Micah. These two prophets echoed each other's prophecy declaring that the King will serve as both lawgiver and judge:

> Out of Zion the law shall go forth, and the word of the LORD from Jerusalem. He shall judge between many peoples, and rebuke strong nations afar off (Micah 4:1-3; see also Isaiah 2:2-4).[28]

Both Micah and Isaiah shared a powerful vision of a future that will stand in stark contrast to humanity's distasteful experience with failed governments, leaving the righteous longing for the coming day when King Jesus will at last change the world.[29] Mount Zion will become the Supreme Court of the world. And the Davidic King will rule as suzerain over all the nations, for He alone will hold all legitimate power to govern and judge (see also Psalms 2; 47; 82; 95; 96; 98; 99).[30]

Isaiah compelled his readers to

> look upon Zion, the city of our appointed feasts; your eyes will see Jerusalem, a quiet home...there the majestic LORD will be...(For the LORD is our Judge, the LORD is our Lawgiver, the LORD is our King; He will save us) (Isaiah 33:20-22).

A judge is usually perceived as one who brings condemnation to the guilty, but during the millennial kingdom, Christ's presence will be welcomed as Savior.

Isaiah also proclaimed the Davidic King's tireless passion for justice:

> He will bring forth justice for truth. He will not fail nor be discouraged, till He has established justice in the earth; and the coastlands shall wait for His law (Isaiah 42:3-4).

Jesus recited this passage to the multitudes whom He was teaching in Matthew 12 (see verses 18-21). He did so to reveal Himself as this prophesied divine Lawgiver. Therefore, when reading Isaiah 42, we can feel assured interpreting this passage with Christ in mind because it is irrevocably stamped with Matthew's canonical recitation of it.[31] We can take away three main reflections from Christ's teachings in Matthew 12: (1) His compassionate miracles, (2) His silence imposed on the cured, and (3) His withdrawal from the plotting Pharisees.[32] Jesus modeled justice tempered by gentleness and restraint, with a policy toward the weak and vulnerable, and He did so in an extraordinarily merciful, tender, and evenhanded way.[33] The life of Christ was meant to provide us with a template for what our lives will be like when we are truly living in truth and justice, just as we will be during the millennial kingdom.

CHARACTERIZED BY THE EXALTED KING

Isaiah also pointed out that those who will one day stand in the millennial court of the Lord will exhibit the same awestruck wonder as those who once stood before the exalted courts of King Solomon:

> Behold, My Servant shall deal prudently; He shall be exalted and extolled and be very high...Kings shall shut their mouths at Him (Isaiah 52:13, 15).

And yet, as Wycliffe Bible translator Kenneth Litwak noticed, "The Servant's exaltation is without precedent."[34]

Isaiah wasn't merely prophesying Judah's remnant one day returning home from Babylonian captivity under Cyrus; rather, God was presenting something greater in mind: an ultimate deliverance from the Lord—one that He will bring about through the mysterious character known only as "My Servant."[35] The suffering of My Servant had made Him worthy of such great exaltation, a glory prescribed only to God.

Remember that during Jesus Christ's earthly ministry, He was looked upon as homely, weak, and an outlier. Other than His ride into Jerusalem on Palm Sunday, Jesus rarely received His due exaltation by the masses. And yet, due to My Servant's selfless actions in bringing salvation to humanity, the citizens of the millennial kingdom will equate Christ as being one truly worthy of receiving the same glory as the God of the universe. Those who appear before the Servant's courts will simply marvel at this transformation. We will wonder open-mouthed, amazed by Christ's gracious and divine justice, and will exalt Him with all the praise due such a righteous liege.

RULED OVER BY AN OMNISCIENT LIEGE

Another reason we will gaze in wonder at the righteous Judge is because He can read the thoughts of those who stand before Him in His courts.

> I know their works and their thoughts. It shall be that I will gather all nations and tongues; and they shall come and see My glory (Isaiah 66:18).

This passage resides in the section of Isaiah 49–55 that includes poems about both the future Servant who will mete out justice to the nations (42:1-9; 49:1-7; 50:4-11; 52:13–53:12) and the fact that during His future reign, every knee will bow before Him (45:20-25; 49:26; 52:7-10).[36] There will be children born to the tribulation saints, potentially billions of them, and at times, they will fall into sin due to their fallen nature. And when they find themselves accused before the Judge, their wicked thoughts will be laid bare by the King's uncanny ability to read their minds so that their very thoughts will bear witness against them. But those who have been forgiven by the shed blood of the Suffering Servant and are saved will, much like a child accepting discipline from their loving parent, receive their fitting temporary punishment, and can still look forward to inheriting the untold wonders that await them in a new creation after the millennium has passed (Isaiah 60–62).

THE WONDERS OF DIVINE JUSTICE

Isaiah wasn't the only prophet who proclaimed the wonders of the divine justice that will define the millennial kingdom. Zechariah also had much to say. He emphatically declared, "The LORD is one, and His name one" (Zechariah 14:9).

We learn in Zechariah 14 that the Lord will come in all His majesty to reign in Jerusalem, not only as a divine warrior, but also as a just judge who will purify the nations in the same way He will do with Israel.[37] Theologian Paul Tarazi noted that this passage falls into the genre of apocalyptic literary "especially devised to express the direct intervention of God to realize fully His reign of justice within the confines of His people."[38] Because this passage is portrayed as God's ultimate intervention, the Lord is spoken of as implementing His kingship over all creation. Therefore, this conquering hero can only be equated with God Himself, as Zechariah meant for us to understand.

The Davidic King will exhibit the divine justice of Father God, for the two are the same (John 10:30). When Jesus stunned His audience with this truth during His earthly ministry, the enraged people were ready to stone Him to death for equating Himself with Yahweh. But upon Christ's return, people will know fully well that the

Father, Son, and Holy Spirit are all God, and so will bow in amazement before the Just Judge.

LET US REVIEW

Let's summarize the attributes that will characterize the Messiah's coming reign. The Messiah will fulfill the unique role of prophet, priest, and king. He will wield such amazing divine power that He can destroy a planet but then promptly restore it back to life again. His coming reign is assured repeatedly throughout the Scriptures. His kingdom can never ever be destroyed. As King, He will rule in perfect righteousness, truth, and justice. As the omniscient Judge, He can read the minds and hearts of everyone, and so knows their motives. And His subjects will stand amazed by His sacrificial love and mercy, and so will rightly exalt their Savior.

All these attributes characterize the reign of an absolute and divine ruler who epitomizes perfect truth, righteousness, and justice. So I say, "Bring it on!"

CHAPTER 8

THE WORLD KNOWS THE LORD: THE CHARACTER OF ITS CITIZENS

No longer will every country on earth be permeated with criminal activities. No longer will Israel be criminally targeted for destruction by Hamas or any other group. Righteousness will prevail everywhere.[1]

RON RHODES, *Israel on High Alert*

We learned that the divine sovereign who will rule over the millennial kingdom is characterized by His perfection. Now let's look at what the Bible has to say about the character of the kingdom's citizens. Scripture characterizes them with three attributes: (1) as imbued with personal knowledge of their king, (2) they communally join together in His worship and adoration, and (3) they praise rather than revile His majestic name. Let's look at each attribute in more detail.

THE FOUNDATIONAL CHARACTERISTIC

It's important to understand that the singular, foundational characteristic on which these three attributes rest is the fact that all who enter the millennial era will be saved. All of them! Those who had placed their faith in Christ after the rapture, survived the tribulation, and passed through the sheep-goat judgment will enter the kingdom in their earthly bodies. Likewise, the resurrected faithful from all of human history will enter the kingdom in their glorified bodies. The mortal will dwell with the immortal. And this is key: Every citizen will have been saved by grace through faith in Christ Jesus, thanks to His atoning sacrifice on the cross and victory over death. Salvation will characterize the kingdom's citizens (at least in the initial years—more on that in a later chapter).

The fact the kingdom's citizens will be pure reflects back on the Davidic King's accomplished salvific work. Certainly, no human government can bring about mankind's salvation nor rescue society from all the ills caused by our fallen nature. The prophesied disarmament of the nations and the peace that will naturally follow is a change only God could engineer.[2] The societal characteristics of true strength, wisdom, peace, and community remain completely out of reach of fallen man. Those sadly misguided individuals who today believe such an altruistic society can be brought about by meager human efforts, as theologian Rick Byargeon chided, have climbed the "false hope of another mountain called Babel," for "true unity comes not from our efforts alone, but through the work of God."[3]

WORLDWIDE KNOWLEDGE OF THE LORD

Looking at the first attribute, all the citizens of the kingdom will possess firsthand knowledge of their king.

The central passages that describe this enlightened state are Isaiah 11:9 and Habakkuk 2:14 (see also Numbers 14:21; Psalm 72:19; Isaiah 6:3):

> They shall not hurt nor destroy in all My holy mountain,
> for the earth shall be full of the knowledge of the LORD
> as the waters cover the sea (Isaiah 11:9).

> The earth will be filled with the knowledge of the glory
> of the LORD, as the waters cover the sea (Habakkuk 2:14).

Habakkuk 2 tells the story of how the citizens who enter the Davidic kingdom will recite a riddle against the defeated end-time dictator, taunting their old tormentor who had caused them so much suffering during the Day of the Lord. They will publicly excoriate the deposed despot who had terrorized them for seven long years.[4] Having rejected the ultimate leader of all failed human governments, the tribulation saints will celebrate with great joy and praise the Messiah for His victory over the beast. The citizens will rejoice in this reversal of fortunes, for the strong king had been made weak (Isaiah 14), and the plunderer had been plundered (Habakkuk 2).[5] Much celebration and the praising of Jesus' name will occur during the opening days of Christ's newly established reign.

Scriptural ignorance appears to be on the rise in our day. The name of Jesus Christ is either forgotten or reviled by those living in rebellion against Him. But, as we have learned, the Bible foretells that during the millennial kingdom, every single person on the planet will know Jesus Christ, and personally. We're told that the nations will flow to the King's court year-round so that Jesus can teach them His ways and His subjects can learn to walk in His paths (Isaiah 2:2-4 parallels Micah 4:1-3). These passages demonstrate the universal appeal of God's teachings, as they are for *all* the nations.[6] God's moral law will no longer be given solely to Israel, or to the church only. Rather, during the kingdom, Christ's law will become acceptable to all the nations, for at least initially, every one of its citizens will possess a new heart onto which God's moral law will be written (Jeremiah 31:31-34).

The fact that everyone will know Jesus personally and receive the good news of salvation directly from Him leads me to conclude that in the millennium, there no longer will be any need for mission work and the spreading of the gospel. The Davidic kingdom will commence with the Great Commission having at long last been completed (Matthew 28:19-20; Acts 1:8). Why? Because

> no more shall every man teach his neighbor, and every man his brother, saying, "Know the LORD," for they all shall know Me, from the least of them to the greatest of them (Jeremiah 31:34).

WORLDWIDE PRAISE AND ADORATION OF THE KING

Looking at the second attribute, we see that the citizens of the millennial kingdom will communally join together in the worship and adoration of Jesus Christ. Imagine the entire world worshipping together in one big church service!

The point is made repeatedly throughout Scripture that this aspect of the kingdom is not meant for a mere remnant of believing few who are scattered across the nations, as if engaging in Sunday morning gatherings, but rather, for *all* the people worldwide, who will join in singing God's praises. King David prophesied this global church service:

> All the ends of the world shall remember and turn to the LORD, and all the families of the nations shall worship before You (Psalm 22:27).

In commenting on this passage, theologian Mark Heinemann clarified that though David was truly a great king, to be rescued by an earthly ruler "would not result in the dominion of God over the whole earth," nor would it achieve "the enlistment of posterity for the purpose of proclaiming His righteousness to future generations."[7] No single man or missions organization could ever bring about such universal praise of God. God's redemptive work alone will have achieved this righting of the relationship between God and man.

When it comes to the worship of the King by those outside of Israel, the word "all" is used four times in Psalm 22, making it clear that David was specifically making the point that the praising of God would no longer be reserved for the Jewish people, or only the church, but rather, in that future time, the formerly once-pagan Gentile nations will join with the Jews and together, as one chorus, the entire earth will worship God and God alone. Other psalms build upon the fact the Lord will be exalted by those who were once heathens but during the tribulation will become saved:

> There is a river whose streams shall make glad the city of God, the holy place of the tabernacle of the Most High... Be still, and know that I am God; I will be exalted among the nations, I will be exalted in the earth! (Psalm 46:4, 10).

Many other psalms reiterate the universality of kingdom worship. "To You all flesh will come" (Psalm 65:2). "All the earth shall worship You and sing praises to You; they shall sing praises to Your name" (Psalm 66:4). The land of Israel will not only see the cities of Judah come to worship, but the whole earth will be filled with His glory (Psalms 69:35-36; 72:2-4, 7-11, 16, 19). When all the nations come and worship King Jesus "from the rising of the sun to its going down" (Psalm 113:3), praise for the name of the Lord will be enjoined by both kings and saints (Psalms 102:13-16, 18-22; 138:4-5; 145:10-11).

The book of Isaiah likewise adds to the weight of evidence that worship during the millennial kingdom will be global in scope. People who were formerly afflicted "shall increase their joy in the LORD" once the glory of the Lord has been revealed to them in person (Isaiah 29:18-19; 32:3-4, 15-17; 40:5). The people will long to be claimed by the Lord, even writing His name on their hands (Isaiah 44:3-5 NIV). We are told that every knee will bow before the Lord (Isaiah 45:8, 14, 23-24). Why? Because Jesus provided salvation for all generations (Isaiah 51:3, 5-6, 8). The Lord will call out His redeemed to worship in unity before Him (Isaiah 62:2-3, 12). God declares that He will "gather all nations and tongues; and they shall come and see My glory," and ever praise Him (Isaiah 66:18-19).

Christ will send Jewish messengers to distant lands to declare to the Gentiles God's glory. The children of the tribulation saints will form all new nations, and Jews will be sent to gather these nations to join together on Christ's holy mountain in Jerusalem to worship as one people.[8] No longer will people be divided by race or class, for the entire population will exist as we were always meant to, as one race—the human race. Mankind's long fight against racism and classism will at long last be realized in the millennial kingdom.

Turning to the New Testament, the fact that the whole world will one day be gathered before King Jesus to worship Him is a point made frequently throughout Paul's two letters to the church in Thessalonica (1 Thessalonians 4:13-18; 5:1-11; 2 Thessalonians 1:3-12). Looking at 2 Thessalonians 1:7-10 in particular, Paul declared that when the Lord Jesus is revealed from out of the heavens in great power, God will punish the unbelievers by depriving them of the presence of His majesty. This righteous act of justice will result in Christ being glorified and marveled at by those believers who survive the tribulation and enter His kingdom.[9]

In Paul's letters to the Thessalonians, the biblical concepts of suffering followed by glory provide today's persecuted believers with the ultimate hope. They unveil the purpose and plan for suffering in the Christian life and promise that our current sufferings will ultimately be replaced by the joyous worship of our Deliverer.[10] The kingdom will no longer exist in part, as it currently does under the first three folds of the four kingdoms concept, but in its fullness as the Davidic kingdom, where Christ will remove all suffering and receive the global adoration long due Him.[11]

PRAISING HIS MAJESTIC NEW NAME

Do you remember the third commandment? Moses read from his God-inscribed tablet:

> You shall not take the name of the LORD your God in vain, for the LORD will not hold him guiltless who takes His name in vain (Exodus 20:7).

And yet, the name of our loving Creator has been used as a curse word since Lucifer first rebelled, thereby terribly maligning Yahweh's holy name. You'll notice the world never curses in the name of Buddha or Confucious or Vishnu, and especially not in the name of Allah or risk a violent death. Rather, people from every corner of the globe and in every language continually and vilely curse using the name of Jesus Christ. As tragic as this is, the fact this sin is a global phenomenon demonstrates to me that there must be a God and that His Son's name is indeed Jesus Christ. That people curse in the name of Jesus shows that every person has the truth of His existence embedded in their hearts, a truth made manifest in the general revelation given by the Creator so that no one will be without excuse upon the day when they finally face judgment (Romans 1:18-23).

The name of Jesus may be reviled in our day, but during the millennial kingdom, the Son's name will at last receive the honor due Him by the worldwide populace. The prophet Jeremiah foretold, "Now this is His name by which He will be called: the Lord our righteousness" (Jeremiah 23:6). In the Masoretic Text of the Hebrew Bible, the phrase "the Lord our righteousness" in Hebrew is *Yahweh Tsidkenu.* Theologian Hugo McCord noted that this name signifies a Davidic scion who is as divine as Yahweh, and as a name becomes important as predictive evidence of the deity of Jesus.[12]

During the millennial kingdom, Jesus Christ will become known and praised by this brand-new name—*Yahweh Tsidkenu.* You may want to practice saying the name a little to get the hang of it, for we're going to be saying it for at least 1,000 years.

CHAPTER 9

JERUSALEM THE CAPITAL CITY: THE SEAT OF HIS AUTHORITY

Some have referred to Jerusalem's history as one of tragedy and triumph. What an apt description. The biblical teaching of Jerusalem's future in the short term is bleak indeed. More war and turmoil are inevitable. Her ultimate destiny, however, is secure. It rests in the hands of our sovereign God. Jerusalem will know peace for an extended time and triumph in the end. The religions and politics of the world are on a collision course with God. Nothing can prevent it.[1]

MARK ROBINSON, *Israel My Glory*

Which city will become the new capital of the earth? Let's find out!

THE SEAT OF GLOBAL AUTHORITY

The book of Zechariah identified the specific city the Lord will rule from, which will become the global seat of His authority.

> Therefore thus says the Lord: "I am returning to Jerusalem with mercy; My house shall be built in it," says the Lord of hosts (Zechariah 1:16).

To reiterate His point, the Almighty declared yet again:

> Thus says the Lord: "I will return to Zion, and dwell in the midst of Jerusalem. Jerusalem shall be called the City of Truth, the Mountain of the Lord of hosts, the Holy Mountain" (Zechariah 8:3).

From these two passages, along with many others, we learn exactly where Jesus plans to establish His new government—in Jerusalem. Not in Brussels, Rome, Dubai, nor any of the other great cities of the world; no, Jerusalem alone will become the seat of global authority during the millennial kingdom.

It's no wonder the governments of today keep fighting over who should control Jerusalem. The Vatican lusts for control of Jerusalem. Islam demands their authority over Jerusalem. The United Nations issues resolutions so it can control Jerusalem. All the nations of the world obsess over this comparatively small yet world-famous city.

But why such a fervent obsession over such a seemingly insignificant locale, especially when compared to this era's megalopolises of power, culture, and trade? The reason can only be satanic in origin. Satan knows Scripture, and the Bible reveals that when Jesus Christ returns, He has destined Jerusalem to become His seat of global authority. The dark spiritual forces that wield the true power behind our failed human governments (again, see Ephesians 6:12) crave to possess that which the Lord claims dominion over. These demonic forces covet Jerusalem and yearn to usurp what has rightfully been promised to the Son of God.

Jerusalem is the city where the throne of the Lord will be established.

The prophecies concerning the Davidic King restoring the "tabernacles of David" signify that any claim to the Davidic throne must be made in Jerusalem (Amos 9:11-12; see also Jeremiah 3:17).[2] And, the Davidic throne is not in heaven, but on the earth, in Jerusalem. Jesus, in His Sermon on the Mount, differentiated between God's heavenly throne and His earthly footstool in Jerusalem, calling Jerusalem "the city of the great King" (Matthew 5:35).[3]

The Lord taught through His prophets about the coming age when the Davidic King will dwell in the midst of His people (Zechariah 2:10-11). His people will, in turn, seek out and worship the King. They will even confer with Israel's patriarchs, such as Abraham and Isaac, as they, too, will be making Jerusalem their home (Zechariah 8:20-23; 14:8, 9, 16; Matthew 8:11). Only from Jerusalem will Jesus Christ rule the regathered tribes of Israel and on into "the ends of the earth" (Zechariah 9:1, 10). Jerusalem is set apart as Jesus' chosen earthly home.

The book of Isaiah provides many interesting details concerning Jerusalem's role during the kingdom.[4] From that famed major prophet, we learn that it is from Jerusalem that the Lord will teach His moral law to the peoples of many nations (Isaiah 2:3), for it is there in that Holy City that the Prince of Peace will reign forever on the throne of David (Isaiah 9:6-7). God's faithful Jewish remnant will all gather together to live in that city, and they will make it their home (Isaiah 11:10-11). No longer will the Jews face any more challenges to their claim of ownership from the Gentile nations. The Gentiles from Egypt and Assyria, as well as many other nations far off, will one day begin making their annual pilgrimages to Jerusalem (Isaiah 19:19-25; 66:18-22). Isaiah foretold how these pilgrims will enjoy the King's lavish banquet (Isaiah 25:6). They will be filled with gladness and joyful shouting, and so festive harmonies will be carried upon the winds in Zion (Isaiah 35:10). The people will shout from the rooftops the good news that there, in Jerusalem, the Lord

God omnipotent reigns (Isaiah 40:5; 52:7; 60:1-2). They will praise Him for having forgiven their sins (Isaiah 52:13–53:12).

It has also been foretold in the book of Isaiah that even with the millennial Jerusalem's greatly expanded dimensions, far beyond the meager acreage of today, the city will still not be large enough, for Zion will be so full of people that there will not be enough room for the world's inhabitants to visit all at once (Isaiah 54:1-17; 60:3-17). This amazing level of activity led one commentator to conclude, "Following the Second Coming of Jesus Christ, Israel and Jerusalem will truly be a holy land and a holy city that will be the focal point of all earthly activity (Isaiah 65:18-23)."[5]

JERUSALEM'S NEW NAME

The book of Ezekiel, especially chapters 40–48—nine whole chapters—greatly adds to our knowledge about Jerusalem's role during the millennial kingdom. We learn that not only will Jesus Christ be called by the new name of *Yahweh Tsidkenu*, but also during that time, Jerusalem, meaning the "City of Peace," will forevermore be called *Yahweh Shammah*, meaning "the LORD is there" (Ezekiel 48:35).[6]

The city's change in name is meant to express the Lord's forgiveness of the Jewish people and their restored solidarity with Him. The Jews will forevermore be dedicated to living as God's people and will call to Him alone to be their God. Bible scholar Frank Gaebelein noted, "This [new] name would characterize God's city just as in Hebrew thought any new name gave a new character to its recipient."[7] Theologian Soo Kim interestingly pointed out how the old Jerusalem of Scripture was often referred to as a former wife of Yahweh, but during the kingdom of Christ, the newly named city will have no gender connotation.[8] He reasoned that the city therefore cannot possibly fall into adultery or idolatry, but will retain its holy status because there dwells the very presence of Yahweh incarnate.[9]

How significant that the city of Yahweh Shammah will serve as a gateway for pilgrims to enter into the presence of the Father, for this city exists in duality—with the Son on the earth and the Father in heaven—as access to the Father is reserved to the eternal state.[10] So, while the pilgrims entering the gates of Yahweh Shammah may not see the exact first person of the Trinity, they will see Him through the second person—the Son (John 10:30).

THE HIGHEST MOUNTAIN

The book of Micah provides some very interesting details concerning both Jerusalem's importance and topography during the millennial kingdom.

> Now it shall come to pass in the latter days that the mountain of the LORD's house shall be established on the top of the mountains, and shall be exalted above the hills; and peoples shall flow to it. Many nations shall come and say, "Come, and let us go up to the mountain of the LORD, to the house of the God of Jacob; He will teach us His ways, and we shall walk in His paths." For out of Zion the law shall go forth, and the word of the LORD from Jerusalem. He shall judge between many peoples, and rebuke strong nations afar off (Micah 4:1-3; parallel passage in Isaiah 2:2-4).

Is this prophecy meant to convey that Jerusalem will be raised up to rest upon the highest mountain on the planet? After all the radical changes to the geography due to the massive tribulation-era earthquakes, this well could be the result. Or is this prophecy only meant to be taken metaphorically, in that Zion will become the most significant of mountains because Christ's seat of authority is universally recognized there? Or possibly both?

Those who take the position that there will be a literal change in elevation to the city look to the aforementioned prophecy of a river of people flowing upstream to the mountain of the Lord.[11] The lowly of the earth will find it necessary to climb to the heavenly in the sky. The nations will receive the Lord's teachings not only at the center of an earthly structure built upon a plateau, but by physically climbing to the top of a mountain, where God and man commune together.[12] Zechariah 14:1-9 appears to support a geographical change in elevation, as Jerusalem is cast as "the navel of the world" and "the highest point on earth," and everything outside of Jerusalem is merely level ground that the nations must traverse before they can ascend to speak to the King.[13]

Those who reject the position that there will be a literal change in elevation to the city claim that Isaiah and Micah's prophecies about Zion being elevated above all the other mountains of the world was merely a "traditional way of stressing the supremacy of Yahweh and His royal residency over any divine or political rival."[14] In other words, the prophecy is meant to be taken as an elevation in esteem rather than in height.

As for those who support the position of "both," they explain that today's comparatively insignificant Mount Zion will one day be exalted and rise to a position of dominance over the earth, and that all the nations will stream up to a literal latter-day Everest.[15] Because we are using the golden rule of interpretation in this book, we are guided by a literal rendering of Scripture, and so to me, the arguments for a significant increase in Jerusalem's importance as well as the literal rise in elevation are both compelling.

Further geological changes to the currently landlocked city of Jerusalem are mentioned in Isaiah 33:20-23. This passage notes that one day Jerusalem will become a place flowing with broad rivers and streams. Theologian Harold Holmyard pointed out these passages are in accord with other eschatological prophecies that speak of waterways being produced due to changes in the earth's surface surrounding Jerusalem (Ezekiel 47:1-12; Joel 3:18; Zechariah 14:4-11).[16]

No ships will patrol these waters in defense of the King's city, for though the Mighty One in Jerusalem will be surrounded by great rivers, His awesome power will assure the new Israelis that they need not be concerned with a maritime invasion.[17] The high elevation and surrounding waters will make the city of Yahweh Shammah impregnable so that its inhabitants can enjoy absolute safety. And, from the unassailable and lofty heights of Yahweh Shammah, the Davidic King will render God's verdicts to the nations as they seek out His arbitration and wisdom.[18]

THE HOLY CONDITION

The prophet Isaiah declared that Yahweh Shammah would be known for the city's most holy condition:

> It shall come to pass that he who is left in Zion and remains in Jerusalem will be called holy—everyone who is recorded among the living in Jerusalem (Isaiah 4:3).

Likewise, the prophet Zechariah described in colorful detail the holiness inherent to Yahweh Shammah:

> In that day "holiness to the Lord" shall be engraved on the bells of the horses. The pots in the LORD's house shall be like the bowls before the altar. Yes, every pot in Jerusalem and Judah shall be holiness to the LORD of hosts (Zechariah 14:20-21).

I find it quite mysterious that Zechariah singles out the bells of the horses. In examining Zechariah's passage concerning Jerusalem's future holiness, biblical linguist Albert Wolters titled it the "penultimate verse of the book of Zechariah," not only because it so colorfully describes the holy condition of the city of Yahweh Shammah, but because the passage provides us with a linguistic challenge, for "bells is a translation of mere modern lexicographical consensus," meaning it's a modern-day rendering.[19] Wolters believed there's a better translation of this Persian loanword, one that points to a musical instrument resembling the tambourine, though one used by horses, hence better translated as the "headstall of a bridle."[20] Think of those jingle bells used on a one-horse open sleigh.

Whether jingle bells or bridle, regardless of what these "bells" truly are, the important point Zechariah was making is that even what we would consider the least impressive of everyday items will still be reserved as holy. And not only will the priestly vessels be consecrated to the Lord, but even every pot and bell that's to be found in Jerusalem, from the least to the most important object. They all will become fit to receive sacrificial offerings.[21]

This future sanctification of Jerusalem will even spill over to the city's inhabitants, for Zechariah 14:21 proclaimed, no Canaanite will dwell there. "Canaanite" can be interpreted as a "zealot, merchant, or huckster." The reference is a nod to the Gospels' account of the greedy moneychangers who were selling in the house of the Lord. They had raised Christ's ire, causing Him to accuse the merchants of turning the temple into a "den of thieves," and leading Him to flip over their tables with great zeal (Matthew 21:13; Mark 11:17; Luke 19:46).[22] This degree of purity was unheard of in the Jerusalem of antiquity, and that is true of today, showing this blessed holy condition remains yet future.

THE FEAST OF TABERNACLES

Isaiah prophesied that the institution of the Feast of Tabernacles will expand beyond the Jewish people and become celebrated on a global scale.

> Look upon Zion, the city of our appointed feasts; your eyes will see Jerusalem, a quiet home, a tabernacle that will not be taken down; not one of its stakes will ever be removed, nor will any of its cords be broken. But there the majestic LORD will be (Isaiah 33:20-21).

According to Leviticus 23, seven feasts were appointed to Israel. Christ, all through His earthly ministry, kept every one of these feasts without fail, even celebrating Passover on the night before He was crucified. Believers in Christ now live under the new covenant, and so we are not responsible for keeping these feasts.[23] According to messianic Jewish expert Zola Levitt, the loss of the temple when it was destroyed and the subsequent ending of the daily sacrifices has left the church with little to no understanding of the meanings or importance of these feasts in connecting God to His people.[24] But during the millennial kingdom, the world will well understand and engage in at least one of these ancient feasts—the Feast of Tabernacles.

How has the Feast of Tabernacles been celebrated for the past 3,400 or so years? On the fourteenth of Tishri, according to the Jewish calendar, the Jewish people pour into Jerusalem and stay within a Sabbath day's journey.[25] Then, on the fifteenth day of the seventh month at the seventh full moon of the year, they set up little shelters, called booths, and there they worship God for seven days (Leviticus 23:42-43). According to Jewish tradition, the fifteenth of Tishri is said to be the very day when the pillar of cloud and fire first appeared to Israel, leading them through the wilderness during the exodus and resting on the tabernacle once it was raised among them.[26]

Historian Alfred Edersheim noted that during Jesus' triumphal entry into Jerusalem, palm branches were laid before Him, which happens to be one of the chief ceremonies involved in the Feast of Tabernacles.[27] Tabernacles not only looks back at the time when the Lord had sheltered with His children during their long desert journey to the Promised Land, but it also looks forward to when God will once more come down from the highest heavens and manifest Himself as the Son of David and bring salvation to the world.[28] The Jews symbolize this outpouring by the pouring out of water, which the messianic Jews interpret during this church age as the outpouring of the Holy Spirit, but they also look to the future when the Davidic King will dwell physically in Jerusalem.[29]

Isaiah adds that when the Davidic King once again tabernacles with His people, inhabitants from all nations will stream up the slopes of Mount Zion to likewise tabernacle with their King (Isaiah 2:2). Once they've reached Jerusalem, there, they will "behold, My Servant" who "shall deal prudently; He shall be exalted and extolled and be very high...kings shall shut their mouths at Him" (Isaiah 52:13, 15).

Bible scholar Peter Bynum called Isaiah's vision "a perfectly organic phenomenon" when describing a current of people who will run their "course in harmony with the proper order of things, even as it seems to defy that order by running uphill."[30] He noted that this human flow will run two ways. The nations will stream up to the heights of Zion to meet their King face to face to receive His wisdom and instruction and blessings, then they will rush back down the slopes to refresh and restore the world below.[31] Because the Feast of Tabernacles will be instituted on a global scale, a "torrent of blessings [will be] cascading down from Zion to cleanse and renew the world."[32]

And so the purified citizens of the millennial kingdom will stream up to a purified Yahweh Shammah and tabernacle with their perfect King. And much like the days when Jesus taught the crowds from the hillsides, the citizens of the kingdom will hang on to every word our Lord utters, learning and growing and fellowshipping with their Savior. It'll be a great day for everyone to tabernacle together!

CHAPTER 10

THE ROLE OF KING DAVID: THE SUB-REGENT

David was Israel's greatest king. The nation was at its zenith of power during his reign. The reason that he reigned so long is David administered justice and ensured equity to all his people. That is not found in the rulers of this world today. They are more concerned with getting reelected and fixing it so they remain there. But one greater than David is coming and He not only will reign over Israel, He will rule over all of mankind.[1]

Jack Wellman, pastor of Heritage Evangelical Free Church in Udall, Kansas

Not only has God made kingdom promises to the city of Jerusalem, but He's also destined a special role to that capital's most famed ruler in all of Israel's history—King David. Once David is resurrected, along with the other Old Testament saints upon Christ's glorious return (Daniel 12:1-3), he will have a position to fill during the kingdom of Christ as sub-regent to King Jesus.

Though David's future role happens to be a highly debated subject within Bible prophecy circles, I look to Jeremiah's prophecy for guidance about this matter, which says that during the millennial kingdom, people "shall serve the LORD their God, and David their king, whom I will raise up for them" (Jeremiah 30:9). Likewise, Ezekiel also foresaw the day when

> I will establish one shepherd over them, and he shall feed them—My servant David. He shall feed them and be their shepherd. And I, the LORD, will be their God, and My servant David a prince among them (Ezekiel 34:23-24).

Notice how in each of these prophetic passages, two separate and distinct personages are listed: the Lord God and the servant/prince David.

THOSE WHO DISAGREE

To my surprise, I've found quite a number of commentators who believe the original King David will play no active role during the millennial kingdom. For example, Andrew Steinmann pointed out, and correctly so, that the divine Messiah's identity in the Old Testament is so closely associated with the man David that at times the prophets simply called the promised savior "David" (see Ezekiel 37:24-25; Hosea 3:5).[2] Yet another theologian, Orville Nave, substantiated this biblical association with a list of verses that portray David as a type of Christ not only in the Old Testament (Psalms 2; 16; 18:43; 69:7-9, 20-21, 26, 29; 89:19-37), but in the New Testament as well (Matthew 9:27; 12:23; 15:22; 20:30-31; 21:9; 22:42; Mark 10:47-48; Luke 18:37, 39).[3] Certainly, many of the prophecies concerning David and the messianic kingdom appear to be interchangeable.[4]

And then there's the Jewish point of view. Though numerous rabbis regard, with some nostalgia, David's reign as the golden age of Israel, they still consider David to have been a mere prototype of the coming Messiah. They are instead anticipating the coming of the "great David's greater Son."[5]

Other commentators take the middle-of-the-road approach in this debate. They admit that the prophecies in Jeremiah 30 and Ezekiel 34 differentiate between Christ and David. But they conclude these prophecies don't refer to the actual resurrected David, the son of Jesse. Rather, they argue, the name David must be considered symbolic of a contemporary human king who hails from the Davidic line.[6]

They reason that this David cannot be the actual resurrected King David because he will offer sin offerings for himself (Ezekiel 45:22), and he has sons (Ezekiel 46:16). They say that at the time of David's resurrection along with the other Old Testament saints, he will have been given a glorified and sin-free body, meaning he will no longer sin nor sire children. This rather human condition would then exclude the resurrected King David from being the prophesied millennial David, lending credence to the argument that this David is, in actuality, a mere mortal of modern-day Davidic descent (also see Matthew 22:30; Mark 12:25).

THE PROPHECY OF THE MESSIAH'S GATE

Let's step back from this debate for a moment to get a different perspective. Way back in 1542, when the famed Ottoman sultan Suleiman the Magnificent ruled Jerusalem, he heard about a prophecy that gave him goosebumps. He summoned the scant few rabbis who had remained living in the city and ordered them to tell him all about the following prophecy found in Psalm 24:

> Lift up your heads, O you gates! And be lifted up, you everlasting doors! And the King of glory shall come in.

> Who is this King of glory? The LORD strong and mighty,
> the LORD mighty in battle (Psalm 24:7-10).

The rabbis spooked Suleiman with the fact that one day, Jerusalem's Eastern Gate—the priestly gate that had formerly led up to the temple—would once again welcome the God of Israel.[7] Not wishing that any Jewish Messiah should try to retake what had become an Islamic stronghold, Suleiman ordered that Jerusalem's Eastern Gate be walled up. The troubled sultan then went so far as to place a Muslim cemetery in front of the gate so that no kosher Jews would dare desecrate themselves by passing through the dead and so become ceremonially unclean.[8] Not only could the Jews no longer enter through the Eastern Gate, but Catholics and the Eastern Orthodox who made their pilgrimages to Jerusalem were now prevented from celebrating their ongoing festivals commemorating the recovery of the Holy Cross.

Suleiman must have believed with some satisfaction that he had effectively prevented the Messiah from ever returning. But his efforts did little to discourage Jerusalem's Jewish residents, because Suleiman's actions instead fulfilled part of the Psalm 24 prophecy. The gate had to be sealed before the Messiah returned! The Jews have long given special observance to the Eastern Gate because they yearn for the day when the prophesied King of Glory will blow that blockade away and enter triumphantly into the city to take up His throne, all in fulfillment of Bible prophecy.[9]

A FUNNY LITTLE STORY

With the Eastern Gate prophecy in mind, I believe another prophecy from Ezekiel has cast a shadow on the supposed cut-and-dry conclusion that the resurrected David will play no role during the millennial kingdom. And it ties nicely into the Psalm 24 prophecy concerning the Messiah's point of entry into Jerusalem.

> He brought me back to the outer gate of the sanctuary which faces toward the east, but it was shut. And the Lord said to me, "This gate shall be shut; it shall not be opened, and no man shall enter by it, because the Lord God of Israel has entered by it; therefore it shall be shut. As for the prince, because he is the prince, he may sit in it to eat bread before the Lord; he shall enter by way of the vestibule of the gateway, and go out the same way (Ezekiel 44:1-3).

Remember that according to Psalm 24, the Messiah, upon His return, will blast His way through the closed Eastern Gate, opening it once again, and entering triumphantly into Jerusalem. Notice how in the Ezekiel 44 prophecy a differentiation is made—in verse 3—between the King (*melek*, see also Ezekiel 37:24) and the prince (*nasiy'*), noting two distinct personages.[10] Therefore, this passage must be telling us that during the kingdom age, only the Messiah can come and go through the Eastern Gate. He alone can use it. As for the prince, he may instead use an interior vestibule, which is kind of like a private little side gate, in his comings and goings in his service to the King. Through the Eastern Gate, this prince must not pass, for Yahweh has already entered through it, but the prince is welcome to sit in his little gate and eat lunch with the King.

I've always found this little aside about where the prince will one day eat his lunch to be rather amusing. To think that the Bible has even prophesied where David is going to take his lunch breaks!

THE SUB-REGENT'S RESPONSIBILITIES

We can learn a little bit about the sub-regent's list of responsibilities as described in that great exposition of what life will be like living in Yahweh Shammah during the millennial kingdom—Ezekiel 40–48.

David was given some requirements that essentially describe him as the future mayor of Jerusalem.

First off, the King will insist that his sub-regent must keep his house and holdings at a significant distance away from His own house, which we will learn in the next chapter to be the Millennial Temple, to maintain an order of purity and holiness.

> He said to me, "Son of man, this is the place of My throne and the place of the soles of My feet, where I will dwell in the midst of the children of Israel forever. No more shall the house of Israel defile My holy name, they nor their kings, by their harlotry or with the carcasses of their kings on their high places...Now let them put their harlotry and the carcasses of their kings far away from Me, and I will dwell in their midst forever" (Ezekiel 43:7, 9).

Ezekiel even revealed where David's family's land allotment will be:

> The prince shall have a section on one side and the other of the holy district and the city's property; and bordering on the holy district and the city's property, extending westward on the west side and eastward on the east side, the length shall be side by side with one of the tribal portions, from the west border to the east border (Ezekiel 45:7).

Ezekiel even noted how the King will schedule the occasions as to when the prince can enter and exit the house of God in concert with the visiting people:[11]

> The prince shall then be in their midst. When they go in, he shall go in; and when they go out, he shall go out (Ezekiel 46:10).

This biblical mystery surrounding King David's future role may not be resolved until Christ's kingdom commences. But to me, it seems highly likely that David's role in biblical history is far from over. God still has promises to keep that He had made to David about becoming sub-regent under His Son over Israel during the kingdom age. True, maybe it's one of David's human Jewish descendants who will instead fill this role as mayor of Jerusalem in his service to the eternal Davidic King. But whomever it will be, we will find this prince around noon each day sitting in his little vestibule on the eastern wall of Yahweh Shammah enjoying his lunch.

CHAPTER 11

THE MILLENNIAL TEMPLE: THE HOUSE OF WORSHIP

For almost two millennia, there has been no Temple in Jerusalem. The Jews have attended synagogue services around the world to pray, read the Scriptures, and perform various ceremonies. Yet, deep in their hearts, they have had a longing for the messianic age and another Temple to be built in Jerusalem.[1]

Fred Hartman, *Israel My Glory*

If King Jesus alone may pass through the Eastern Gate (Ezekiel 43:4), then it stands to reason that on the other side of that gate, there must also be a temple. Indeed, so will it be!

THE DIVINE CARPENTER BUILDS THE TEMPLE

Sure enough, Zechariah 6 prophesied that the divine carpenter will be the very one to build His temple:

> Thus says the LORD of hosts, saying: "Behold, the Man whose name is the BRANCH! From His place He shall branch out, and He shall build the temple of the LORD; yes, He shall build the temple of the LORD. He shall bear the glory, and shall sit and rule on His throne; so He shall be a priest on His throne, and the counsel of peace shall be between them both" (Zechariah 6:12-13).

CHRIST IS BUILDING THE CHURCH

Some theologians spiritualize the prophecies concerning Christ building the temple. They conclude that the "temple of the LORD" will not be a physical building, but is a reference to Jesus gathering the body of church-age believers from Pentecost up to the rapture into the "structure" known as the church.

Charles Spurgeon is one of the great theologians who took this position, as revealed in his commentary *Christ in the Old Testament.* He believed the Zechariah 6 prophecy referred to Christ building the church because as the "promised Builder of the spiritual temple, [He] will inhabit and build it in His double character as Priest and King."[2] No mere human carpenter could possibly fulfill this dual role, not even King David or King Solomon. Only the divine Son of Man can act in the capacity as both King and High Priest for His people. The purpose for Christ building the church, Spurgeon pointed out, works toward fulfilling what the Holy Spirit promised in Psalm 66:4—that on that day, "all peoples shall adore their Maker with hearty praise and joyful song."[3]

Others, such as biblical linguist Adam Kubis, concurred with Spurgeon. He noted how Zechariah's prophecy foretelling the future rebuilding of the temple by the messianic King perfectly dovetails with what he calls the Johannine Temple-Christology, whereby the resurrection of Jesus stands as the work of construction that rebuilds the temple bodily through the Messiah-King.[4] Remember when we noted that Jesus drove the moneychangers out of the Second Temple due to His great zeal for the house of Yahweh (John 2:13-22)? Well, others, such as theologian Cecil Roth, claimed Christ went out of His way to do this as a symbolic fulfillment of Zechariah 14, where not only the ordinary domestic utensils in Jerusalem would be consecrated as holy vessels, but also there will be no more "Canaanite" (verse 21), meaning "foreigner," defiling the house of the Lord of Hosts.[5] In cleansing the sanctuary of sacrificial animal traffickers, Jesus presented a symbol of the purified condition of our souls once redemption was made possible, and once we are saved, He then dwells in our hearts. Roth also pointed out that during this act, Jesus had made the first public assertion of His messianic claims that He would construct a better temple than the building He'd just cleansed—one made from His own body—and so usher in the messianic eschatological era.[6]

CHRIST BUILDS THE MILLENNIAL TEMPLE

I believe these theologians' interpretation to be partly correct in that Christ has indeed instituted the church, but incomplete due to their ignoring of Cotton's fourth fold of the kingdom of Christ—the Davidical Kingdom. Remember, our guiding light for interpretation is the golden rule of interpretation, and that requires a literal reading of Scripture, not spiritual.

For example, has the church era seen "all the earth" coming to adore their Maker (Psalm 66:4)? No, clearly not. The majority of the world currently stands in open rebellion against our Creator. The scope of the prophesied activities surrounding the rebuilt temple remains global in scale—a condition that can be met only during the Davidic kingdom.

Other theologians agree that the temple prophecies can find their fulfillment only during the millennial kingdom. For instance, commentator John Taylor contested Spurgeon's symbolic interpretation of the rebuilt temple due to the wealth of details and precise measurements prophesied about the Millennial Temple as recorded in Ezekiel 40–48.[7] Likewise, commentator John Whitcomb also agreed that spiritualizing the prophecies concerning Christ building His temple would leave one's understanding of this momentous event falling short.[8] After all, Ezekiel 40–48 must confirm the future existence of a literal temple because the prophet provided innumerable specifics concerning the building's dimensions, parts, and contents. Whitcomb poignantly added, "The fact that its structure and ceremonies will have a symbolic significance cannot be used as an argument against its literal existence, for the Tabernacle was an actual structure, regardless of the fact of its typical significance."[9]

When it comes to properly understanding the Millennial Temple that Christ will build, the spiritualizers can be countered by three interpretive views.[10] First, a literal prophetic interpretation concedes the detailed blueprints that were given to Ezekiel can only signify an actual physical temple structure. Second, a dispensationalist interpretation sees a literal and future temple, even if those who hold to dispensationalism struggle to reconcile Ezekiel's revelations concerning future temple sacrifices, feast days, and the return of the priesthood. And third, the apocalyptic view focuses on the symbolism, numerical symmetry, and futurism surrounding the temple and so differentiates it from the church.

One would have to spin some pretty nifty interpretive cartwheels to conclude that Ezekiel 40–48 is talking about the church. Only a literal interpretation remains true to the messianic prophecies that fit so perfectly into the millennial era, as if a hand in a glove.

THE BLUEPRINT

As we are engaging in our exploration of the plain-sense meaning of what the Bible has to say about the kingdom of Christ, let's go on a tour of the Millennial Temple by first reading Ezekiel 40–48.[11] A warning: This is no small task, for as Charles Feinberg illuminated, the last nine chapters of this prophecy exist as an "inseparable unit" that forms a "continental divide" in the area of biblical interpretation, making any of our mere human understandings of the Millennial Temple simply "unworthy of the book and the Author behind the text."[12]

Controversies over interpretation aside, the task should not be unsurmountable for us as students of the Bible. As author Adriane Leveen so colorfully noted, "The vision in Ezekiel 40–48 is strangely exhilarating—dramatic, densely detailed, concrete, and visual."[13] Ezekiel ventured to take us along on his tour of the Millennial Temple—not of a resurrected body, but a physical structure, and one described in precise detail. Let's explore!

In chapters 36–39, Ezekiel revealed that a tremendous transformation of the Jewish people is coming. The Jewish exiles would be restored to the land of Israel, and that has been happening right before our eyes over the last 100 years. The nation was miraculously reborn in May of 1948. And Ezekiel foresaw that the peoples of this new nation of Israel would be given a heart for Yahweh and His Son, which we learned will happen by the end of the tribulation.

God gave Ezekiel another climactic vision in his book's final nine chapters, 40–48. An angel shining with the appearance of bronze and carrying a line of flax and a measuring rod approached Ezekiel. The angel then took the prophet on a guided tour of a future version of the city of Jerusalem and the temple within. Chapters 40–42 provide the actual blueprints for this temple of the future.[14] Starting their tour at the Eastern Gate—the gate that historically provided access to the temple complex—the angel painstakingly began taking measurements of the complex's buildings. The well-remembered lines of Solomon's Temple are meant to be brought to mind, but on a much grander scale, patterned on the spacious sanctuaries and fortress walls that the prophet had long dreamed of seeing every day during his exile in Babylon[15] Everything the angel measured was in cubits, from the gateways to the outer and inner courts, to the chambers and vestibules, and to the sanctuary and walls. Upon translating cubits to feet, we realize that the measurements demonstrate that this Millennial Temple will be far, far more massive in scale than any of the three structures that previously stood on the Temple Mount.[16]

Theologian John Bergsma brought up an interesting point. He noted that the 40 times cubits were used in measuring the dimensions of the Millennial Temple (and that's 40 times just in chapter 40 alone), the count always pointed to the number 50.[17] The angel repeatedly explained that the dimensions of this visionary temple consisted of multiples of 25 (half a jubilee) and 50 (a jubilee).[18] This number is significant to the Jewish people, for 50 points to the Israelite institution of the jubilee, known as the year of liberation, meant to be celebrated every 50 years.[19] Because the people of Judah had failed to celebrate 70 consecutive Sabbath rest years every seventh year so that the land could lay fallow and rest, God had them exiled to Babylon for 70 years (Leviticus 25:2-7; 26:34-35, 43). While in exile, Ezekiel received this vision "in the twenty-fifth year of our captivity" (Ezekiel 40:1), on the Day of Atonement midway through a 50-year jubilee cycle. This was meant to suggest to the disheartened exiles that the future restoration of the temple would stand in some sense as Israel's jubilee, when at last the proper worship of Yahweh would provide her true freedom.[20] The Jewish people, having been exiled to a strange land and in great need of hope, would correlate the jubilee buried within the temple measurements to their anticipated year of freedom. In doing so, they would joyfully realize that they had not been forever set apart from God's presence; but rather, they would as a people one day enter into Yahweh's restored house to again be called God's children. With this divine nod to the future and final restoration of Israel to Yahweh God, as Leveen pointed out, "Thus does the book end with a grand and climactic solution to the dilemma with which it began."[21]

RETURN OF THE SHEKINAH GLORY

Earlier in Ezekiel's ministry, the prophet had, with great sorrow, described the shekinah glory of God—the Holy Spirit—abandoning the First Temple and leaving His wayward people behind (Ezekiel 10:18). But the prophet was also granted the blessed opportunity of bringing the exiles the good news that, in the future, once God's people are reconciled to Him, the shekinah glory does plan on returning to the Millennial Temple. Ezekiel actually got to watch the future return of the Holy Spirit as He traveled back through the Eastern Gate, passed through the temple courts, and then resided within the Holy of Holies so as to fill the temple with God's presence once more (Ezekiel 43:1-12; 44:1-8).

Isaiah also described the glorious return of the shekinah glory:

> The Lord will create above every dwelling place of Mount Zion, and above her assemblies, a cloud and smoke by day and the shining of a flaming fire by night. For over all the glory there will be a covering (Isaiah 4:5).

So, too, did Zechariah prophesy Yahweh's Spirit dwelling once more among His people. Zechariah described the shekinah glory as suddenly appearing in the likeness of a divine, flaming wall (Zechariah 2:5). He will arrive at the institution of a global extension of God's reign, coinciding with the King rebuilding and restoring the temple and bringing holiness to the city of Jerusalem (Zechariah 14:9, 21).[22] And God's glory will be seen as all the nations come to worship the King in Jerusalem (Zechariah 14:16-19).

You've likely already made the correlation between the flaming cloud description of the shekinah glory in Ezekiel to the same imagery present during the exodus. Remember that the newly liberated Hebrew slaves were led through the wilderness by "the Lord [who] went before them by day in a pillar of cloud to lead the way, and by night in a pillar of fire to give them light" (Exodus 13:21-22).[23] We tend to think of the Holy Spirit as being present in the hearts of those who are saved, but as an invisible presence. And yet God's Spirit showed up as a pillar of cloud and fire to the Hebrew sojourners, as the thunder and lightning-filled cloud at the giving of God's commandments at Sinai, and as the atonement and transfiguration cloud during Christ's first advent. This same cloud will again surround Christ at His second coming. Wherever the shekinah glory resides, there, too, will be the Almighty's divine presence offering reassurance and comfort in the fact that He has arrived to at last provide for, protect, lead, and guide His children.[24]

TEMPLE SACRIFICES

For those of us now living in this church age, the Old Testament prophets left us with a conundrum. What the Old Testament temples were historically known for was the carrying out of the Mosaic sacrificial system, whereby the blood of the sacrificed animals served as a temporary atonement for the people's sins and foreshadowed the ultimate and perfect sacrifice to come (Leviticus 17:11). Because Jesus Christ provided that ultimate sacrifice on the cross, we now live in an era when mankind receives salvation by God's grace through faith in Christ (Ephesians 2:8). The sacrificial system became no longer necessary as a temporary covering for one's sins requiring endless ongoing sacrifices, for when Christ shed His blood, He permanently atoned for and removed our sins "as far as the east is from the west" (Psalm 103:12; see also Hebrews 9:12-18). After this church age ends, we've established that a massive physical Millennial Temple will be built by the Davidic King, and that it will serve in the dual role as the King's throne room as well as His house of worship. And yet, the prophets prophesied that animal sacrifices are going to return during the Millennial Temple era. How strange and confusing!

Read what the prophet Isaiah revealed about this quite surprising aspect of worship at the Millennial Temple:

> Even them I will bring to My holy mountain, and make them joyful in My house of prayer. Their burnt offerings and their sacrifices will be accepted on My altar; for My house shall be called a house of prayer for all nations (Isaiah 56:7).

If the final atonement for mankind's sins was made possible by Jesus Christ's sacrificial death and resurrection, and the new covenant of grace nullified the Old Testament sacrificial system, then why are there so many verses describing priests making animal sacrifices at the Millennial Temple?[25] With the institution of five official offerings, four of which require bloodletting (Ezekiel 43:13–46:15), were the prophets saying that an animal's blood still must be shed, in addition to Christ own blood already having been shed, so that the citizens of the millennial kingdom can be saved from their sins?

The prophesied return of burnt offerings and sacrifices has caused quite a dilemma for the biblical interpreter of this age. If the passages about the Millennial Temple sacrifices are to be taken literally, and that's exactly how we're approaching Scripture, then they stand at odds with the book of Hebrews' clear teaching about how Christ's sacrifice put an end to all sacrifices (Hebrews 9:11-15; 10:1-4, 18).[26] To reject the apparent return of the sacrificial system seems at odds with the literal interpretation of prophetic literature.

How do we explain this apparent contradiction? Biblical expositor Jerry Hullinger offered a few possible explanations that may provide us with some insight. The first he called the memorial view, whereby "the sacrifices offered during the earthly reign of Christ will be visible reminders of His work on the cross," having only the efficacy of memorializing Christ's death, just as the Lord's Supper has done for the past 2,000 years.[27] In other words, the sacrifices could merely serve as a memorial that reminds people of Christ's ultimate sacrifice on the cross, similar to why we Christians observe communion today.

Hullinger, in his second view, though he neglected to name it, emphasized that nowhere does Ezekiel state that these sacrifices will be memorial in nature. Rather, he reminded us that these offerings are said to be made specifically for the atonement of the kingdom's citizens (Ezekiel 45:15, 17, 20).[28] Therefore, should this view be proven correct, during the millennial kingdom, salvation for those in their earthly bodies will require both Christ's sacrifice plus animal sacrifices.

Hullinger, in his third view—the one he holds—suggested that animal sacrifices during the kingdom will "serve primarily to remove ceremonial uncleanness and prevent defilement from polluting the Temple," for "this will be necessary because the glorious presence of Yahweh will once again be dwelling on earth in the midst of a sinful and unclean people."[29] These blood sacrifices would then be used only to ceremonially sanctify Israel, and specifically her restored priesthood, because God's holy presence will again be dwelling among the people.[30]

Does this mean that we should accept, at face value, this additional requirement to Christ's completed work of salvation for those living in their mortal bodies during the millennial kingdom? The Old Testament sacrificial system was always meant to be provisional, and never to be restored and required for blood-bought believers in Jesus Christ. And yet, we are left taking the Davidic kingdom for what it is—a whole new era—and therefore we should accept the fact that it requires new rules and regulations.[31] Regardless of which view is correct, the mystery of the return of the sacrificial system, and to what extent, will remain a mystery until the millennial kingdom is realized.

CHAPTER 12

THE JEWS EXALTED: A PRIESTLY PEOPLE

It's important to keep in mind the directional sense of history that is idiomatic to the Jewish mind. To the Jew, history is not a spattering of stuff-that-just-happens. Neither is it a never-ending cycle. It's going somewhere. As the Talmud puts it, the six millennia of time lead toward "a day that is entirely rest and serenity for eternal life."[1]

Rabbi Tzvi Freeman, *Chabad*

Thousands of years of recorded history reveal that no other people group has been more beaten down and abused than the Jewish people. Four hundred years of slavery in Egypt, two mass exiles from their homeland, countless pogroms, numerous genocide-level events, several major holocausts, endless daily persecutions, and rabid antisemitism confronting them from every corner of the globe—it's frankly quite miraculous that there's even a single Jew alive in our day.

God has preserved the Jewish people because He's not finished with them. God meant for the Jewish people to serve as a priestly people, and though they initially failed at the task, His purpose still stands. The prophesies concerning the millennial kingdom include a glorious future for Jacob's descendants.

THE EXALTED NATION

The Bible foretells how a believing Jewish remnant will at last become the exalted and priestly nation God has always meant for them to be. The relationship between Yahweh and His chosen people will, at last, be reconciled and restored. God foresaw this day when He said,

> I will heal their backsliding, I will love them freely, for My anger has turned away from him...their scent shall be like the wine of Lebanon (Hosea 14:4, 7).

Cotton Mather believed that a glorious future awaited the Jewish people. Why did he believe this? Simply because the Bible said it would be so. He wrote:

> A distinct body of the Jewish Nation shall be exalted unto a most particular acquaintance with our Lord Jesus Christ... Indeed, they shall know Him: yea, then shall they be so converted and advanced by our Lord Jesus in the world.[2]

Mather's teachings concerning the future exaltation of the Jewish people greatly influenced Puritan ideology, which later became foundational to Western thinking. The Puritans strongly believed that the Jews would one day return to their land, and Christ, along with His saints, would set up the kingdom's seat of authority in a restored nation of Israel.[3] This belief even influenced other historic biblicists, such as German poet Heinrich Heine, who, while reflecting on the currently exiled and downtrodden state of the Jewish nation, exclaimed that Israel would indeed rise again: "The Jews are the people of the spirit, and whenever they return to the spirit, they are great and splendid."[4]

Zechariah Revealed

Mather and Heine built their view when reading the prophecies of Zechariah, who like Hosea, also revealed that the Lord's plan for the Jewish people in the kingdom would be for them to finally fulfill their priestly role. Zechariah prophesied:

> Thus says the LORD of hosts: "In those days ten men from every language of the nations shall grasp the sleeve of a Jewish man, saying, 'Let us go with you, for we have heard that God is with you'" (Zechariah 8:23).

By taking up the mantle of serving Yahweh as intermediaries between the Gentile nations and the Davidic King, the Jewish people will once again become what they were always meant to be yet had failed to become—a chosen kingdom of priests and a holy nation (Exodus 6:7; 19:5-6; Deuteronomy 29:12-13).[5]

In his exposition of Zechariah's messianic prophecies, theologian J. Duncan Derrett explained the Semitic cultural nuances involved when one person takes hold of another person's garment.[6] While Zechariah 8:23 is often translated as the grasping of a "sleeve," in ancient Hebrew culture, the garment would actually be grasped by the border at the feet. Such an act demonstrates humility and the making of a request for refuge. If accepted, the one grasping would be placed under the power and protection—the *mana*—of the garment's owner (other examples: Ruth 2:12; Psalms 17:8; 36:7; 57:1; 61:4; 63:7).

Bear in mind that at the onset of the millennial kingdom, the Jewish people will all be believers. At the start, there will not be a single unbelieving Jew, for the Jewish remnant will have been saved out of the fires of the tribulation. They will have been healed from their backsliding and so purified to serve their Davidic King as a priestly people to the world. The Lord will bless them, and in turn, the Jewish people will become a blessing to all nations by guiding the growing Gentile populace to "tabernacle" with their King.

Zephaniah Revealed

The prophet Zephaniah also foretold the future exaltation of the Jewish people:

> "At that time I will bring you back, even at the time I gather you; for I will give you fame and praise among all the peoples of the earth, when I return your captives before your eyes," says the LORD (Zephaniah 3:20).

Biblical studies expert Greg King noted in his exposition of this passage that the book of Zephaniah is resplendent with comparisons between Israel's former shame and Israel's future remnant receiving international fame and honor.[7] Zephaniah weaved this theme of future Jewish exaltation throughout his writings by making the following comparisons.

Whereas Yahweh once punished Israel for her sin and rebellion, a day will come when a remnant will at last respond to His wrath with repentance. God will respond, in turn, by granting the penitent forgiveness, restoration, and inevitably, exaltation before the Gentile nations.

Whereas the Jewish people were once taunted and reviled by the other nations (Zephaniah 2:8, 10), the redeemed remnant will one day command respect (3:19-20). Instead of being the object of Yahweh's wrath (1:18), the remnant will become the object of His love (3:17).

Whereas the Jews formerly were threatened by enemies from all directions, they will get to witness the elimination of their enemies (3:8). Instead of continually suffering the loss of their possessions and territory by plunder (1:13), they will become the recipients of increased territorial and material wealth (2:7, 9).

Whereas the Jews were formerly threatened with the horrors of war (1:14-16), their land will at last find peace and security (3:13). Instead of facing destruction as a race (1:4), the Jews will receive what Greg King called "the most magnificent salvation" (3:14-20).[8]

And instead of bearing shame and reproach throughout the Diaspora (2:8, 10), the saved remnant of Jewish people will be honored by the nations as a priestly people (3:19-20). As Greg King concluded, "Their fortunes will be reversed, their well-being restored."[9]

Isaiah Revealed

The prophet Isaiah also foretold the future exaltation of the Jewish people:

> Kings shall be your foster fathers, and their queens your nursing mothers; they shall bow down to you with their faces to the earth, and lick up the dust of your feet (Isaiah 49:23).

When elaborating on this very humbling passage from the book of Isaiah, professor John Willis explained how the Jewish people are to be progressively restored into a national priesthood and tasked with being intercessors between the Gentile nations and King Jesus.[10] First, Christ will restore to the Jews two millennia's worth of lost fortune caused by Roman exile by calling on the Gentiles to financially contribute their newfound wealth to assist in restoring war-torn Jerusalem (Isaiah 45:13-14; 60:8-16; 62:6-12). Second, because the Messiah gloriously rescued the Jewish people at the climactic ending of the "time of Jacob's trouble" (Jeremiah 30:7), this substantial act of deliverance will reverberate down through the succeeding centuries, teaching subsequent generations that Jesus is indeed the Son of God and that worship is for Him alone. And third, the saved Jewish remnant will be tasked with carrying the Davidic King's instruction out from Zion and into the nations of the world. The exalted Jewish priesthood will then lead the Gentiles back to Jerusalem to pay homage to the King and His priestly people.

The Church's Objection

Unfortunately, not every Christian engages in using a literal interpretation when it comes to the verses that foretell the future exaltation of the Jewish people. For much of church history, Christianity has erroneously claimed these prophecies for itself. We call this misapplication replacement theology.

Jewish studies expert Randy Weiss shared that he often has to remind Christians today how, over the centuries, Christendom forgot that first-century Christianity was mainly comprised of Jewish converts.[11] Even Emperor Claudius in AD 49 had expelled all Christians, along with the city's Jewish residents, from Rome because he saw no difference between the two groups.[12] Judaism and Christianity were not always as different as they appear today because they share what Weiss labeled as "the same taproot," for "the God of Israel and the Hebrew Bible form the infrastructure of both."[13]

As Christianity drew more Gentile converts from paganism, it increasingly rejected the faith's Jewish origins, and many forms of replacement theology began to be adopted. The church more and more became fervent in promoting its claim that once the Jewish people failed to accept Jesus as their Messiah, they, in turn, forfeited all the blessings of the old covenant, yet oddly retained all the curses.[14]

The fact that Israel is tangibly a nation once more, just as prophesied, should make today's Christians disagree strongly with the errant claims of replacement theology. The fact is that the New Testament does not cancel or replace the Old, but rather, builds upon it. Likewise, everything written in the Old Testament is assumed by the New to be faithful and true, and that includes all the promises God made to the nation of Israel.[15]

Under the old covenant, a new covenant was promised, whereby a new heart and spirit for the Jewish people would be coupled with God's unconditional promise that the Jewish remnant would one day live safely in the land of Israel. There alone would the seat of the kingdom be established, and there alone would the Son of David sit upon His majestic throne (Jeremiah 31:31-37; Ezekiel 36:22-36). These extra-salvific promises made specifically to the Jewish people mean that the Jews as a race have never been canceled in the name of some mystical fulfillment by the church. Rather, by fulfilling the law, Jesus provided the assurance that God's irrevocable promises must come to pass (Matthew 5:17).[16]

THE LAND EXPANDED

In connection with Israel's final spiritual restoration, God also made promises about the Jewish nation being physically given the entirety of the Promised Land. The long-ago established boundaries stretch "from the river of Egypt to the great river, the River Euphrates" (Genesis 15:18-21; see also Ezekiel 37:21-22).

Commentator Timothy Demy noted four major stages to this final land restoration, all of which rest upon God's covenants and are expanded upon by subsequent prophecies.[17] The first stage, as previously explained, starts with the national regathering of the Jewish people back into the land God promised to them. Once Israel and Judah are reunited as one people, their resettlement of the land will be total and permanent. No king or nation will ever be able to uproot the Jewish people from the land of Israel ever again—not even by the massive coalition of Gog during the Gog-Magog War (Ezekiel 38–39), nor by the global military commanded by the Antichrist (Isaiah 29:5-8; 31:4-5; Zechariah 14:1-2). The regathering also includes aspects that currently do not exist in Israel in this day and age—the resettled Jews are never to be persecuted or dispersed, and the wrongs they suffered throughout history will be righted, as Balaam's third prophecy revealed (Numbers 24:5-7).[18]

The second stage to the total restoration of the Promised Land, Demy noted, coincides with the spiritual regeneration of the Jewish people on a national scale.[19] The totality of their land will be restored to the Jewish remnant at the time when these survivors of the tribulation at long last acknowledge the new covenant (Jeremiah 31:31-34). This believing remnant will then confess Israel's national sin of rebellion against God and their rejection of His Son (Jeremiah 3:11-18; Hosea 5:15). This pivotal event will happen, as previously mentioned, upon the return of the Messiah (Isaiah 53:1-9; Zechariah 12:10; Matthew 23:37-39). The Messiah will then rescue the Jewish people in their darkest hour, both physically and spiritually, so that as a nation, they will, at last, be saved (Romans 11:25-27).

The third stage to Israel's final restoration centers on the reclamation of the land of Israel in its entirety.[20] The saved remnant will take permanent possession of all the land promised to Abraham (Genesis 12:1-3; 13:14-17), but it will have been ravaged by the wars and judgments of the tribulation. We today have lived to see the desolate and forlorn country, long neglected for centuries by the Ottomans and other overlords, bloom to life. But today's Israel has experienced only a foreshadowing of this final restoration of their land. Over the last century, those who have made aliya have terraformed the wastelands and made them bountiful again.

But the complete realization of the land reaching optimum productivity—along with a state of permanent peace and security—has yet to happen. The Israel of the twenty-first century governs only a sliver of the massive amount of land that God promised, which would extend from a river in Egypt (possibly the Nile) to the Euphrates River. Israel does not, at this time, possess the lands currently held by the modern-day nations of Egypt, Gaza, Jordan, Lebanon, Syria, and Iraq. Land for peace? In truth, these nations are the ones squatting on Israel's promised lands! But during the millennial kingdom, Israel will have peacefully settled in and govern over the entirety of the Promised Land, and the deserts will bloom richly once more.

The fourth stage to Israel's final restoration—the Messiah sitting upon David's throne over a fully restored Israel—rests on the previous three (2 Samuel 7:11-16; 1 Chronicles 17:10-14).[21] The Davidic covenant promised Israel and her King an eternal kingdom, throne, and ruler—all of which have not yet been realized, but will be upon the return of the ultimate Davidic King (Isaiah 9:6-7; Jeremiah 23:5-6; 33:17-26; Amos 9:11-12; Luke 1:32-33). The reign of Jesus Christ, who will rule from the throne of David, will extend from the fully restored nation of Israel outward to the Gentile nations and their descendants. When Christ sits upon His throne, the restoration of Israel's lands to the Jewish people will be completed.

Bible prophecy has revealed that this global recognition of King Jesus and His fully restored Jewish nation will happen at a time when all the people living in that era will know Jesus Christ and see Him face to face. That is when the Jewish people will, at long last, fulfill their role as God's priesthood, and in turn they will receive the respect and exaltation that God promised would come from the nations.

CHAPTER 13

THE SAINTS REIGN: THE ADMINISTRATIVE BODY

You Christians own everything. So, relax. You don't need it now. Kids get themselves in trouble. They're called prodigals. They get themselves in trouble by demanding inheritances ahead of time. You have an inheritance. It's called everything. Everything—all spiritual blessings in the heavenly places. The world, life, death, fellow heirs with Christ who made the world—[Christ] owns the world. It's coming![1]

JOHN PIPER, *Desiring God*

In connection with the fully restored Israel, Isaiah prophesied that "kings shall be your foster fathers, and their queens your nursing mothers" (Isaiah 49:22-23). *Who are these kings and queens who will bow before the Davidic King and His priestly people?*

THE REIGN OF THE SAINTS

Daniel provided the answer to this perplexing question:

> The saints of the Most High shall receive the kingdom, and possess the kingdom forever, even forever and ever... and the time came for the saints to possess the kingdom... Then the kingdom and dominion, and the greatness of the kingdoms under the whole heaven, shall be given to the people, the saints of the Most High (Daniel 7:18, 22, 27).

Six centuries after this prophecy was made, the apostle John was taken up in the spirit to God's throne room and saw these very saints worshipping the Almighty. As they were awaiting Jesus Christ's second coming, with great exuberance they rang out in unison, "[You Jesus] have made us kings and priests to our God" (Revelation 5:10).

Later in Revelation, John pointed to yet another body of saints—those who were martyred during the tribulation:

> I saw thrones, and they sat on them, and judgment was committed to them. Then I saw the souls of those who had been beheaded for their witness to Jesus and for the word of God, who had not worshiped the beast or his image, and had not received his mark on their foreheads or on their hands. And they lived and reigned with Christ for a thousand years...they shall be priests of God and of Christ, and shall reign with Him a thousand years (Revelation 20:4-6).

When the various accounts of God's eyewitnesses to the future kingdom of Christ are inspected altogether, we learn that those saints who will be given the kingdom and rule under the King of kings are comprised of three orders of the redeemed. The first are the resurrected faithful from the Old Testament era, the second are the raptured church-age saints, and the third are the martyred and resurrected tribulation saints.[2] If Christ's role is the perfect king, then these saints' roles are to become the purified administrators of that kingdom. They will rule the government under the King. If you are saved, then you will be one of those rulers!

Who will we be ruling over? The citizens of the millennial kingdom will consist of three groups of human beings. The first is the reestablished Jewish priesthood who remain in their earthly bodies, the second is the newly born Gentile nations comprised of people in their earthly bodies, and the third is the resurrected saints in their glorified, eternal bodies.[3] All three groups will dwell together on an earth that King Jesus will have restored from the ravages of the tribulation. We may even see an angel or two now and then visiting from their abode among the stars (Ephesians 3:10; 6:12). So, the Gentile nations will be the subjects, the Jewish people will serve as the priesthood, and the glorified saints will function as the administrative body.

Some theologians point to the church-age saints as being the only ones ruling and reigning with Jesus during the millennial kingdom, and so exclude the Old Testament and tribulation saints. After all, when Jesus preached the kingdom during His first advent, He often promised His followers that they would one day become the inheritors of the kingdom (see, for example, the parable of the minas in Luke 19:11-27). These followers did indeed become the inheritors, at least of the spiritual fold of the kingdom of Christ.

But, as author Shaye Cohen reminded his readers, Judaism and Christianity share a common root, for "the history of Christianity's beginnings is part of the history of Judaism in antiquity."[4] In other words, salvation did not begin with the church age. Faith in God also existed long before Christ's sacrifice, though that sacrifice was necessary to make final atonement for the sins of the Old Testament overcomers (see Hebrews 11). Likewise, salvation did not end with the church age either, for as one anonymous author wrote, "Pentecost was only a few drops of the coming shower."[5] That "shower" will become a downpour during the tribulation, when a "great multitude" from "all nations, tribes, peoples, and tongues" will repent and so be saved to rule over the earth (Revelation 7:9).

Still others argue that the Jewish people alone will reign over the Gentiles during the millennial kingdom. In expounding on Daniel 7, those saints who receive the kingdom will certainly include the believing Jewish remnant, but the ruling sainthood designation must also incorporate church-age saints comprised of both Jews and Gentiles.[6] After all, Paul explained that the church has been grafted like a vine into Israel's olive tree (Romans 11:17-29). So the church has not replaced Israel, as we've discussed, but will share in Israel's covenant blessings (Ephesians 3:6). The promises that Gentiles, too, will also become heirs and receive the honor of reigning with the Son over His kingdom are prolific in Scripture (see, for example, Romans 8:14-17; Revelation 20:6).[7] Therefore, all the resurrected redeemed from each era are promised that they will rule and reign under King Jesus.

THE DUTIES OF THE SAINTS

As we—the kingdom's resurrected citizens—rule over the saved tribulation survivors and later their children, what will be our duties? What exactly does it mean to reign with Christ? And what will our future careers entail?

Government

The first role we will fill apparently involves serving in the new government. Jesus, being the ultimate Judge, will, of course, possess ultimate authority over His kingdom and so "rule all nations with a rod of iron" (Revelation 12:5; see also 2:27; 19:15). Jesus as King will hold the supreme position over the executive, legislative, and judicial branches. But it appears that Christ still plans to delegate positions of authority to His glorified saints.[8]

When it comes to the judicial responsibilities of the kingdom's government, Jesus promised the 12 apostles, "You who have followed

Me will also sit on twelve thrones, judging the twelve tribes of Israel" (Matthew 19:28). By this we learn that the Supreme Court of Israel of today will be replaced by the judgeship of the 12 apostles (whether Paul or Matthias replace Judas Iscariot, we will find out). While the apostles' authority to make rulings over Israel and the Jewish priesthood will stand, the seats of the judges over the Gentile nations will be filled by the remaining glorified saints.

When it comes to the legislative responsibilities of the kingdom's government, there can be only one divine Lawgiver. As we have learned, Jesus Himself will teach His perfect law from the Millennial Temple to His visitors as well as via His Jewish priesthood. Therefore, it stands to reason that no human legislators will be necessary. A national congress will not be needed to write up laws for the people, for that duty will reside with the King, who long ago already wrote His moral law.

This arrangement will solve one of the fatal flaws in today's failed human governments—corruption. During the kingdom, there will be no fallen earthly body of legislators passing corrupt laws that merely serve their own selfish agendas. Rather, only those who are no longer beholden to a sin nature will enact God's perfect law and see to it that the nations obey His precepts. The role of lawmen enforcing the King's law will rest on the glorified saints. No wonder the nineteenth-century clergyman Phillips Brooks, while looking forward to this marvelous time when the failures of human government will have been replaced by the ongoing successes of a glorified governmental body, advised believers today, "Be such a man, and live such a life, that if every man were such as you, and every life a life like yours, this earth would be God's paradise."[9]

Finally, when it comes to the executive responsibilities of the kingdom's government, every role from presidents down to city councilors will be filled by the glorified saints. No longer possessing a sin nature, the resurrected redeemed will hold the earth's citizens to the letter of the King's law. They will not waver from doing their duty, be corrupted by bribes, or seek their interests over the King's interests. Rather, they will institute the perfect government of the benevolent Davidic monarchy. Peace, righteousness, and justice will at last prevail!

Councilors

The second role we glorified saints will fill during the kingdom will be as councilors who provide godly wisdom to its earthly citizens. As our example, we have only to look heavenward to Yahweh's divine council, where the Almighty calls upon the angels and the 24 elders (Revelation 4:4, 10; 5:8, 14; 11:16; 19:4).[10] Not that the omniscient God has any need for the advice of angels or we mere mortals, but the Lord, in part, governs through leadership councils. Based on this model of the heavenly council, God will convene an earthly council made up of glorified saints, for the "Lord of hosts will reign on Mount Zion and in Jerusalem and before His elders" (Isaiah 24:23).

This means that we, the glorified saints, will sit in positions as kings and queens, rulers and enforcers, governors and mayors, and even teachers and instructors. It appears that in all positions involving leadership and education, there will sit a resurrected saint, perpetuating a government consisting strictly of God's faithful sainthood.

This model of government isn't capitalism, parliamentarianism, socialism, communism, or any other "ism" of today. Rather, the millennial kingdom will be defined essentially as a theistic monarchy.

THE LENGTH OF THE KINGDOM

While the bulk of information concerning the various aspects of the millennial kingdom is spread throughout the Old and New Testaments, Revelation 20 alone provides us with the exact length of time that Christ's kingdom, specifically on the earth, will last.[11] John repeated six times the length as being "[a or the] thousand years" (Revelation 20:2, 3, 4, 5, 6, 7).

Those of us who take a literal approach to interpreting the Bible, and so believe that the earthly kingdom of Christ will last for exactly a thousand years, meaning 1,000 years, are called chiliasts, from the Greek word *chilia*, meaning "the number one thousand."[12] Chiliasm is one of the oldest terms the church has used for this belief, along with millenarianism (*milli* + *annum* = millennium or thousand years), or as Calvin preferred to call it, premillennialism.[13] Increase Mather confirmed that chiliasm was the belief of the early church "for divers hundreds of years," and that it was the general belief of the great Christian scholars and New England clergy of Mather's day.[14]

When it comes to interpreting Revelation 20's six references to a thousand years, oddly, great controversy swirls around whether to take the phrase "[a] thousand years" literally, as we premillennialists do, or to see the term as being yet another symbol from a book seemingly engrossed in symbolism, as the non-premillennialists do. I would argue that interpreting "thousand years" as being merely symbolic is fallacious, because the symbols presented in the book of Revelation are invariably explained by Revelation or other passages peppered throughout the Bible.[15] After all, other increments of time found in Revelation—such as 1,260 days, 42 months, and three-and-a-half years—are almost universally taken literally, so why wouldn't a "thousand years" mean "1,000 years"? And why would Revelation specify 1,000 years as many as six times unless God truly wanted the reader to take that length of time seriously?

To not take the phrase "[a] thousand years" as a literal notation of time will invariably result in misinterpretation. As Arnold Fruchtenbaum warned: "The desire to spiritualize the text always places the burden of proof on the interpreter. Without objective proof, it will result in a subjective interpretation."[16]

The answer to this controversy may be found in an actual biblical symbol—God's use of the creation week—as a historical type. Genesis 1–2 tells us that God created the universe in six days and rested on the seventh.[17] We can look to the rabbinic interpretation of the creation week pattern of six days of toil and a seventh day of rest as the template for defining the total length of human history.[18] Based on James Ussher's chronology of 6,000 years of human history followed by a sabbath millennium, Cotton Mather concluded, "The six days wherein the world was making, were a type of the six thousand years, after which the Church is to enjoy a blessed Sabbatism."[19] For 6,000 years humanity would toil, followed by a sabbath 1,000 years.

God again substantiated this historical type with His command to allow a day of rest, whereby the toiler works for six days and then rests on the seventh day (Leviticus 23:3). This type can be found yet again in the Jewish feasts, whereby six feasts are related to working the agricultural cycle, and the seventh—the Feast of Tabernacles—stands apart as a feast offering rest for seven days upon the completion of the agricultural cycle (Leviticus 23:34-36).[20] Such prevalent typology presents a strong case substantiating that the length of the kingdom of Christ must be taken as a literal 1,000 years.

If indeed the kingdom of Christ is to last exactly 1,000 years on this earth, as Revelation has repeatedly stated, then the common label "millennial kingdom" can be justly applied to the kingdom of Christ. Going forward, then, we can feel comfortable using both terms interchangeably.

The fourth fold of the kingdom of Christ—the Davidic kingdom—is then the millennial kingdom. But, what about the aforementioned promise that Christ's kingdom will be eternal? Eternal is a whole lot longer than 1,000 years. If you've ever wondered about that, the nuances between *millennial* and *eternal* will be addressed in detail in the concluding chapter.

CHAPTER 14

A TIME OF JOY: THE MOOD OF THE ERA

Joy to the world, the Lord is come!
Let earth receive her King!
Let every heart prepare Him room,
and heav'n and nature sing,
and heav'n and nature sing,
and heav'n, and heav'n and nature sing.
Joy to the earth, the Savior reigns!
Let men their songs employ,
while fields and floods, rocks, hills, and plains
repeat the sounding joy,
repeat the sounding joy,
repeat, repeat the sounding joy.[1]

Isaac Watts, "Joy to the World"

If there's one word that most perfectly describes the overall mood of the millennial kingdom, it would have to be *joy*. It's that same kind of matchless joy I remember my little daughter having when, at the petting zoos, she'd snatch up a baby bunny or ducky to blissfully snuggle. It's that type of love unburdened by any trace of sorrow or regret.

A KINGDOM DEFINED BY JOY

The kingdom era will be just like that—a glorious time when all the citizens will be filled with these many wonderful emotions: bliss, cheer, comfort, delight, elation, glee, satisfaction, wonder, exultation, festivity, gladness, jubilance, liveliness, merriment, refreshment, rejoicing, and solace. I think you get the picture.

The joyousness of this era will, in reality, have commenced some seven years earlier with a celestial wedding in heaven. As the tribulation rages on the earth, the heavens will instead celebrate with great joy the spiritual union of Jesus Christ with His bride, the church. The jubilant atmosphere will continue at the wedding reception of the marriage supper of the Lamb. Then we will experience a family reunion at the reunification of the resurrected and glorified saints from all ages at the onset of the 1,000-year kingdom. The celebration will finally move down to the earth at Christ's second coming with the institution of His Davidic kingdom.

Imagine the exuberant exaltations that will erupt from every corner of the cosmos as the angelic beings, glorified saints, and earthly tribulation survivors celebrate in the commencement of the Davidic King as He sits for the very first time upon His majestic throne in Zion. What joy will burst forth as King Jesus ushers in a new era for His people to dwell!

It's a fact that the millennial era will be defined by its great joy. And the rejoicing will echo down through the centuries, for as the prophet Jeremiah foretold of the delight of God's people in the kingdom:

> Then shall the virgin rejoice in the dance, and the young men and the old, together; for I will turn their mourning

to joy, will comfort them, and make them rejoice rather than sorrow (Jeremiah 31:13).

The book of Isaiah includes a sampling of verses that poetically chronicle the great joy and unending rejoicing of the citizens of the kingdom. The personal presence and bountiful provision provided by the Son of God will cause[2]

- the angels in heaven and the peoples of the earth to break out in song because of the Lord's overflowing comfort and mercy (Isaiah 49:13)
- the ransomed inhabitants to wear everlasting joy on their heads and obtain fulfilling gladness, for sorrow and sighing will flee from them (Isaiah 51:11)
- these "millennials" in their earthly bodies to find their wombs to be fruitful, and families will grow and prosper, so that the world will be filled with the cooing of babies (Isaiah 54:1)
- the faces of the King's fishermen to become radiant as their hearts swell with joy at the abundance of their catch (Isaiah 60:5)
- the souls of the people to greatly rejoice in the Lord because righteousness will bud like a spring garden (Isaiah 61:10-11)
- God's servants to break into song due to the ample joy overflowing from their hearts as they eat and drink and are satisfied (Isaiah 65:12-14)
- the inhabitants of Jerusalem to be glad and rejoice in the city's newfound esteem, and weeping and crying will no longer be heard in her streets (Isaiah 65:18-19)

- the world to drink deeply from the consolation of Jerusalem's bounty and the abundance of her glory because her source will flow from her King (Isaiah 66:10-11)

THE ANNUAL CELEBRATION

In a previous chapter, we explored the worldwide celebration of the Feast of Tabernacles. This feast will be held by the world's inhabitants as they make their annual pilgrimage to Jerusalem to visit King Jesus. God declared, "It shall be that I will gather all nations and tongues; and they shall come and see My glory" (Isaiah 66:18). Once the inhabitants of the world reach their King, tremendous joy and blessings will flow out of Zion to each pilgrim, who will then carry their excitement back to their homelands. Prophets such as Zechariah added further details about this annual pilgrimage:

> It shall come to pass that everyone who is left of all the nations which came against Jerusalem shall go up from year to year to worship the King, the Lord of hosts, and to keep the Feast of Tabernacles (Zechariah 14:16).

As explained earlier, during the millennial kingdom, the Lord plans to institute the Feast of Tabernacles, but on a global scale. Zechariah 14 confirms the prophetic significance of Sukkot as being the only one out of the seven Jewish feasts where all the nations will be commanded to celebrate the dwelling of the Son of God with mankind.[3] Tabernacles, also called the Feast of Booths, marks the final festival in the cycle of seven holy days (Leviticus 23), and stands apart as the third of the aliya ("going up") festivals (Deuteronomy 16).[4] As the Jewish people in their messianic hope have been "going up" to Jerusalem over the past millennia, in their hearts, they have been acting out a dress rehearsal for the soon-coming kingdom, during which the entire world will be "going up" to celebrate with Immanuel—"God with us" (Matthew 1:23). Jewish studies expert David Brickner explained:

> One could travel from the top of Mount Everest to Jerusalem, and it would still be "going up" because God chose to place His holy name in that city and He will, in the Messiah, return someday.[5]

Zechariah tacked on a warning to those who unwisely choose to decline attending the annual joyous reunion between mankind and their Creator:

> It shall be that whichever of the families of the earth do not come up to Jerusalem to worship the King, the Lord of hosts, on them there will be no rain (Zechariah 14:17).

The prophet noted that God will turn off the rains in their locality as a reminder that the King desires their presence in Jerusalem, not for selfish reasons, but to share in His great joy. At one point, likely near the end of the 1,000 years, the entire nation of Egypt will need to be reminded with a drought just how important this annual fellowshipping is with their Savior (Zechariah 14:19).

Our Creator desires to fellowship with His creation and to share in His joy. And that joy, in part, will so well define the millennial kingdom.

CHAPTER 15

A TIME OF PEACE AND NO WAR: THE POLITICS OF THE NATIONS

We look forward to the time when the Power of Love will replace the Love of Power. Then will our world know the blessings of peace.[1]

William E. Gladstone, former British prime minister

How long has mankind tried to live in peace without war, and failed?

We can look as far back as 1500 BC, when humans had begun to consistently record their various acts of warfare, and it's shocking to learn that war has raged across all the centuries since, minus a scant 268 years.[2] That means over the last 3,500 years, 92 percent of those years have seen armed conflict, while a mere 8 percent have achieved "universal" peace.[3] That figure takes into account the standard definition of war as an active conflict that has claimed more than 1,000 lives. Count in those skirmishes that have resulted in less than 1,000 deaths, and factor in civilian casualties, along with the repercussions of war causing even more deaths due to hunger and disease, and the number of years this globe has been without the ravages of war approaches a dismal zero percent. Why, in the 1800s alone, more than 37 million people worldwide died from actively fighting in some war or conflict.[4] And during the 1900s, the death toll due to fighting resulted in a staggering 110 million people dead![5]

THE GREATEST FAILURE

So the question should be rephrased, "Has the world ever known peace?" No, never—at least not since the Fall. Only in those earliest days before Cain slew his brother Abel, and the factions soon after began fighting, has the world been without a war.

I believe the failure of achieving peace and security by putting an end to war has been one of the greatest, if not *the* greatest, failures of fallen human governments. For, rather than desiring peace, our leaders have continually perpetuated war in order to serve their bloated egos and lust for more land, money, resources, and power. Their moral failings will always stand in the way of brokering any lasting peace. We mere mortals are simply not capable of perpetuating unity.

THE TRIUMPH OF PEACE

But I can report with great excitement that one day, this futile condition will all be behind us. Once the King of kings sits upon the Davidic throne and institutes His earthly kingdom, He will usher in the long-desired era of true peace with no war. Why no war? Because the government of the kingdom will be ruled over by the divine King Jesus and administrated by His redeemed children. Everyone serving in that government will have the mind of Christ—the one and only Prince of Peace—and so naturally peace will reign supreme.

Think of it: no soldiers, no weapons, and no hatred of one's fellow man. Consider what today's national budgets would look like if governments instead invested their monies in the betterment of their citizens rather than devoting vast sums to creating instruments of destruction such as guns, missiles, nuclear bombs, chemical and biological weapons, and other horrific world-annihilating devices. If these monies were instead invested in infrastructure, we would be able to build the cities, highways, and advanced technologies that would leap society far, far beyond today's levels.

Peace between all people will define the politics of the nations during the millennial kingdom. The result will be the greatest flourishing of society the world has ever known.

THE PROPHETS' PROMISE

We know that this future era of global peace must become a reality because God Himself promised through His prophets that such a day will come. Prophets such as Isaiah, Joel, and Micah looked longingly for the day when

> they shall beat their swords into plowshares, and their spears into pruning hooks; nation shall not lift up sword against nation, neither shall they learn war anymore (Isaiah 2:4; Micah 4:3-4; see also Joel 3:10).

Hosea detailed God's promise to take "bow and sword of battle" and "shatter [them] from the earth," with the wondrous result of making all people "lie down safely" (Hosea 2:17-18).

This prophesied era of perpetual peace will find at last its fulfillment during the millennial kingdom. Peace will come because all citizens will heed King Jesus' commandment to "love one another as I have loved you" (John 15:12). Isaiah foretold that once we truly know how to love our neighbors, that's when true peace will flow "like a river, and your righteousness like the waves of the sea" (Isaiah 48:18).

THE COLLECTIVE HEARTS

What condition must change to make true peace among our fellow brethren a reality?

Former US president Herbert Hoover knew the answer when he stated, "Peace is not made at the council tables, or by treaties, but in the hearts of men."[6] Hoover accurately pointed out that the collective hearts of mankind are what first must be changed. The only way the heart can be changed, as one author identified so well, is when "peace rules the day when Christ rules the mind."[7] The personal presence of the great Lawgiver and Judge must rule directly over the hearts and minds of His subjects, thereby synchronizing His people with His moral law. Once that occurs, Christ's subjects will, in turn, respond in faith. Their hearts will transition from selfishness to selflessness, which will empower a desire to keep a lasting peace.

Former US diplomat John Foster Dulles once noted:

> The world will never have lasting peace so long as men reserve for war the finest human qualities. Peace, no less than war, requires idealism and self-sacrifice and a righteous and dynamic faith.[8]

The very righteous character of the Davidic King will inspire His people to attempt by faith to seek to attain His perfect righteousness. And the Prince of Peace will provide worldwide peace through the example of His perfect character, along with the strict enforcement of His moral law.

SHADOWS OF A LOST PEACE

I was struck by the longing that Harvard's greatest colonial president, Increase Mather, expressed for the peace of Christ's millennial kingdom. He wrote:

> It will be in vain to expect a lasting peace throughout the earth, until such times as the righteous kingdom of Christ shall obtain a great footing among the nations…It is possible that there may be a peace patched up among the nations, but we may boldly prophesy from the Word of God that it will not be lasting peace.[9]

Mather understood the biblical assurances that until Jesus Christ returns to institute His kingdom, true and lasting peace will remain an impossibility due to mankind's fallen human nature. And yet buried within humanity's long genetic memory are traces of the peace that had once prevailed in the Garden of Eden. These shadowy memories continue to stoke humanity's vision of a better society. Our very DNA yearns to return to life under the long-lost relationship with the Father that had preceded humanity's fall into sin. This once-peaceful reality was lost, rejected, and violated due to humanity's selfishness.

Nevertheless, humanity still longs to restore this paradise lost in some future form of human-engineered utopia.[10] As we've witnessed, many would-be secular messiahs have sparked such utopian-thinking movements, only to see their efforts inevitably fail miserably due to human shortcomings. Utopianism is built into our collective genetic memory, but it will always remain out of reach when attempted apart from the work of the divine Peace-giver.

THE FIRES OF TRANSITION

We faithful Christians long to see the age of Christ's peace be ushered in, but we do so with a hint of sadness. Why the sorrow? Because we know, from God's prophetic Word, that the world simply does not transition from one age to the next without passing through the refining fires of God's cataclysmic judgment.

With an awareness of the tribulation judgments that lie between the church age and lasting millennial peace, theologian W. Sibley Towner, through his studies of the rich spectrum of prophetic scriptures, discovered that humanity has historically transitioned from war to peace in three stages: (1) the ending of an age results in (2) a cataclysm, beyond which lies (3) a limited time of shalom, meaning "peace."[11] The biblical writers did not look upon such transitional cataclysms with eager anticipation; nevertheless, they accepted the necessity of them and sought God's divine help to at least endure them. The biblical prophets understood that once the people made it through these prophesied times of great upheaval and judgment, on the other side lay an infinitely more desirable age.

Looking at an example of this difficult transition, we have learned that the millennial kingdom is when God's people, having become a purified and reconciled community, will at last rejoice in the shalom God will provide. But before that peace can be achieved, those left behind after the rapture will endure the world-shattering trials of the seven-year tribulation. And those who come to faith during that trying era will end up dwelling in the true peace of the millennial kingdom.[12]

Once all of God's children are living securely in the kingdom, as St. Augustine concluded, "Peace [will be] our final good."[13] This bringer of good can only come by the "second Melchizedek"—the King of Righteousness—once He ascends the throne of David. Jesus Christ will become our forever priest as the Prince of Peace. It is He who will bring all nations to a saving knowledge of the Father so they can rest in His shalom (Psalm 110:1-4).[14]

THE JEWISH LONGING FOR SHALOM

The Jewish people long for true peace and a final rest from the oppression four excruciating millennia of warfare, exile, and persecution have brought them. They have long looked to the kingdom prophecies found in Isaiah and Micah that serve to whisk Israel away to what one commentator called "a vastly different place, an other-worldly vision of righteousness, justice, and unending peace."[15] These servants of God leave the Jewish people dreaming of their city standing high upon a hill above everything else, where the people stream upward to attain its blessings and to receive its greatest reward—peace.[16]

From the divine ruler of this city, the citizens of the kingdom will learn a new trade—they will become like blacksmiths, beating their swords into plowshares and their spears into pruning hooks. God's use of these two interchangeable pairs of tools is meant to present Israel with an important parallelism: the metal instruments will be transformed, metamorphosizing from implements of warfare to agriculture, taking the world from wartime to peacetime.[17] The symbolism reinforces God's promise to Israel that a transition is indeed coming. The dark days of evil forces haunting and hunting down the Jewish people will transition into a new era during which God protectively rules from His throne in their holy city. That is when Yahweh will, as one author noted, "Wipe away every injustice and put an end to the destructive pain of war forever."[18]

The newly returned and anointed Davidic King will most assuredly defeat the Gentile nations that have long threatened Israel—that is, once the aforementioned remnant of Jewish people ultimately recognize Jesus as their Messiah and cry out to Him for deliverance.[19] Due to Christ's victory at the second coming, Israel will have at last attained, as English cleric Charles Caleb Colton described, the long-desired condition where "peace is the evening star of the soul, and virtue is its sun; and the two are never far apart."[20]

SITTING UNDER A VINE

Following God's hope-filled promise that during the millennial kingdom, "nation shall not lift up sword against nation, neither shall they learn war anymore" (Micah 4:3), we are told the result of all the nations laying down their arms: "Everyone shall sit under his vine and under his fig tree, and no one shall make them afraid; for the mouth of the LORD of hosts has spoken" (verse 4). Micah 4:4 is one of my most cherished passages, for it stands on a beautiful promise declared by our trustworthy Savior.

Oh, how this verse often reminds me of that tranquil scene from the first Lord of the Rings movie, the one where young Frodo sits restfully under a towering tree. He's there reading a book, unaware of the chaos that lies outside of the Shire, simply resting and at peace. I find this scene to be the closest to a perfect modern-day representation of Micah's idyllic promise that one day, we, too, will sit under our own trees, living blissfully without any fears, and will finally be at rest.

Oh, how I long to live in a world where we no longer have to be fearfully looking over our shoulders anymore! Where the threat of being assaulted by our countrymen, or being attacked by another nation, is no longer even a possibility. Wouldn't it be great if we could all cease stockpiling guns and bullets and knives, no longer shadowed by the possibility that we may be forced to use them to prevent ourselves or our loved ones from getting hurt or killed? I wait expectantly for the time when governments will no longer salivate over the opportunities war provides them to make money and increase their power. And I yearn for the day when all countries will at long last lay down their arms and embrace true peace, the kind only the Davidic King can provide.

What will motivate us to embrace this peace? The mouth of the Lord will command it. Come, O Prince of Peace!

CHAPTER 16

ANIMALS AT PEACE WITH MANKIND: SERENITY IN THE ANIMAL KINGDOM

The "dog eat dog" world of "nature red in tooth and claw" will no longer prevail...The vision of a world in which wolves and lambs, calves and lions all lie down together clearly moves beyond the possibilities of the present age. The description seems to partake of elements common to fables and fairy tales, but something else is at stake here...Judgment and promise, sin and grace are not only for humans, but their consequences, good and bad, are felt by the entire creation.[1]

ANONYMOUS, "ISAIAH 11:1-9—THE PEACEABLE KINGDOM"

Shortly after Noah and his family had disembarked from their great seacraft and set foot upon the soggy ground, God established the first covenant with our great-great ancestor. He ordered Noah and his descendants to "be fruitful and multiply, and fill the earth" (Genesis 9:1). But the Flood had radically changed the earth's environment, and mankind could no longer be sustained and thrive solely on a diet of fruits and vegetables. After centuries of vegetarianism, mankind would need to eat meat in order to survive the newly transformed world. And so, humanity was permitted to kill and eat the animals.

The expected response from the animal kingdom quickly became apparent:

> The fear of you and the dread of you shall be on every beast of the earth, on every bird of the air, on all that move on the earth, and on all the fish of the sea. They are given into your hand. Every moving thing that lives shall be food for you. I have given you all things, even as the green herbs (Genesis 9:2-3).

God then added His promise that He would never again destroy the earth by water (verse 11). The Almighty went on to seal this unconditional covenant with a beautiful reminder of His merciful peace—the rainbow. As stated earlier, this promise is what we today call the Noahic covenant (Genesis 9:1-17).

NATURE FINALLY AT PEACE

While God will never again destroy the earth with water, we learned that He will nearly destroy it with His wrath during the tribulation. As the earth teeters on the brink of extinction, the Prince of Peace will return triumphantly to restore peace. But that peace doesn't refer only to relations between the nations. One of the many glorious aspects we can anticipate about the millennial kingdom involves a radical change in our relationship with the animal kingdom. Nature will, at long last, be at peace with itself, as every animal will no longer live in fear of mankind, but in solidarity with us.

The prophet Isaiah described this future idyllic scene:

> The wolf also shall dwell with the lamb, the leopard shall lie down with the young goat, the calf and the young lion and the fatling together; and a little child shall lead them. The cow and the bear shall graze; their young ones shall lie down together; and the lion shall eat straw like the ox. The nursing child shall play by the cobra's hole, and the weaned child shall put his hand in the viper's den. They shall not hurt nor destroy in all My holy mountain (Isaiah 11:6-9; see also 65:25).

In considering this amazing passage, professor John MacKay remarked, "[An era is coming when] the animal world, in its relations with itself and with mankind, will put aside cruelty and bloodthirstiness."[2] After five long millennia, that terrible yet understandable fear animals have of mankind—that we will harm them for sport, or hunt them for food, or by our careless violence annihilate entire species—will finally pass away.

And for us people, who are always keeping a wary eye out for so many dangerous predators lurking about, we will find only fellowship with the animal kingdom. The enmity between mankind and the animals that was imposed by God's covenant with Noah will at long last be removed.

Even our fear of snakes—which comes from that old curse set between humanity and serpents—will be removed. A child will be able to live together with an asp without fear of death.[3] I'm reminded of Edward Hicks's painting "The Peaceable Kingdom," which portrays an arcadian scene of peace, safety, and security as a human child, predator, and prey lull together peacefully on a hillside.[4] This will be the harmonious condition of life during the millennial kingdom.

A RETURN TO VEGETARIANISM?

When it comes to eating, what will have changed in the millennial kingdom compared to the world of today?

Isaiah told us that all animals will adopt a vegetarian diet once more.[5] Animals will no longer eat one another but will return to the condition known in the Garden of Eden, when edibles consisted of plants alone. That means predators will no longer spend every waking hour on the hunt, and prey will no longer warily eat and drink in anticipation of a predator's surprise attack. With no threat of aggression, predator and prey will dwell together at the watering hole without fearing one another.

This return to vegetarianism in the animal kingdom could well mean that the world's most dangerous predator—mankind—will also put aside its hunting and meat-eating and join in the vegetarian lifestyle. After all, Adam and Eve and their descendants up until the time of Noah had enjoyed a meat-free diet, and so maybe we will once more. Just like the Flood radically transformed the living requirements for all species, the world's restoration after the tribulation could return life to what it was like before the Flood.

Whether Isaiah was merely intending to convey the idea that vegetarianism would become the lifestyle of the future or not is the subject of much debate. Theologians such as Michael Jinkins questioned whether these texts are instead meant to depict not the future peaceable behavior of wild beasts, but rather, represent a "deep human longing for peace, security, safety, and justice."[6] In John Calvin's commentary on Isaiah 65, we read, "The lion shall eat harmlessly, and shall no longer seek his prey," and "the serpent, satisfied with his dust, shall wrap himself in it, and shall no longer hurt by his envenomed bite."[7] Calvin said this means "all that is disordered or confused shall be restored to its proper order."[8] Perhaps Isaiah was presenting the ideal of all of creation brought into harmony?[9] It could be that Isaiah was offering a vision of the restoration of peace and gentleness, when innocence and trust will no longer be abused.[10] For example, the holiness of a naive little child will grant him the power to rule over the fiercest of God's creatures, for the child will hold neither guile nor evil intent.

Seminarian Edward Wheeler took Isaiah's vision even further down the speculative hole, concluding that Isaiah was prophesying the fulfillment of mankind's millennia-old dream of a new golden age when conflict would cease; and the world freed from suffering, pain, and alienation would at last know true peace.[11] Such a dream serves as a gift from God, providing us with a lasting hope.[12] Jinkins foresaw an additional gift given by the Almighty, whereby the "creation restored to God's original vision places humanity in a radical position of freedom in the presence of God."[13]

I don't find Isaiah's description of the peace between mankind and animal-kind to be merely symbolic. After all, to truly create a condition of peace, safety, and security, the threat of harm and death at the hands of an attacker must be eliminated. Trust can grow only when no fear of harm is present. When we interpret Isaiah's words literally (as always), we see the prophet was presenting the conditions necessary for such a peaceful world to exist—animals will no longer eat other animals, nor will they attack people. Isaiah clearly took this condition literally, and at the same time, he used this imagery to depict a world that will have at last found true peace.

There are grey areas I sometimes ponder when it comes to whether mankind will return to vegetarianism during the millennial kingdom. For one, the Bible doesn't explicitly say that mankind will fully return to vegetarianism. That idea is only inferred. And two, we must deal with what the major prophets described as animal sacrifices being performed at the Millennial Temple. Under the Old Testament sacrificial system, the priests lived on the meat that was sacrificed. Will the Jewish priests at the Millennial Temple do so again during this coming age?

If vegetarianism is our destiny, I will truly miss a thick cut of steak smothered in onions, mushrooms, and A.1. Sauce. Will our glorified bodies even need such sustenance? Probably not. But then the resurrected Jesus ate fish, and He's our template for glorified living (Luke 24:42-43).

So during the millennial kingdom, can we enjoy eating meat yet keep the peaceable condition with the animal kingdom? I don't know. I can only conclude that some elements of the Davidic kingdom, such as what we will eat, will remain shrouded in mystery until that age arrives. But, as the next chapter shows, there will certainly be plenty to eat.

CHAPTER 17

THE BOUNTIFUL LAND: THE RESTORATION OF THE PLANET

Widespread peace and justice, spiritual blessing, and a bountiful supply of food in every land will result in a general era of prosperity such as the world has never known... The many factors which produce poverty, distress, and unequal distribution of goods will to a great extent be nonexistent in the millennium. Labor problems which now beset all nations will be solved, and everyone will receive just compensation for his labors... Thus, the curse which creation has endured since Adam's sin... will be in part suspended as even the animal creation will be changed...[1]

John Walvoord, *"The Doctrine of the Millennium"*

The Bible presents a resplendent array of verses so bountiful that they rival the great bounty of food that will also characterize the millennial kingdom. Bounteous days are coming to the earth!

AN ABUNDANCE OF FOOD

Amos prophesied that during the kingdom of Christ, crops of food will grow in largess and with stunning rapidity:

> The plowman shall overtake the reaper, and the treader of grapes him who sows seed; the mountains shall drip with sweet wine, and all the hills shall flow with it (Amos 9:13).

Zechariah embellished Amos's idyllic description of the coming era of tremendous agricultural bounty:

> The seed shall be prosperous, the vine shall give its fruit, the ground shall give her increase, and the heavens shall give their dew (Zechariah 8:12).

The prophet added that by these the Davidic King will bless His subjects, giving "the remnant of this people to possess all these."

Isaiah also credited the ample agricultural bounty to "the Branch of the LORD":

> [He] shall be beautiful and glorious; and the fruit of the earth shall be excellent and appealing for those of Israel who have escaped (Isaiah 4:2).

The Creator will make the world teem with life, and nothing will live in constant fear of death.

Likewise, the psalmist also foretold of the glorious days when the earth will yield its increase (Psalm 85:10-12). Those in past ages who once sowed their seeds in sorrow, wary of producing a meager crop, will instead reap their sheaves with great rejoicing, for in the kingdom, there will be no end to the harvesting of food (Psalm 126:5-6). The land will truly be blessed by "My Anointed"—the Davidic

King (Psalm 132:17; see also verses 15, 18). As Jesus suffered on the cross, He spoke the words of Psalm 22, revealing how His sacrifice would make it possible for His faithful to one day eat "the fat of the earth" in a time when humans and animals alike will be amply nourished, finding great satisfaction and pleasure in the prosperity His kingdom will provide.[2]

The prophet Ezekiel longed for the days when rivers would bubble clean and water the trees, which will bring forth fruit to feed God's people and healing leaves useful for making medicines (Ezekiel 47:3-5, 7-9, 12). Those citizens who are still in their earthly bodies will continue to need cures for cuts and broken bones and whatnot, but with such an abundance of flora, medical discoveries will likely outpace anything we have experienced up to this time.

Joel likewise foresaw the days when the mountains and hills of the Holy Land will be watered by a river flowing from the Millennial Temple. This will result in the earth being flooded with the fruit of the tree and the vine:

> It will come to pass in that day that the mountains shall drip with new wine, the hills shall flow with milk, and all the brooks of Judah shall be flooded with water; a fountain shall flow from the house of the LORD and water the Valley of Acacias (Joel 3:18).

All these Old Testament prophets anticipated the days when the Davidic King will make the evils of hunger and poverty relics of the past. Such agricultural bounty can be achieved only during a state of peace, for as one anonymous writer so sagely noted, "Where there is no peace, there is no feast."[3] The peaceful conditions that will so beautifully characterize the millennial kingdom will provide the essential mechanism that makes the failure of human governments' long desire to end world hunger a reality. The absence of war and strife will mean no massive military budgets diverting funds from agricultural production. No wartime destruction will mean no need for incessant rebuilding. Only true peace can create unlimited prosperity, and only the Prince of Peace can provide what mankind has long failed to achieve.

Newly restored by King Jesus, the earth will yet again become a garden paradise rich in all its bounty. And some of this magnificent bounty will be shared between King and millennial citizens at the annual great feast—the Feast of Tabernacles—during which Christ's people will share in the fullness of His love with thankfulness, gladness, and expectancy.[4]

THE DEAD SEA BROUGHT BACK TO LIFE

Once Jesus has revitalized the planet from the devastation wrought by the tribulation, one of His most epic transformations will involve bringing the Dead Sea back to life. Not only is the Dead Sea, located southeast of Jerusalem at the tail end of the Jordan River, the lowest land-based elevation on the earth, but it is 9.6 times saltier than an ocean, and it possesses an environment too harsh for plants and animals to survive its depths.[5] The Dead Sea is aptly named!

And yet Zechariah prophesied how, during the kingdom, Christ will fill the Dead Sea with living waters:

> In that day it shall be that living waters shall flow from Jerusalem, half of them toward the eastern sea and half of them toward the western sea; in both summer and winter it shall occur (Zechariah 14:8).

Ezekiel likewise revealed where these living waters will flow:

> This water flows toward the eastern region, goes down into the valley, and enters the sea. When it reaches the

> sea, its waters are healed. And it shall be that every living thing that moves, wherever the rivers go, will live. There will be a very great multitude of fish, because these waters go there; for they will be healed, and everything will live wherever the river goes (Ezekiel 47:8-9, see also verses 1-12).

Labeling this healing river the Temple River, Frank Gaebelein explained that the basic purpose of this divine brook will be to bring life back to what once was dead.[6] This river of life will stream out from under the throne of the Giver of Life, flowing down out of Yahweh Shammah and into the Dead Sea and the Arabah, so that the entirety of these waters will be healed. Ezekiel foresaw the day when fishermen will cast their nets across the entire length of the Dead Sea, from En Gedi to En Eglaim. Interestingly, Ezekiel also noted how the King will leave the swamps and marshes unhealed so that the salt could still be harvested by His people. The land that reminded Lot of the Garden of Eden, but which God had blighted due to Sodom's sin, will be brought back to life (Genesis 13:10-12).

THE REDEMPTION OF THE EARTH

Some theologians look at these prophecies concerning the coming great agricultural abundance and the healing of the Dead Sea and say that they apply only to the land of Israel. They argue that the curse God placed on the ground (Genesis 3:17-19) will be partially lifted in the Holy Land, but not across the rest of the earth.

If that were true, then a troubling question remains. Will the millennial kingdom at last provide the full redemption of the earth from its "bondage of corruption" that Paul had been anticipating, or will Christ heal only a small region of the planet during that time? Let's look carefully at what Paul prophesied:

> The earnest expectation of the creation eagerly waits for the revealing of the sons of God. For the creation was subjected to futility, not willingly, but because of Him who subjected it in hope; because the creation itself also will be delivered from the bondage of corruption into the glorious liberty of the children of God. For we know that the whole creation groans and labors with birth pangs together until now (Romans 8:19-22).

Hebrew scholar Katheryn Darr is among the theologians who believes the prophecies concerning the redemption of the creation do not apply to any land but Israel. She noted Ezekiel's silence concerning "any paradisiacal transformation of land lying beyond the perimeters of Israel's territory."[7] In pointing out Ezekiel's supposed silence concerning the rest of the earth, she concluded that the transformation of Israel's barren lands cannot be a foretaste of a universal return to Edenic conditions, but rather presents merely a manifestation of God's blessings poured out upon Israel alone, and does not extend beyond Israel's borders.[8]

I believe such a strict interpretation limiting Christ's restorative work as being only within the bounds of Israel's borders falls short of the larger context presented by the scriptures we've observed so far. Why would Christ leave the world a barren, wrath-torn, radioactive wasteland? Why would the King wish to rule over a decimated planet? And why would the King grant the struggling survivors of said badlands one annual respite to travel to Israel to enjoy His great wealth, only to then send them back into the harsh wilderness once more empty-handed?

For the Lord to exhibit such blatant hostility toward His subjects goes against His loving nature, and such a notion defies the near-Edenic nature characteristic of the kingdom. No, these prophecies cannot apply to Israel alone. Rather, they prophesy a world entirely transformed into a garden paradise, one repaired quite speedily soon after Christ's return.

Despite this near-total restoration, there will still be some limits that keep the world from being fully released from its bondage of corruption. As Gaebelein pointed out, "The Millennium is [merely] the doorway to the eternal state."[9] In other words, the river Ezekiel foresaw flowing out of the Millennial Temple is quite different and more limited in its restorative nature than the river we read about in Revelation 22, which will flow from the throne of God in the New Jerusalem. Humanity, therefore, will have to look past the millennial kingdom and on into the eternal state to experience the full redemption of the creation and the total realization of Romans 8:19-22. The millennial kingdom will provide a taste of that eager expectation, one that should be quite fulfilling. But the total redemption of creation lies beyond the millennial kingdom (more on that later).

THE PLAINS OF THE EARTH

One of the more striking descriptions of the earth during the millennial kingdom concerns its geography. Isaiah foresaw the day when the call will come to

> make straight in the desert a highway for our God. Every valley shall be exalted and every mountain and hill brought low; the crooked places shall be made straight and the rough places smooth (Isaiah 40:3-4).

Could this mean that if we were to do a study of the geography of the millennial era that it would reveal Jerusalem had become the highest—and only—mountain on the planet? And would the rest of the earth consist merely of plains? Are we talking about there being no mountains save one during the millennial kingdom?

Several rabbinic texts throw their historical support to a literal interpretation of the earth becoming all plains. The rabbinical traditionalists claim that God performed a similar deed during the exodus when, as a pillar of cloud and fire, the shekinah glory went before Israel to prepare the way for them by raising the depressions and lowering the elevations (Exodus 13:21).[10] This highway in the wilderness, stretching from Egypt to the Promised Land, was created during the exodus and could foreshadow the prophesied millennial highway that will run from Egypt to Assyria, with its center at Christ's seat of authority in Jerusalem (Isaiah 19:23).[11]

The flattening of the world into plains would have already happened during the Day of the Lord, as the four great earthquakes of the tribulation will have leveled the earth so that the rough places will indeed have been made smooth.[12] Just as in the days of the ancient Babylonian monarchies, whose kings had their roads cleared ahead of them to ease their passage, the whole earth will be cleared so that no obstacle can stand in the way when the King's subjects make their yearly journey to Jerusalem.[13]

The Essenes, who during the final centuries leading up to Christ's first advent lived on the shores of the Dead Sea at Qumran, had set up their community in that desolate wilderness to prepare the way for Yahweh.[14] These ancient scholars believed that interpreting Isaiah 40 literally would be too prosaic in thinking that Yahweh was merely referring to the creation of a futuristic desert superhighway. Rather, they interpreted the passage figuratively to mean that the Lord desired for the Essenes to establish a place in the wilderness for studying the Torah and preparing for the soon coming of the Messiah.[15] Judeo-Christian beliefs certainly owe the Essenes a great deal of thanks for being the guardians of the Torah and for producing the Dead Sea Scrolls, but their theological understanding of the wilderness as being a place of "eschatological testing" from which deliverance will come seems too localized in light of the global scope of the millennial kingdom.[16]

I favor the grandeur of mountains, so the possibility our world will be flattened into plains rather saddens me. Likewise, it's believed the great oceans of today will be divided into countless lakes spread out over enlarged continents. For our world to have no mountains or oceans almost seems like the earth will become as alien a planet as one taken straight out of a science fiction novel. And yet we can be sure that the sight of majestic Mount Zion rising up out of the plains in all its splendor, with the nations streaming down the multilane highway and up into Yahweh Shammah, will be absolutely breathtaking!

CHAPTER 18

LONG LIFE: THE REJUVENATION OF HUMANITY

Throughout history, fairly arbitrary lines drawn on maps have determined who prospers and who needs, who eats and who starves, who attacks and who is attacked, who lives long and who dies young. Oh, we have been slaves to those lines for so long.[1]

Gavin de Becker, billionaire

If the word *bounty* stands out as one of the most prolific characteristics of the millennial kingdom, and well it does, then its citizens will experience a plethora of different types of bounties. Another one of these bountiful blessings will involve the counting of the lifespans of its citizens, not in decades, but in centuries!

THE BOUNTY OF LONG LIFE

The prophet Isaiah foresaw this glorious day when humanity will be rejuvenated and people's lives prolonged:

> No more shall an infant from there live but a few days, nor an old man who has not fulfilled his days; for the child shall die one hundred years old, but the sinner being one hundred years old shall be accursed...For as the days of a tree, so shall be the days of My people (Isaiah 65:20, 22).

Isaiah's stunning prophecy reminds me of what is said in a stanza from Horatius Bonar's hymn "He Liveth Long Who Liveth Well":

> He liveth long who liveth well;
> All other life is short and vain;
> He liveth longest who can tell
> Of living most for heavenly gain.[2]

The residents of the millennial kingdom will endure as if they'd found the fabled Fountain of Youth, for indeed they will live both long and well.

NO MORE INFANT MORTALITY

Isaiah 65 reveals several extraordinary conditions related to mankind's seemingly unbeatable nemesis—time. For one, infant mortality will be no more. Isaiah's vision holds out the promise that a child dying in infancy will be unheard of during the kingdom. No longer will babies be born with congenital defects, or neonatal hemorrhages, suffer from complications, or die of Sudden Infant Death Syndrome (SIDS). And, after birth, the most vulnerable in society will receive the proper nourishment and medical care so that they can grow to maturity and live out their lives without infirmities.[3]

LIFESPANS THE DAYS OF TREES

Isaiah 65 revealed a second wondrous condition: People will live to become an astounding number of years old—"as the days of a tree" (verse 22). Remember how Methuselah lived to be a staggering 969 years old (Genesis 5:27)? This isn't a scribal error. The inhabitants of the earth before the Flood really did live for centuries. But, soon after the Flood, God set a limit on how long a person could live—He reduced their lifespans first to 120 years, and then later to 70-80 years (Genesis 6:3; Psalm 90:10). God shortening mankind's years is meant to be temporary, for the lifespans of the earthly residents of the kingdom will be lengthened once again to pre-Flood levels. As Isaiah revealed, if a 100-year-old is considered a mere child in the kingdom, then humanity's lifespans will be counted not in decades but in centuries. Humans could possibly even live as long as the entirety of the millennial kingdom—the full 1,000 years!

Theories vary as to why the kingdom's residents will live such exceedingly long lives. Isaiah identified one compelling reason: "The inhabitant will not say, 'I am sick'; the people who dwell in it will be forgiven their iniquity" (Isaiah 33:24). Because sin will be so tampered down during the kingdom, the ravages of sinful living and imbibing in excesses will no longer eat the years away from human lives.

Isaiah also described the end of bodily infirmities:

> Then the eyes of the blind shall be opened, and the ears of the deaf shall be unstopped. Then the lame shall leap like a deer, and the tongue of the dumb sing (Isaiah 35:5-6).

It also appears that the aging process will slow down greatly—so much so that its length will negate what philosopher W.H. Channing observed: "Life is a fragment, a moment between two eternities."[4] God will create environmental conditions paralleling those of the pre-Flood era, which will decelerate the aging process. With ample food, no poverty, no wars, practically no killing by man or animal, no sickness or infirmity, and a repaired biosphere, it's no wonder that the earthly residents of the millennial kingdom will live on and on for centuries.

EARLY DEATH DUE TO SIN

The third condition is rather sad. Isaiah reveals in chapter 65 that the earthly, non-glorified residents of the kingdom will still be capable of sinning (verse 20). Those who get caught up in a lifestyle of sin will be punished by having their long lives revoked. They'll be lucky to make it to 100 years old, and when they die, others will consider them to have died in their youth. Again, sin robs mankind of life.

The prophet's revelation that sin and death will still exist during the millennial kingdom sounds most unfortunate. Sure, sin will be greatly curtailed, as the evil influence of Satan and his demons will be absent, and we the glorified saints will ever be there to lovingly guide sinners to their Savior. But because human nature is a fallen nature, those in their earthly bodies will still commit sins. Sin will have yet to be fully eradicated from the earth during that era. What's so different compared to today, though, is that sin during the kingdom will be dealt with, and dealt with swiftly, by Christ's rod of iron. Justice and punishment for sinners during that era will have to come swiftly because sin offers a terrible appeal to our fallen human nature, and so multiplies rapidly across a population, much like a virus.

Such a sin-tarnished reality has created a stumbling block for those theologians who place Christ's kingdom solely within the eternal state, an era when sin and death will at last be conquered (Revelation 20:14-15). Other theologians jump through hoops as they try to explain away the sin and death aspects of the millennial kingdom by claiming that Isaiah 65 is merely using "longevity language" (such as in Exodus 23:26).[5] Still others even grant contemporary significance to Isaiah's revelation by interpreting long lives as really being about our society's attempts to one day attain a more just society.[6] When theologians like these deny the six references to the millennial kingdom as lasting a literal 1,000 years, then they fall prey to making these faulty conclusions—and as one anonymous author observed, "Our lives are a manifestation of what we think about God."[7]

Returning to a literal interpretation of the Bible, we come to the wondrous realization that for 1,000 years, the earthly citizens of the millennial kingdom will enjoy God's bounty of centuries-long lives.

CHAPTER 19

SATAN BOUND

God made bees, and bees made honey,
God made man, and man made money,
Pride made the devil, and the devil made sin;
So God made a coal-pit to put the devil in.[1]

William Cowper, eighteenth-century English poet and hymn writer

Let's pause for a moment and circle back to another bounty we've only briefly touched upon so far—a world without demonic influence. As we learned earlier, the powers that are truly behind our fallen human governments are spiritual in nature. When Christ arrives in victory at His second coming, He will banish Satan to the bottomless pit and cast the demonic realm far away from this planet. As Satan's chained form falls swiftly out of view, the world will collectively take a great sigh of relief, sharing in the same kind of elation as if they were cancer patients just informed that they were now cancer-free. During the millennial kingdom, the earth will be cured of the cancerous machinations of the demonic realm.

THE NEFARIOUS WORK OF SATAN

I hardly believe I have to take time to cover this, but in this day and age of skeptics, it's important to affirm that there is indeed a devil. The Bible makes it abundantly clear that the nefarious work of "the god of this age"—Satan—continues unceasingly and at a frantic pace. Satan desires to blind people to the saving knowledge of Jesus Christ, "lest the light of the gospel of the glory of Christ, who is the image of God, should shine on them" (2 Corinthians 4:4). In his diabolical efforts, Satan is compared to a roaring lion "seeking whom he may devour" (1 Peter 5:8).

In his harried task to send as many of those made in God's image to hell, Satan will lie (John 8:44) and tempt people to sin (1 Corinthians 7:5; Ephesians 4:27). Our enemy disguises himself as an angel of light for the purpose of deception (2 Corinthians 11:3, 13-15). For those who love their sin more than their Creator, Satan will influence people to lie (Acts 5:3) until they become so debased that they become ensnared under his persuasive power (Acts 26:18; 1 John 3:8-10; 5:19). The devil deceives and entraps unbelievers, holding them captive with their vices so that they will become enslaved to his wicked will (2 Timothy 2:26).

For those seekers who initially hear the gospel, Satan attempts to snatch away the truth, leaving doubts and questions in their hearts (Matthew 13:19; Mark 4:15; Luke 8:12; 1 Thessalonians 3:5; 1 Timothy 1:20; 4:1-2). And for those who do accept the gospel, Satan's not done distressing them. He takes advantage of believers (2 Corinthians 2:11), torments the servants of God (2 Corinthians 12:7), thwarts their evangelistic efforts (1 Thessalonians 2:18), seeks to destroy believers' faith (Luke 22:31), and wages an all-out war against the church (Ephesians 6:11-17).

THE REALITY OF SATAN

Satan's incessant and ongoing mission to destroy humanity during this church age should leave no one doubting Satan's existence.

And yet many people today deny that such an evil being could exist. They deny that Satan exists as a personal entity and instead relegate him as some force of nature or merely the personification of unfortunate events.

Cotton Mather, in his *Discourse on the Wonders of the Invisible World*, nailed the reason for why the existence of Satan is so lightly dismissed:

> That there is a Devil is a thing doubted by none but such as are under the influences of the Devil. For any to deny the being of a Devil must be from an ignorance or profaneness worse than diabolical.[2]

There are even Christians who, though they concede the existence of the evil angel known as Satan or the devil, claim that Christ bound Satan at the cross, and so the devil's damnatory work has been severely curtailed. When cataloging the rampant evil that defines our day, Matt Waymeyer laughed at such a ridiculous conclusion and stated, "It is impossible to reconcile this portrayal of Satan's activities in the present age with the view that he is currently sealed."[3] I even heard one preacher—who sensibly agrees that the notion of the devil being curtailed today is preposterous—remark that if Satan is indeed leashed, then why is he always nipping at his heels?

THE BOUNDING OF SATAN

It is quite evident by the devil's numerous visible and nefarious works, along with the Bible's detailed personal descriptions, that an evil entity entirely bent on attempting to thwart God at every turn does indeed exist, and his name is Satan. But was Satan truly bound at the cross, as if a dog tethered on a short chain, or will he instead be bound at the onset of the millennial kingdom? Revelation 20 answers the questions as to how and when Satan will be bound:

> I saw an angel coming down from heaven, having the key to the bottomless pit and a great chain in his hand. He laid hold of the dragon, that serpent of old, who is the Devil and Satan, and bound him for a thousand years; and he cast him into the bottomless pit, and shut him up, and set a seal on him, so that he should deceive the nations no more till the thousand years were finished. But after these things he must be released for a little while (Revelation 20:1-3).

In the debate over the timing and nature of Satan's role during the millennial kingdom, this passage in Revelation 20 has been labeled the "crux interpretum."[4] And while New Testament expert Sydney Page believed Revelation 20 contains a "veritable battleground of conflicting interpretations," I disagree, for quite a lot of details concerning Satan's bounding are revealed, especially in verses 1-3. They explain how and when Satan is to be bound and imprisoned in an abyss for 1,000 years (if interpreted literally, of course).[5]

From the Beginning

For the initial detail, in the first of four visions John witnessed in Revelation 20, he saw Satan bound at the beginning of the millennial kingdom. This reference debunks the notion that Satan was bound at the cross. Jesus may have defeated Satan and death at His first advent, but Christ still needs to return to claim His victory. Only then will Satan be rendered completely inactive. As one theologian so rightly commented, "It is difficult to imagine how this could have been portrayed more clearly."[6]

That means all of Satan's work in lying and tempting, thwarting and scheming, persecuting and causing suffering, will not be present during the millennial kingdom. Because the kingdom age is described as a virtual paradise on earth, this time the old serpent will not be skulking around Christ's garden.

For 1,000 Years

The second detail in Revelation 20 concerns the length of time that Satan will be bound—1,000 years. While one could interpret the phrase "[a] thousand years" figuratively, John went out of his way six different times to note the length of the kingdom age. This 1,000 years of exile jives harmoniously with Revelation's other descriptions concerning the length of the kingdom as being a literal 1,000 years. The world will rejoice when Satan becomes bound and gagged and remains harmless for the entirety of the 1,000-year period.

In the Bottomless Pit

The third detail Revelation 20 provides is the exact location where Satan is to be bound—the bottomless pit. Also known as the abyss, the bottomless pit exists even today as an inescapable prison that binds the worst of the worst evil angels, preventing them from carrying out their horrific demonic activities on the earth—that is, until their time to be released comes (Luke 8:31; Revelation 9:1; 20:1, 3).

In earlier chapters, the book of Revelation describes the bottomless pit as the holding place of the locust-like demons and their demonic ruler *Abaddon* (Hebrew), also known as *Apollyon* (Greek). Abaddon's eventual release and rampaging across the earth will serve as the fifth trumpet judgment during the tribulation. He and his demonic followers will torment those loyal to the Antichrist for five whole months by inflicting painful stings that cannot be relieved even by death (Revelation 9:1-12).

The fifth trumpet judgment describes the abyss as bottomless, filled with acrid smoke, emanating the heat of a furnace, and equipped with an entryway that can be locked with a key and so be sealed. This bottomless pit is where the Davidic King will banish Satan for the entire duration of the millennial kingdom.

Therefore, it will be impossible for the devil to tempt the kingdom's inhabitants. Can you even imagine a world where Satan and his miscreants are no longer causing so much pain and suffering? That will be one of the many blessed conditions we will all enjoy during the millennial kingdom.

CHAPTER 20

SATAN DEFEATED

I'm not afraid of the Devil. The Devil can handle me—he's got judo I never heard of. But he can't handle the One to whom I'm joined; he can't handle the One to whom I'm united; he can't handle the One whose nature dwells in my nature.[1]

A.W. Tozer, twentieth-century pastor

For 1,000 years, the subjects of the kingdom will know a world of peace, righteousness, and justice. At least once a year, the Davidic King will lovingly greet His children in Jerusalem, where they will flock to look upon His shining face and listen intently to His wise teachings. No poverty or want will plague mankind, and both the human and animal kingdoms will share in the bonds of mutual friendship. This will be a world enjoying its sabbath rest.

SATAN RELEASED

But then John shatters this scene of idyllic utopian serenity with the following revelation:

> When the thousand years have expired, Satan will be released from his prison and will go out to deceive the nations which are in the four corners of the earth, Gog and Magog, to gather them together to battle, whose number is as the sand of the sea. They went up on the breadth of the earth and surrounded the camp of the saints and the beloved city (Revelation 20:7-9).

This scripture plainly states that once the 1,000 years have passed, Satan will be inexplicably released, but only for a short amount of time. Satan doesn't break the seal and escape out of the bottomless pit. All his demons will already have been sentenced to their final judgment, so his minions cannot aid in his prison break. No, in a stunningly confusing move, God Himself will command the release of the devil. The angel who stands guard over the abyss will obey God's command, breaking the seal and unlocking the great barrier that has held the devil at bay for a millennium. The most powerful enemy of both God and man will burst forth from out of that pit, raging in ferocious fury, and will immediately set out to resume his evil work.

In describing Satan's malignant work, President John Adams's youngest son, the inventor Thomas Adams, commented:

> The devil is no idle spirit, but a vagrant, runagate walker, that never rests in one place. The motive, cause, and main intention of his walking is to ruin man.[2]

Thus, the old serpent will be let loose in a garden once more, deceiving not just one couple, but that couple's descendants in numbers as uncountable as the sands of the sea. Many of the peacefully naïve children of the tribulation saints will all too easily fall for the deceiver's deceptions and will gladly follow him instead of their King. Satan will marshal his newfound followers into a colossal army, marching them toward Yahweh Shammah for one last desperate attempt to overthrow the Son of God.

Why our omniscient God frees Satan from his prison and allows him to incite the kingdom's earthly inhabitants to rebel presents one of the more puzzling mysteries of the Bible. Gregory Harris, a Bible scholar, in attempting to solve this puzzle, concluded that God will release Satan so that he can incite one last rebellion in mankind to cause the deaths of every human who has still rejected their Messiah.[3]

Another theologian, Robert Govett, presented four reasons as to why Satan must be released.[4] One, God will wish to demonstrate to unregenerate mankind that if left to their own devices, they will almost always choose to sin, even in the most favorable of circumstances. Two, God will establish to a new generation the fact that He possesses foreknowledge of mankind's actions. Three, Satan's own actions upon release will demonstrate that he remains unrepentantly and incurably evil. And four, the crime of rebellion further justifies God's just sentence of eternal punishment.

Even when living in a near-perfect society, the heart of an unregenerate man will remain bent on rebellion. The renowned Renaissance scholar Petrarch identified what he called "the five great enemies of peace" that inhabit mankind's souls—avarice, ambition, envy, anger, and pride—saying, "If these were to be banished, we should infallibly enjoy perpetual peace."[5] But the sinful heart of man seldom wishes to remain at peace. Instead, our fallen nature causes humanity's longing to overthrow the one true God and replace Him with the idol of self.

Here's the problem for those dwelling in the millennium in their earthly bodies: Every selfish attempt at sin will be thwarted instantly. The omniscient King will rule directly over the earth, and He will enforce His peace and justice through the glorified saints. So while the earthly residents of the kingdom can still choose to commit evil, they will be swiftly punished by Christ's "rod of iron."[6] I imagine that we will witness many of the children and grandchildren of the tribulation saints greeting their King each year with forced words of praise, but in their fallen hearts, they will be seething to throw off Christ's yoke of authority so they can live out the lusts of the flesh.

Into their frustration will enter Satan, freshly released from his imprisonment. As English poet John Dryden noted, "When to sin our bias'd nature leans, the careful devil is still at hand with means."[7] Satan will indeed provide those means, deceiving these closet rebels with the same old promise that if they would only overthrow the Man in Jerusalem and install the devil upon the King's Davidic throne, then he would grant his followers all the desires of their wicked hearts. Reverting to the devil's tired, worn-out strategy of assembling an army large enough so that at an initial glance it appears it could have a chance of overthrowing the city, Satan will march his rebels toward Yahweh Shammah. As the seventeenth-century author John Clarke wrote, "'Tis an ill company where the Devil bears the banner."[8]

THE FINAL REBELLION

Satan's massive army of wayward "millennials" will encamp around the defensive waters that surround the great capital of Yahweh Shammah. That "prince of expositors," G. Campbell Morgan, described this scene: "Man in his rebellion is gathered to oppose Him. The battle is immediately joined."[9]

But will there actually be a battle? John describes Christ's swift response, the outcome of this rebellion, and so, too, the rebels' fate:

> Fire came down from God out of heaven and devoured them. The devil, who deceived them, was cast into the lake of fire and brimstone where the beast and the false prophet are. And they will be tormented day and night forever and ever (Revelation 20:9-10).

For all the terrible, consuming rage brandished by the adversary, and the looming menace coming from what will likely be the largest army ever fielded in human history, these rebels will end up defeated. As Martin Luther sang, "The prince of darkness grim, we tremble not for him; his rage we can endure, for lo! his doom is sure; one little word shall fell him."[10] Morgan further narrated the quick and decisive action taken by Yahweh Tsidkenu in defeating His enemies with an act so simple that it's stunning in its simplicity—by calling fireballs to blaze down from heaven to incinerate the rebels:

> There is no indecision, no varying fortunes. It is quick, sharp, decisive, terrible. The king and His armies are supernatural. It is the hour when heaven is touching earth. The spiritualities which men have refused to acknowledge are carrying out a judgment due to blasphemous denial... Victory having thus been obtained over all the manifestations of godlessness on earth, Satan is arrested and imprisoned.[11]

The reason the Davidic King puts down this sudden rebellion with such a speedy, immediate, and decisive response can be explained by a condition of the Davidic covenant. The Messiah's earthly reign must be defined as having no end to peace (Isaiah 9:7).[12] Therefore, there can be no actual fighting in this final battle, as revealed in Revelation 20:7-9, but only an allowance for an assemblage to battle. If an actual battle was allowed to occur, it would undermine the Messiah's promise of everlasting peace.[13] Thus, God must vanquish the assembled enemies with a preemptive strike—only then can He fulfill all His covenantal promises.[14]

With the human rebels incinerated, at long last, the Son of God will judge Satan. This curse on all humanity will be forced to kneel before his maker. He will be the last of the demons to receive his due punishment. Revelation 20 outlines the overthrow of the devil as occurring in stages.[15] First, Satan will be bound and sealed in the abyss for 1,000 years. Next, he will be released and given a short amount of time during which to deceive the nations. Then Satan will marshal the rebellious to confront the King and His saints, only to face an inglorious and swift defeat. And finally, the devil will be cast into the lake of fire to suffer everlasting punishment. Once this final sentence against Satan has been carried out, there will remain one last enemy for God to vanquish—death itself (Revelation 20:14).

Satan will finally and forever be defeated! All creation will cry out in relief with a heartfelt amen.

THE KINGDOM'S ONE FLAW

Now that we've learned much about the content and character of the millennial kingdom, and have reached its epic conclusion in our narrative, we can afford to take a short pause and ask a vital question. *Because a rebellion will break out at the end of the 1,000 years, should we consider that the millennial kingdom will fail at resolving the problem of evil as it relates to failed human government?*

Let's first address this: Will the final rebellion be due to some flaw inherent in the head of the kingdom's government? The Sovereign who will rule over this kingdom is the very definition of perfection (Matthew 5:48). Jesus Christ is all-loving, all-giving, all-compassionate, all-providing, all-holy, and all-wise. As the psalmist wrote:

> The law of the Lord is perfect, converting the soul; the testimony of the Lord is sure, making wise the simple; the statutes of the Lord are right, rejoicing the heart; the commandment of the Lord is pure, enlightening the eyes; the fear of the Lord is clean, enduring forever; the judgments of the Lord are true and righteous altogether (Psalm 19:7-9).

Christ will rule over His kingdom with a rod of iron, and that may be perceived as harsh by some of His subjects, but the King's precepts will still remain perfect. After all,

> he who looks into the perfect law of liberty and continues in it, and is not a forgetful hearer but a doer of the work, this one will be blessed in what he does (James 1:25).

That means if the millennial kingdom were to be considered a failure, the fault most definitely would not lie with its King.

Second, will the final rebellion be due to some flaw inherent in the administrators of the kingdom's government? Remember that every administrator at every level of authority under the King will be a resurrected believer. With the glorification of their bodies upon their resurrection, the old sin nature will have been done away with so that it no longer clouds their thinking with selfish ambitions and corrupt desires. The glorified officials of the kingdom will obey the precepts of the Davidic King to the letter, and because His ways are perfect, so too will be the carrying out of His commands. Therefore, any apparent failure connected to the millennial kingdom will not lie with the glorified administrators of that kingdom.

Third, will the final rebellion be due to some flaw inherent in the societal conditions of the millennial kingdom? The philosophers of this age argue that mankind is inherently good, and so conclude that environmental factors must be the cause of society's ills. But during the millennial kingdom, the environment will be utopian, so the earth cannot be blamed.

In summary, we've established that the King will be perfect, the administrators will have been perfected, the world will be at peace, and no poverty or want will exist—therefore, the perfect environment. Also, Satan and his demons will have been locked away and so cannot tempt anyone, at least until the very final days of the millennium.

And the surviving tribulation saints, who will have learned the hard-knocks lesson about what a nightmare a world rampant with sin can become like, will in no way join the final rebellion.

The only remaining citizens left to evaluate are the children and children's children born to the tribulation saints. Still residing in a fallen earthly body, they will continue to possess sin natures. But with no negative environmental influences to adversely affect their decision-making, these "millennials" will have no one but themselves to blame and so will be fully responsible for their own actions. The problem inherent with the millennial kingdom, then, must lie solely with these fallen subjects. So while the millennial government will be perfect, and society will be perfect, the non-glorified subjects will remain imperfect.[16] Their fallen, imperfect state is the one flaw that will cause the millennial kingdom to fail in the end—not the government, mind you, for it is perfect, but the ability of its earthly citizens to remain living in a utopian society.

WHY UTOPIANISM FAILS

Because a utopia is, by its very definition, an ideal or a perfect society, free will and personal responsibility would have to be jettisoned, because to have these would inherently create conflict, and an idealized society cannot tolerate conflict.[17] Any change to the ideal status quo must be regarded as a fall from perfection, and thus free will becomes a deadly threat to the society's integrity and survival, resulting in obedience and conformity becoming the ultimate personal good.[18]

While God does indeed desire obedience and conformity to His perfect will, He also desires His subjects to make the choice to obey, and that choice demands that humanity's free will remain unmolested. God's original intention for His creation entails freedom, even if said freedom subjects God's plan to the cataclysmic risk that humanity may or may not choose to adore and trust in Him. God, in elevating free will at the moral level, revolutionizes humanity's worship of our Creator, turning worship into an act of freedom.[19] Choice has always been essential to God's plan of salvation, or people would simply serve as mindless robots with no choice but to obey their programming to "love" and worship their Creator. God has always wanted to populate His kingdom with individuals who freely desire to live with Him forever. Nobody wants to spend eternity with those who disdain them.

The trouble with fallen man's utopian expectations is that we want perfect holiness to coexist with few, if any, moral constraints, causing our expectations to become both unrealistic and misguided.[20] Mankind's longing for a utopia, and the frustration at its failure to achieve one, have caused two diametrically opposed responses throughout human history.[21] First, when we take into our own hands the personal responsibility for creating a new world order apart from God, mankind will always pursue its establishment through revolutionary actions, often violently. The resulting destruction thwarts any achievement of that initial goal of a peaceful society. You cannot build a peaceful society through violence. Or, second, believing that the material world is so evil that it is beyond redemption, mankind will then seek to create a spiritualized form of utopia through transcendence into a higher form of life or plane of existence, as is being attempted in today's radical race to force our "evolution" via transhumanism.

Historically, these failures lead societies down the dark path of pessimism and resigned to fatalism, which inevitably leads to nihilism. And once nihilism has grabbed hold of a society, it's not long before the culture and then the entire civilization commit suicide.[22] Therefore, every human government will inevitably fail at producing a utopian society, which leads its citizens to reject their society, and whose nihilism further regresses their culture into killing itself. This is the current state of the Western world today. We are witnessing with great dismay so many of our nations, quite frankly, committing suicide.

As one philosopher observed, inevitably, all philosophies, religions, and political and military institutions will fail to overcome the difficulties that beset humanity in every generation.[23] The societal problems that we seek to eradicate through education, revolutions, and governmental power are merely offshoots of our true problem—ourselves. This means that the solution to mankind's real problem in solving the failures of government will forever lie outside the secular orientation that dominates modern thought, because we cannot possibly create a utopia as long as humanity remains in a fallen state.[24]

This must be the lesson God has long been trying to teach humanity. Even living in a utopian society, with the perfect King and government—which the millennial kingdom will achieve—the problem of sin will remain. Over the centuries, God has persistently tried again and again to pound this truth into the minds of the Jewish people, and later, the church, but people continue to cast the blame for their failure to perpetuate a utopian society on outside forces, such as their environment, rather than on their sinful hearts.[25] The Bible stands, then, as a record of God's instructional process, where He is teaching us that mankind can never bring about heaven on earth as long as people remain in their fallen nature. We can only conclude, then, that the apparent failure of the millennial kingdom will stand as God's lesson to fallen man about the consequences of sin.

LOOKING BEYOND THE MILLENNIAL KINGDOM

If the millennial kingdom ends without fully fulfilling all the kingdom promises, especially concerning its stated perfection and everlasting qualities, then what is the answer?

If the kingdom of Christ is destined to fulfill all the covenants (Abrahamic, Davidic, and new), as well as the kingdom promises, how, then, can a mere 1,000 years fulfill a "forever promise"?[26] We know it cannot.

Our answer resides, then, in the final phase of the Davidic kingdom. Yes, there still remains one more phase to the Davidic kingdom, one that comes after the millennial kingdom, and it's called the eternal state.[27] God's solution to mankind's problem of evil as it relates to failed governments is to be found yet again in the Messiah, but fully realized in that final phase of the kingdom of Christ.

We come to understand, then, that the millennial phase of the Davidic kingdom will exist merely, as one commentator whimsically observed, as the "kickoff party" to God's "forever kingdom."[28] Because the first 1,000 years will serve to foreshadow the eternal state, we are to look to this final phase for the complete fulfillment of all the promises related to the Davidic kingdom. It is in the eternal state that we will fully and finally find the solution to mankind's problem of evil—our own fallen humanity. So let's venture beyond the millennial kingdom and explore that blessed final phase of the Davidic kingdom.

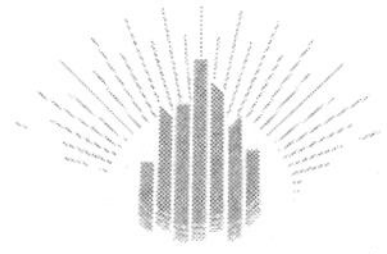

CHAPTER 21

FINAL JUDGMENT

It is all too easy to become discouraged and disheartened by the rampant presence of evil and injustice in our world today. It leaves us wondering: Will anything ever be done to bring to justice those who have perpetrated such wickedness? Will anything ever be done to reward those who are righteous? *The answer is Yes!*[1]

Sam Storms, professor and preacher

At this point in our narrative, the millennial kingdom phase of the Davidic kingdom has, at last, come to an end. Its final act will be when King Jesus banishes Satan to the lake of fire to burn forever and ever (Revelation 20:10).[2] Even with this most satisfying act of judgment completed, the sentencing of Satan will not have divinely eradicated all evils, as death won't have been abolished forever—at least, not yet. One closing, forever judgment remains—the fate of the eternally damned. The final gavel must fall before the new heavens, the new earth, and the New Jerusalem arrive to usher in the terminal, everlasting phase of the Davidic kingdom.

THE GREAT WHITE THRONE JUDGMENT

John shared how this climactic judgment will commence:

> I saw a great white throne and Him who sat on it, from whose face the earth and the heaven fled away. And there was found no place for them. And I saw the dead, small and great, standing before God, and books were opened. And another book was opened, which is the Book of Life. And the dead were judged according to their works, by the things which were written in the books. The sea gave up the dead who were in it, and Death and Hades delivered up the dead who were in them. And they were judged, each one according to his works. Then Death and Hades were cast into the lake of fire. This is the second death. And anyone not found written in the Book of Life was cast into the lake of fire (Revelation 20:11-15).

The Inevitability of Judgment

J.I. Packer noted, "There are few things stressed more strongly in the Bible than the reality of God's work as Judge."[3] Look to the Old Testament (Psalm 96:13; Ecclesiastes 12:14; Daniel 12:2), then look to the New Testament (Acts 17:31; 2 Timothy 4:1), and we discover that the entirety of the Bible is overshadowed by the certainty of a coming day of universal judgment. Just as the moon hangs over the earth, the inevitability of this judgment ever hangs over every verse in the Bible. When it comes to God's plan for the ages, judgment is ever looming.

The book of Hebrews affirms this truth: "It is appointed for men to die once, but after this the judgment" (Hebrews 9:27). Hebrews even listed eternal judgment as one of the elementary teachings in Scripture (Hebrews 6:1-2). Professor David MacLeod called this great court drama "the Great Assize before which all men must appear and at which they will be assigned their eternal destiny."[4]

Jesus, in 12 out of His 36 parables, spoke about the final tribunal. Jesus explained how the rebellious will inevitably be judged, condemned, and punished for their sins to a place called hell (Hebrew *yeevva*), a term Christ used 11 out of the 12 times the word *hell* is found in the New Testament.[5]

The Judge Who Sits on the Throne

Revelation 20:11-15 is the central passage of Scripture that provides the specific details concerning the doctrine of the last judgment of the wicked. Mark Twain, in his manuscript *About Cities in the Sun*, eloquently painted the scene the apostle John was witnessing in this sobering passage:

> John did not know where he was. And as he looked up at the lofty acropolis on the top of this vast pyramidal mountain with the beautiful terraced city sloping far down below it, and Deity and his great white throne and shining acropolis glittering with a million of diamond coronets, and the crystal light of the corona covering all like a canopy of effulgent glory...It is clear from John's statement that the great white throne that was in the midst of the city was on this great central apex or acropolis; and there were the great auditorium and magnificent court of honor in front of the great white throne. And from this throne, or near it, and perhaps in the center of this vast court was a wonderful fountain of the waters of life, "clear as crystal," and from it flowed the beautiful river of life.[6]

John wasn't gazing at Christ's millennial throne in Jerusalem, nor was it the Son's celestial throne in heaven, but rather, the very throne of the Father. The fact that the great white throne is described as "great" could either mean that it is great in size and so conveys the grandeur of its authority, or that the occasion would be great because it finally concludes the affairs of this earth, or both.[7] What we do know is that the throne being white points to the purity and invincible justice of the One who sits upon it. While not identified by John, other scriptures reveal the Judge to be none other than the Lord Jesus Christ sitting upon His Father's throne (John 5:22; Acts 17:31; 2 Timothy 4:1).[8]

The Cosmic Courtroom

It is on this great white throne that all the attention of the universe will be centered, for to the spectators, it will appear as if both earth and sky had fled away (Revelation 20:11). The watchers will then behold one final resurrection—called the resurrection of the wicked. This resurrection will not include raptured believers, for they will have already been resurrected 1,000 years earlier at the resurrection of the just, then evaluated for their rewards at the bema seat of Christ (2 Corinthians 5:10). The believing dead will have been participants in the first resurrection, which will have two phases—first, the church at the rapture before the tribulation, and then later, the Old Testament and tribulation saints at the second coming of Christ.[9]

Revelation 20:12-13 instead points to a completely different and second resurrection for the rest of the dead—that is, the unbelieving wicked. This will consist of all people who throughout human history had hardened their hearts and clenched their fists in rebellion against their Creator, including those who had heard about Christ's salvation but rejected it, and so upon death were consigned to Hades to await final judgment (John 5:28-29).[10]

The Books of Life

Once every sentient being assembles before the great white throne, John noted that books will be opened, including the Book of Life. The Bible recognizes two Books of Life. The verse in Psalms is most likely referring to the Book of Life in which every person who was ever created is listed (Psalm 139:16). This is a different book than the Lamb's Book of Life, in which those who are saved are listed (Revelation 13:8; 21:27). Only those who are written in the Lamb's Book of Life will receive eternal life and live forever with their loving Savior (Revelation 21:27). Those who are not written in the Lamb's Book of Life will be sentenced to the same fate as the villainous Satan, his demons, the Antichrist, and the false prophet, who by this point in Revelation's narrative, had already been thrown into the lake of fire. This final sentence to hell, after already being resurrected from the dead, is fittingly called the second death (Revelation 20:14).

A Judgment by Works

Interestingly, God will judge the resurrected wicked using the same criteria He used at the sheep-goat judgment—their works (Romans 2:6). Alas, human works will always utterly fail to measure up to God's perfect standard of holiness (Matthew 5:48).[11] As noted, all who will stand before the great white throne judgment will be there because, in life, they had been faithless. They had wholeheartedly rejected Christ's substitutionary work of atonement, and so the Lord hadn't absolved them of their transgressions. And because human works are considered to be as if filthy rags to a perfectly holy God (Isaiah 64:6), the defendants' works can only be counted as worthless.

We learn from this ultimate judgment the ultimate biblical truth: The only work that can save the soul is the work of salvation Jesus performed by sacrificing Himself on the cross. "Nor is there salvation in any other, for there is no other name under heaven given among men by which we must be saved" (Acts 4:12). By rejecting Christ and His salvation, the unredeemed will lack the only work that would garner the Judge's decision of "innocent," and so the defendants will have earned their final sentence of "damnation by works."[12]

When our good works haven't been anointed by the shed blood of Christ, they will always fall short of the glory of God (Romans 3:23).

The unregenerate remain facing God's wrath (John 3:36). Christ as the Righteous Judge must judge the wicked to show that their punishment—eternal death in the lake of fire—is well deserved.

The Just Judge will once again scan the pages of His books, and not finding these rebels' names written in the two books of life, will dispense perfect justice by casting them bodily into hell (Revelation 20:15). In their resurrected though unglorified bodies, those sentenced to hell will feel unending heat, severe pain, utter loneliness, and a complete severance from the source of all life—Yahweh God. That severance is why hell truly is a death sentence, and is therefore fittingly called the second death.

The Death of Death

John then reveals something wondrous! Death and Hades will also be cast into the lake of fire to join the unredeemed in serving out their eternal punishment (Revelation 20:14). While death is personified in this passage, Hades is an actual, physical location, but will be no more. As David MacLeod explained, "Hades is the grim receptacle of death's prey, that is, the abode of the dead."[13] Death will have lingered on until the end of the millennial kingdom as humanity's last, inescapable enemy, only to likewise face the same eternal destruction as Satan, his demons, and the unredeemed (1 Corinthians 15:54-55). With Hades and death forever banished to the lake of fire, the last vestiges of human rebellion against God will have at last been destroyed.

THE ETERNAL STATE

With God's enemies having been summarily defeated, it's time for all God's children to celebrate in that long-anticipated victory. Jesus Christ will prepare to fulfill His promises, in totality, as the apostle Paul recorded:

> Then comes the end, when He delivers the kingdom to God the Father, when He puts an end to all rule and all authority and power. For He must reign till He has put all enemies under His feet. The last enemy that will be destroyed is death...Now when all things are made subject to Him, then the Son Himself will also be subject to Him who put all things under Him, that God may be all in all (1 Corinthians 15:24-28).

Thus, the kingdom of Christ will have lasted for 1,000 years, after which evil will summarily be expelled. All of Christ's enemies will have been defeated, including death itself. Then Jesus will hand the kingdom over to the Father. With that final victorious act, the Davidic King and His faithful will enter the ultimate phase of the kingdom. Remember that the promised nature of the Davidic kingdom is its eternality—hence, this new and final phase has been given the theological title—the eternal state.

Revelation 21–22—a mere two chapters out of the entire Bible—provide us with the only details about what the eternal state will be like. We learn that during the eternal state, Christ will continue to reign from Jerusalem on the throne of David over all nations for all eternity. But the earth as we will have known it during the millennial kingdom will be no more. God will melt, transform, and rejuvenate the current earth, creating a whole new one. God will then lower the enormous supercity the Bible calls the New Jerusalem down out of the new heavens to rest upon the new earth.

Everyone dwelling in the New Jerusalem will either be redeemed humans in their glorified bodies or angels. Because the death of our old bodies removes our sin nature, our resurrected bodies will be left without any desire to rebel against God. With sin itself extinguished, mankind's desire to feed a rebellious nature will have disappeared forevermore. The harmonization of free will with a perfected desire will result in both God and man living together forever in perfect harmony. With God and man enjoying a personal, face-to-face relationship once again, a Garden of Eden–like era will have been restored. Human history will have come full circle.

The conclusion of the millennial kingdom will have provided the ultimate proof of mankind's depravity.[14] Every excuse for mankind's sin will have been exposed as just that—bankrupt—for sinners will still rebel and turn their loyalties toward the darkness. But in the eternal state, the final phase of the kingdom of Christ will have at last achieved the perfect environment, perfect economy, perfect education system, perfect legal system, perfect state of health, perfect society, perfect opportunity, and perfect government. The face of God the Father will at last be revealed, and He will dwell with His redeemed children, with no trace of sin to separate them. God the Son will sit upon the Father's throne in the New Jerusalem, and all eyes will behold His glory. And God the Holy Spirit will burn like a flame before the throne.

While 1,000 years have been allotted for the first phase of the Davidic kingdom, the sum and substance of the promises made concerning the kingdom of Christ rest firmly within the eternal state. As if a down payment, the millennial kingdom will have provided only the first 1,000 years of an eternal promise, and as the last salvific dispensation, like all dispensations so far, it will have ended in tragedy. But not so with the eternal state. In that glorious era, from King down to His citizens, all will have been purified and made holy. The sting of sin and death will be no more.

Therefore, the biblical response to the problem of evil as it relates to failed human governments will be fully realized, at long last, with the eternal state.

CHAPTER 22

MILLENNIAL VIEWPOINTS

Truth; that long clean clear simple undeniable unchallengeable straight and shining line, on one side of which black is black and on the other white is white, has now become an angle, a point of view.[1]

William Faulkner, twentieth-century American author

In this book, we have explored what the Bible teaches concerning the kingdom of Christ. Along the way, I have utilized a plain-sense, literal methodology in the reading of the plethora of various kingdom-themed scriptures. My purpose in using this approach has been to answer the questions that had initially been posed:

- When it comes to understanding the Davidic aspect of the kingdom of Christ, who has gotten it right?
- Was God promising a literal kingdom, with a literal descendant of David, who would sit on a literal earthly throne that would last literally forever?
- Or is the Davidic kingdom simply rolled up in the initial three folds Cotton Mather defined?

- How, then, should the kingdom of Christ be interpreted—literally or spiritually?

Any conclusions we could draw from Scripture will have been greatly influenced by whether we chose to use either a literal or spiritualized approach to interpreting God's Word. The methodology we chose to apply tends to result in placing us into one of four main interpretive camps when it comes to our understanding of eschatology, or the end times. So what are the four major millennial viewpoints, and what does each one believe? Let's find out!

THE LITMUS TEST

Before we delve into each of these eschatological camps, I want to provide you with a litmus test. If you took chemistry in high school, you probably remember these specially treated little strips of paper that turned blue when dipped in an alkaline solution or turned red when dipped into an acidic solution. Similarly, the following 12 questions act rather like said litmus test when applied to what we have learned from the Bible about the kingdom of Christ. Using these questions will help you determine whether a particular millennial viewpoint lines up with the authority of Scripture:

1. Have the Jews all been regathered back to the land of Israel?
2. Has the world endured the horrors of the Day of the Lord?
3. Has Jesus Christ returned physically to conquer the Antichrist and banish Satan?
4. Has the Gentile world order been destroyed?
5. Has the world been judged, and only the faithful entered into Christ's kingdom?

6. Does Jesus rule as King and Priest from His temple in Jerusalem?
7. Do King David and the resurrected saints fill roles within the kingdom's administration?
8. Does a remnant of saved Jews serve as an exalted priestly people?
9. Do all of the world's inhabitants personally know Jesus and worship Him?
10. Has all conflict ended between man and beast, resulting in a world that knows only peace and bounty?
11. Are human lifespans counted in the hundreds of years?
12. Has Satan been bound, released, then banished to hell forever?

The following millennial viewpoints, ordered progressively by the corresponding historical eras within the church age in which they were predominantly developed, provide a cursory overview of the various eschatological methodologies commonly used when interpreting what the Bible teaches concerning the millennial kingdom. As you use the above-stated litmus-test questions, my hope is that you will be able to identify the strongest viewpoint, and thereby glean the most accurate understanding of the Bible's response to the problem of evil as it relates to failed human governments.

1. Historic Premillennialism

History and Origins

The origins of historic premillennialism stretch back to the earliest centuries and foundational years of church history, and possibly even earlier. The idea of the coming of a Messiah to rescue Israel from its oppressors was a quite-common notion by the time of Christ's first advent, as evidenced by the wealth of apocalyptic texts found in the Dead Sea Scrolls.[2] Resting on the teachings of Jesus and the apostles, the early church fathers, with only a few exceptions, overwhelmingly held to the eschatological understanding that Christ would return to set up a literal, earthly, 1,000-year kingdom.[3]

Philip Schaff, one of the foremost Victorian-era church historians, noted:

> The most striking point in the eschatology of the Ante-Nicene age...[that being the period following the Apostolic Age of the first century down to the First Council of Nicaea in AD 325]...is the prominent chiliasm, or millenarianism, belief of a visible reign of Christ in glory on earth with the risen saints for a thousand years before the general resurrection and judgment.[4]

Along with church fathers such as Barnabas, Papias, Methodius, and Lactantius, Irenaeus (AD 170) stated that a belief in a future fulfillment of Christ's physical reign was an "indispensable part of orthodoxy to believe that these things shall indeed come to pass on this earth."[5] Likewise, Tertullian (AD 180) believed that a heavenly Jerusalem was about to descend to the earth, and so Christians should expect Christ to appear in Jerusalem.[6] Justin Martyr, in his *Dialogue with Trypho*, when asked if he believed Jerusalem would in the future be rebuilt and the Jewish people regathered together there to be "made joyful with Christ and the patriarchs," responded, "I and many others are of this opinion."[7]

Though the early church fathers were far more focused on ascertaining the church's essential doctrines over developing the finer points of their eschatological understanding, they still held to a futurist eschatological outlook. As Ben Witherington concluded, "[This] explains much about Jesus, about the early Christians' belief system, and the belief system of the author of Revelation."[8]

BELIEFS AND TENETS

Those who embrace the historic premillennial viewpoint hold to a consistent application of historical-grammatical hermeneutics based on a literal, or plain sense, interpretation of Scripture while taking into account genre, literary structure, and the canonicity of the Bible.[9] This results in its adherents being labeled futurists, meaning that they believe that major key prophetic events such as the tribulation, the second coming (equated with the rapture of the church), and the millennium remain yet future.[10] Such a wholly literal interpretive approach results in the interpretation of the six references within Revelation 20 of "[a] thousand years" to mean exactly that—that the millennial kingdom will indeed last exactly 1,000 365-day years on this earth.

The use of the Latin prefix *pre*, meaning "before," indicates premillennialists also hold to the belief that the second coming of Christ will occur *pre*, or before, the millennium, and that the personal reign from Jerusalem of the newly returned Davidic King will commence thereafter for 1,000 years.[11] In doing so, the Davidic King will fulfill the prophecy of the stone that will eradicate all human governments and then grow to fill the whole earth and establish His "kingdom that will never be destroyed," as the prophet Daniel had prophesied to King Nebuchadnezzar (Daniel 2:31-45).[12]

Premillennialists attempt to be consistent with the biblical witnesses by placing the millennium of Revelation 20 after Jesus' second coming to the earth. They acknowledge all four folds of the four kingdoms concept, especially in that the actualization of Christ's Davidic kingdom remains both earthly and future from this present point in history.[13] They reject the preterist conclusion that the fall of Jerusalem, which took place in AD 70, is when Christ's second coming took place. Premillennialists conclude that the fall of Jerusalem in that year served merely as a type pointing to the future eschatological fulfillment of the Antichrist's siege of Jerusalem and subsequent return of the Lord to set up His earthly reign.[14]

The view's adherents have long claimed that their position remains consistent with the biblical worldview that affirms the initial goodness of God's creation and Christ's plan to restore all things material and immaterial to their perfected Genesis state (see also Colossians 1:15-20).[15] Seminarian Michael Vlach identified God's plan to reconcile His fallen "rebel planet back into conformity with His universal kingdom in which His will is perfectly done" as the fulfillment of the scriptural teaching that an "intermediate kingdom" that is distinct from both this present evil age and the coming perfect eternal state—i.e., the millennial kingdom—is necessary toward achieving God's glorious goal.[16]

Premillennialists also believe that after the unspecified length of time of the church age, a seven-year tribulation will follow, which will end with Christ's second coming. And once the 1,000 years of the millennial kingdom are instituted and then over with, the final phase of the Davidic kingdom will continue with God, Christ, and the saints reigning forever in the eternal state (Daniel 7:13-14, 18; Revelation 22:5).[17] Thus, the events in the timeline for the kingdom of Christ, as interpreted by historic premillennialism, line up as follows:[18]

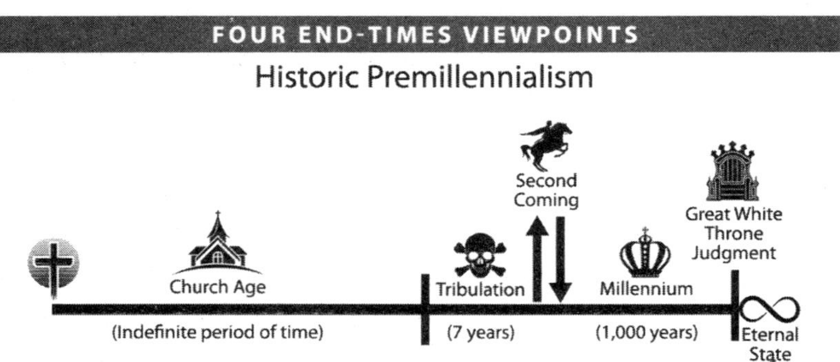

CHART 1

Where Israel Fits In

When it comes to their belief in Israel's inevitable restitution and role in the kingdom, premillennialists tend to be uniform in their view. And yet, ever since the revival of premillennialism during the Reformation, its adherents' beliefs concerning Israel's role in the kingdom have become quite varied, even surprisingly so after the nation of Israel was reborn in 1948 in fulfillment of Bible prophecy.[19]

Arnold Fruchtenbaum noted three main modern-day interpretive camps have risen within historic premillennialism concerning Israel's restitution and role.[20] The first believes that the modern Jewish State is merely an accident of history, and so dismisses its relevancy to the actualization of Christ's kingdom here on the earth. This particular version of premillennialism follows the Anabaptist chiliasm that had already begun to emerge during the second century, when the Jewish elements within eschatology had begun to diminish, when Christian forms of the promised kingdom became elevated over Jewish ideas from the Old Testament, and when Zionism began being denied, claiming instead that there will be no future for national Israel in its promised land.[21]

The second camp acknowledges that the rebirth of the nation of Israel does indeed mark the beginning of the fulfillment of all eschatological prophecies concerning the Davidic kingdom. And yet, they claim the time of tribulation needed to bring about a national spiritual restoration for the Jewish people already happened during the Nazi Holocaust. Therefore, what is being seen in the land of Israel today is an extension of that final restoration.

The third camp follows the traditional historic premillennial interpretation. They believe that increasingly the Jewish people will continue to make aliya until every Jew has returned to Israel. Then a remnant will survive the three-and-a-half year time of testing called the great tribulation, after which the remaining Jews will undergo a national regeneration and salvation. Only then will the Messiah return at last to set up His kingdom and establish the world's seat of authority at Jerusalem.

Analysis

The strengths of historic premillennialism rest on its adherence to the literal interpretation of Scripture. It is compatible with the plethora of Bible passages that place the timing of Christ's earthly reign in concert with His second coming to the earth. And the view holds strongly to the teachings of Christ and the apostles, along with a consensus among the early church fathers that was predominant during the first three centuries of church history.[22] Also, the answer is yes to all 12 of the litmus-test questions that evaluate whether this interpretive view lines up with the authority of Scripture.

Historic premillennialism is not without its challenges, though, which will be especially noted in the next section concerning the amillennial interpretive framework. Some historic premillennialists will admit that the view possesses three serious problems that were identified when the viewpoint was revived during the Reformation.[23]

The first problem that historic premillennialists struggle with is the inherent imminency repeatedly taught throughout the New Testament concerning Christ's return. *Imminency* means that Christ could return at any moment without anything prophetic needing to happen before it occurs. Verses such as Matthew 24:42 state, "Watch therefore, for you do not know what hour your Lord is coming" (see also verse 36). Matthew 25:13 warns, "Watch therefore, for you know neither the day nor the hour in which the Son of Man is coming." And Luke 12:40 counsels, "You also be ready, for the Son of Man is coming at an hour you do not expect." In these passages, Jesus is anticipating His return to be an imminent event.[24]

As seven 360-day years of tribulation judgments—as detailed in Revelation 6–19—act as a countdown and precede Christ's second coming, the exact day of His glorious return would be known, thus negating Christ's many statements about His imminent return. Jesus must then have been talking about another type of return, separate and apart from His second coming at the end of the tribulation. But historic premillennialism does not make a distinction between the rapture and the second coming.

The second problem historic premillennialists struggle with is how children could be born during the millennial kingdom in light of the resurrection granting all believers glorified bodies that cannot reproduce (Matthew 22:30; Mark 12:25). If everybody enters the millennial kingdom in their resurrected, glorified bodies—bodies that, like those of the angels, are incapable of procreating—and all who took the Antichrist's mark will have been banished to Hades, then who will be left in their earthly bodies for the glorified saints to rule over during the millennial kingdom? The only way there could be earthly subjects residing in the millennium is if the rapture was separate from the second coming.

The second problem leads to the third problem that historic premillennialists struggle with, and that is how to justify two seemingly conflicting accounts of Christ's return.[25] In one account, Jesus appears in the heavens, but in the other, He returns to the earth. In one account, Jesus appears to gather His saints, but in the other, He returns to the earth with His saints. In one account, Jesus appears as a deliverer, but in another, He engages as a warrior. In one account, Jesus appears to bring grace, while in the other, He doles out wrath. In one account, Jesus appears as the Bridegroom coming to collect His bride, the church, while in the other account, Jesus returns as King to rule over the earth.[26] (We'll soon look at modern premillennialism, which I believe has the solution to this dilemma.)

2. *Amillennialism*

History and Origins

The amillennial viewpoint originated with one of the initial few dissenters to historic premillennialism—Origen of Alexandria (AD

185–254).[27] Origen rejected the literal interpretation of Scripture and instead adopted one based on spiritualizing and allegorizing the texts in his search for what he believed were Scripture's deeper spiritual truths.

Origen's allegorical interpretive method was picked up many years later by a Donatist, a Christian sect from Africa, by the name of Tichonius (d. AD 400).[28] While little is known about the man, Tichonius's commentary on the apocalypse set the amillennial precedent for interpreting Bible prophecy not as predictive of actual coming events, but as symbols depicting spiritual battles. He considered the events in Revelation as being merely symbolic of spiritual warfare in which the church is presently engaged. Tichonius not only spiritualized prophecy, but he also spiritualized the resurrection by equating it to the moment one becomes saved. He also claimed the 1,000 years didn't mean a literal 1,000 years, but instead, stood for an undetermined length of the church era. Though Tichonius's failed prediction of Christ returning in AD 381 should have discounted his views in the eyes of the church as being a false prophet (Deuteronomy 18:20-22), his commentary continued to exercise a profound influence on all prophetic exegesis throughout the Middle Ages and beyond.[29]

Tichonius's allegorical interpretive method most influenced Aurelius Augustinus (AD 354–430)—Saint Augustine—who would then in his book *City of God* (AD 426) make the allegorical method the de facto interpretive method of the church throughout Europe during the Middle Ages.[30] Augustine went so far as to claim in his book, "The Church even now is the kingdom of Christ and the kingdom of heaven."[31]

Other fourth-century church leaders, such as Eusebius of Caesarea and Jerome, also attacked the idea of a future millennium. They believed Revelation 20's references to "[a] thousand years" were merely symbolic of the struggles Christians will experience living in this present age. They also presented the earthly rulership of the kingdom of

Christ to be Christ's rule through the bishop of Rome, whom they called the Vicar of Christ on Earth, meaning the Pope.[32]

Ben Witherington noted that with this interpretive transition, "future eschatology came largely to be replaced by otherworldly eschatology and mysticism the closer one got to the Middle Ages," so that "the grip of imminentist eschatology on believers gradually loosened."[33] By the time of Eucherius, Bishop of Treves (c. AD 450), the allegorizing of Scripture had made deep inroads into church orthodoxy. So much so that the Roman Catholic Church condemned any futurist interpretations of Scripture, and any contention with its view was punishable by excommunication, and even death![34]

Quite a number of historical occurrences led to the church's transformation from using a literal to an allegorical interpretive method of understanding Bible prophecy. One factor is that once the Roman Empire converted to Christianity during the fourth century, Christians found themselves no longer being oppressed, and so they began to move away from belief in the need for a Messiah to save them from an ever-impending apocalypse of persecution.[35] As the church became infused by Roman culture, a belief in a Messiah who would establish an earthly paradise came to be seen as an "old Jewish fancy."[36]

A second factor involved the "Gentilization" of the church. Over time, far more Gentiles were becoming saved than Jews, and eventually, almost no Jews at all, thereby cutting off the church's historical Jewish roots. This led to the rapid and pernicious growth of antisemitism within Christianity, whose adherents accused the Jews of having committed deicide—the killing of God—by crucifying Jesus. They concluded thus that God must have washed His hands of the Jewish people and replaced them with the church.[37] The church began to see itself as the new Israel, having inherited all the promises God had made to the patriarchs and King David, though receiving none of the curses.

A third factor, and maybe the most impactful, was the growing influence of Greek philosophy as the church became more "Gentilized."

The Greek worldview saw the material world as essentially evil and not needing restoration from corruption, as the Jews claimed, but instead, needing total dissolution into the good of an immaterial, spiritual existence.[38] In that model, Christ could not possibly rule personally over an earthly, material kingdom. This led to the conclusion that Christ must rule in the hearts and minds of men from His abode in heaven.

A fourth factor points to the misinterpretation of Christ's final promise made in Revelation: "I am coming quickly" (Revelation 22:7, 12, 20). After 300-plus years had gone by since the ascension with no bodily return in sight, the church lost its faith in the physical return of Jesus and instead concluded that He must have meant a spiritual return, one within the hearts of those who had become saved.

Beliefs and Tenets

Amillennialism, which in Latin means "no millennium," is the theological interpretive framework that rests on a spiritualized and allegorized interpretation of Scripture.[39] It is so named for its primary premise that rejects the notion that Christ and His saints will ever reign personally over the earth for a literal 1,000 years after Christ's second coming.

In denying the strict literalness of Revelation 20's six references to "[a] thousand years," Augustine was the first to postulate that the number 1,000 is simply the cube of 10, and so 1,000 is only meant to represent the definition of perfection.[40] George Ladd, in his commentary on the book of Revelation, commended Augustine for his interpretation of "[a] thousand years" as being an "obvious symbolic use of numbers in Revelation," and agreed that Revelation was merely referring to "an ideal time."[41]

The classical amillennial belief concerning Christ's reign therefore rejects Cotton Mather's fourth earthly fold of the Davidical Kingdom. It instead supplants it with the third fold—the Ecclesiastical Kingdom—a reign spiritual in nature that had begun at the cross, permeates through the work of the church, actuates at Christ's second coming, and culminates in the eternal state. As Floyd Hamilton, one of the leading amillennialists of the twentieth century, summarized:

> When Christ comes, the dead are raised, the righteous raptured, the wicked destroyed by fire, the great judgment occurs, and the new heavens and the new earth follow immediately.[42]

Thus, the timeline of events for the kingdom of Christ, as interpreted by the amillennialist, would be represented as follows:[43]

CHART 2

Some amillennialists claim their simplified prophetic timeline is more palatable than premillennial interpretive frameworks. Hamilton went on to confess, "By eliminating the alleged millennium, putting the two resurrections into one, the different judgments into one, and declaring that when Christ comes, He comes to end this age and judge the world," the student of the Bible can get rid of "all the difficulties that beset both Premillennialism and Postmillennialism."[44]

Though a postmillennialist in view, Lorraine Boettner agreed with amillennialism's rejection of premillennialism, stating that "frankly, we have no desire for such a state as Premillennialism sets forth, but prefer at death to enter into the heavenly state."[45] Strangely enough, a large segment of Christianity finds the notion of Jesus Christ and His saints physically ruling and reigning over the earth for a literal 1,000 years to be quite distasteful.

Where Israel Fits In

As stated earlier, amillennialism rejects any future role of the Jewish people in the kingdom of Christ, and instead appropriates the promises God made to the Jewish people, claiming them for the church. Fruchtenbaum calls this "a theology of transference," whereby Israel's rejection of the Messiah supposedly caused God to replace Israel with the church in His standing.[46] This view teaches that the responsibility God gave to Israel for bringing His salvific message to the world has been transferred to the church.

The prophesied worldwide regathering of the Jewish people is also interpreted allegorically, pertaining instead to the elect being brought into the church until the kingdom has reached numerical completion, which will then trigger Christ's return.[47] Historically, the Roman Catholic Church has begrudgingly conceded that some Jews might be saved and amalgamated into the larger church body. But amillennialists strongly believe that God couldn't have a future restoration planned for Israel as an ethnic people, or for that matter, anything prophetic related to the Jews. They conclude that the rebirth of the modern Jewish State of Israel is nothing more than an accident of history.[48] This notion is what's called the supersessionist view, meaning the church has replaced Israel, and this view extended well into the Reformation. Great Reformers such as Calvin still maintained the Augustinian framework for amillennialism.[49] These perpetuations of Augustine's teachings have caused many churches to continue to embrace the spiritualization of Scripture to this very day.

The Binding of Satan

How would the amillennial viewpoint explain Peter's warning to Christians, "Be sober, be vigilant; because your adversary the devil walks about like a roaring lion, seeking whom he may devour" (1 Peter 5:8), in light of its commitment to its conclusion that Satan has already been bound at the cross? Matt Waymeyer delineated the amillennialist timeline for Satan going forward from Christ's victory at the cross:

> Satan is bound (Matthew 12:29); he falls from heaven (Luke 10:17-18); he is cast out (John 12:31-32); he is disarmed and conquered (Colossians 2:15); he is rendered powerless (Hebrews 2:14-15); his works are destroyed (1 John 3:8); and he is thrown down from heaven to earth (Revelation 12:7-11).[50]

Therefore, amillennialists will claim that Christ's victory over the devil at the cross parallels the description of Satan being cast into the abyss in Revelation 20:1-3. Thus this "binding of Satan" began at the start of the present church age, an age that they claim also happens to coincide with the tribulation and the millennium.[51] Such an inference has led amillennialist expositor William Cox to conclude:

> Satan, though bound, still goes about like a roaring lion seeking whom he may devour. The chain with which he is bound is a long one, allowing him much freedom of movement.[52]

To the amillennialist, the binding of Satan to the abyss is merely a figurative way of saying that Satan's activities will be limited, but not eliminated, from the earth—that is, until Christ's second coming.[53]

Analysis

Some argue that the strength of the amillennial viewpoint rests on the near universality of the church's acceptance of this view over the last 13 centuries. The fact is that it remains the majority viewpoint held by many Christians today. The framework can also be credited for its simplicity in that it recognizes only two stages: the church age and the eternal state.

For those who go so far as to adopt preterist amillennialism, claiming that all the prophesied apocalyptic events have already taken place in the past, a literal millennium is completely unnecessary. The evangelistic successes of the church, and the knowledge that Christ's return will inaugurate an eternal utopia, leaves the bulk of the Bible's prophetic passages to be dismissed as, "Been there, done that."[54]

Challenges to the amillennial viewpoint center on the view's primary means of interpretation—a spiritualized, allegorical approach to Scripture. Historian LeRoy Froom leveled a charge against amillennialism's principle of concluding that a passage may say one thing while meaning something else as a travesty, and "thus the Bible is emptied of significance, and the reader is at the mercy of the expositor."[55] He also unhappily noted how this view's allegorizing of Scripture, which was almost universally accepted under Augustine, had refocused the church's gaze on the kingdom of Christ as a "then-present reality on earth" instead of where it truly belongs—the future kingdom of Christ to be inaugurated at the second advent. He lamented this refocus as "tragic nearsightedness which [has] blurred his vision of the future kingdom of Christ."[56]

Cotton Mather likewise had nothing good to say about elevating the personal interpretation of man over the intended meaning of the author of the Bible—the Holy Spirit. When it comes to amillennialism's insistence on equating 1,000 years as an indefinite amount of time, Mather contended:

> For anyone to think that it is already come to pass, is altogether as ridiculous as to say that the thousand years of Satan's binding, begun at the days of Constantine. The bare proposal of such cruel and absurd interpretation, is enough to beget in us, a distaste of all the schemes that they give unto us. No, tis a Future State, that is here set before us.[57]

Mather also mourned the papacy's ending of the historic premillennial interpretation by force for the sole purpose of elevating the Pope's role in the kingdom. He saw this usurpation as a sign that the papacy might fulfill the role of the Antichrist:

> If you will believe such men as Justin Martyr, who flourished in the second century (yea, or Irenaeus, the Scholar of Polycarp), it is very certain, that some things concerning the Kingdom of our Lord Jesus, were embraced in the primitive times, by all the Orthodox, which were forgotten, and perhaps forbidden, when the Kingdom of Antichrist came upon the stage.[58]

David Reagan likewise responded with great skepticism to amillennialism's assertion that when Jesus declared, "All authority has been given to Me in heaven and on earth" (Matthew 28:18), Christ meant that He had bound Satan at the cross. Such a claim is highly problematic—though Jesus has indeed been given all authority, He obviously is not yet exercising it, as evidenced by the wretched state in which the world exists today.[59] Reagan added with some humor, "If Satan is bound now, then he is bound on a very long chain, because he is always nipping at my heels, chewing on my leg, and lunging for my throat!"[60]

What happens when we evaluate amillennialism in light of the 12 litmus-test questions? We will see that when we evaluate whether this interpretive view lines up with the authority of Scripture, the answer to all 12 questions is a resounding no. For one, the authority of Scripture is transferred from the inerrant, divine Godhead to fallen, mortal man. Therefore, any interpretation that spiritualizes Scripture over the Holy Spirit's literal and intended meaning can only fall short of the glory of God (Romans 3:23). It appears that in elevating the amillennial view, and forcefully at that, the papacy had sought to usurp Christ's role in His own Davidic kingdom and the Catholic Church had sought to usurp the kingdom itself.

Also, explaining away the modern-day miracle of the rebirth of the nation of Israel as being mere happenstance completely ignores the second fold of Cotton Mather's definition of Christ's power over His kingdom—the Providential Kingdom. And the dire spiritual condition in which the world finds itself today negates any actualized interpretation of the scriptures concerning the world being at peace, bountiful, and with the global population all worshipping Jesus Christ in Jerusalem. Even amillennialists claim that the long duration to which the church has held this view is merely a paper-tiger argument, for the length by which something is held does not imbue it with spiritual truth.

3. *Postmillennialism*

History and Origins

During the seventeenth and eighteenth centuries, the papacy's amillennial stranglehold on the church as the only biblical interpretive framework was challenged by the Great Awakening on one front and a counter-rationalistic revolution called the Enlightenment on the other.[61] While the Reformers still clung in part to amillennialism, historic premillennialism began seeing the light of day once more and gained traction as an influencer on the Christian biblical worldview. The Enlightenment challenged all religious worldviews with its emphasis on humanism and its belief in the general "goodness" of man and the betterment of mankind through education.[62] Out of the synthesis of these two very different worldviews came postmillennialism. It teaches that mankind is perfectly capable of building the kingdom of Christ here on earth without Jesus being physically present. Then one day Christ will return at the end of a millennium to accept the "keys to the kingdom" from the church.[63]

Postmillennialist theologian Mark Toulouse credited the founding of this interpretive framework to Unitarian minister Daniel Whitby (1638–1726) of Salisbury Cathedral and Dutch scholar Campegius Vitringa (1659–1722).[64] It later became espoused by Restoration Movement clergyman Alexander Campbell (1788–1866) and early American Puritans John Cotton and Jonathan Edwards.

In the formation of Whitby's "doctrine of last things" understanding of the Bible, Whitby blanched at what he considered premillennialism's very pessimistic view of the future, as if the unfolding of history was continually a downward spiral caused by the fallenness of mankind, and whose only hope lies in the intervention of a Messiah. Influenced by Enlightenment thinking, as well as imbued with a sense of optimism due to living during a period of unprecedented educational and technological growth in both Europe and America, Whitby presented his "New Hypothesis," which foresaw mankind influencing the world for the better.[65]

Postmillennialism's profound optimism caught the Protestant world by storm during the 1800s, fueling one of the greatest eras for the spreading of the gospel and spurring massively successful evangelistic missionary outreaches. Churches and mission organizations sprung up all over the world, fueled by their anticipation of ushering in the kingdom without any need for supernatural events. The Christians of that era hoped they would build the kingdom of Christ by the power of what Alexander Campbell attributed to as "God with us," and so a millennium would grace the world characterized by religious peace and spiritual fulfillment.[66]

The missionary zeal promulgated by the postmillennial kingdom anticipation lasted throughout the nineteenth century, with many at that time expecting the twentieth century to become the "Christian century" and see the world fully Christianized.[67] Church historian James Moorhead confirmed, "In 1859, an influential theological quarterly asserted without fear of contradiction that Postmillennialism was the 'commonly received doctrine' among American Protestants."[68] The evangelistic efforts of the church would have at last solved the problem of evil as it pertains to failed human government due to the church ushering in an era of global peace and harmony.

But, as Moorhead added, "By the early twentieth century, it [postmillennialism] had largely vanished."[69] During the years after the Civil War, the predominance of the postmillennial view began to slowly diminish. And by 1936, Lewis Sperry Chafer had declared that postmillennialism was without a "living voice."[70] The reason? The world simply was not getting better and better—contrary to the foundational belief that had compelled postmillennial mission fervor. Rather, the world was getting much worse as plagues and wars continued to decimate the population, culminating in the Great War and followed by the Great Depression. Tragedy upon tragedy had pushed the world more toward embracing a secularist mindset, thereby almost eliminating evangelicalism in European countries that had once been known for the intensity of their missionary efforts. A belief in supernaturalism was on the wane, replaced by a belief in science. "In short, experience simply had not sustained Postmillennialism...it became a relic of a lost world."[71]

Except for an almost obscure book by postmillennialist Loraine Boettner written in 1958, the world had largely forgotten postmillennialism. That is, until the view made a sudden comeback during the 1980s. Influential writers such as Earl Paulk (1927–2009), a hyper-faith charismatic, proclaimed Kingdom Now theology with its belief that Christians are all "little gods" who have the authority of Christ over the nations. David Chilton (1951–1997), a non-charismatic Calvinist, proclaimed Dominion theology, which reclaims the traditional postmillennial methods of missions and political activism. These two men and their movements became the primary drivers that brought postmillennialism back to the forefront.[72] Chilton was joined by Rousas John Rushdoony (1916–2001), who is considered the philosophical father of Dominion theology.[73] Today, postmillennialism has been revived in the Restoration, Reconstruction, New Wave, Latter Rain, and Manifest Sons of God movements.[74]

Beliefs and Tenets

Postmillennialism, which in Latin means "after the millennium," is a theological interpretive framework that rests on a combination of mostly spiritualized but some literal interpretations of Scripture.[75] The view's founders based their eschatological understanding upon their belief in the inherent goodness of man and mankind's inevitable progress. As one theologian so accurately observed:

> In spite of all the historical evidence, there are still some who conscientiously suggest that Mankind can reacquire Eden without Jesus Christ reigning as King.[76]

Where Israel Fits In

Early postmillennialists expected the ascendency of the church because it had appropriated the Jewish promises and established the church upon the throne of David. They denied there was still any role for the Jewish people to fulfill in God's salvific and restorative promises, for the church will have brought all Jews to salvation in Christ anyway.[77]

The church age would place a much greater emphasis on the ability of human efforts to bring about the millennium, in contrast to the premillennial view. They would become superficially affirmed by the historical successes of America's efforts in bringing civilization and democracy to the rest of the world.[78] The world would eventually become fully Christianized once the church overthrew every human government and defeated what postmillennialists believed where the four great evils—Mahometanism, papalism, paganism, and atheism.[79] The church would then usher in a new golden age that would serve as a 1,000-year sabbath.

Thus, in Alexander Campbell's understanding, God's ultimate purpose for history would be the triumph of the church (aided by the Holy Spirit) over its enemies, followed by a golden age characterized by unparalleled human happiness due to the church's reign by absolute divine justice.[80] Moorhead pointed out that when it comes to the prophesied tribulation period, the postmillennial theory "postponed history's cataclysmic end until after the millennium and thereby allowed the temporal interval necessary for the gradual evangelical conquest of the world and the triumph of secular progress."[81]

The Binding of Satan

When it comes to the temporary unbinding and release of Satan, the postmillennial view takes what's called a "preconsummationist perspective" in that Satan is released at the end of the millennium but before the second coming.[82] Alexander Campbell, though interpreting the 1,000 years as literal, spiritualized the first resurrection as merely signifying the "revival of the martyrs' spirit within the church," but took the second resurrection and universal judgment upon Christ's second coming literally, followed by the eternal state.[83]

Thus, as interpreted by postmillennialists, the events in the timeline for the kingdom of Christ would be arranged as follows:[84]

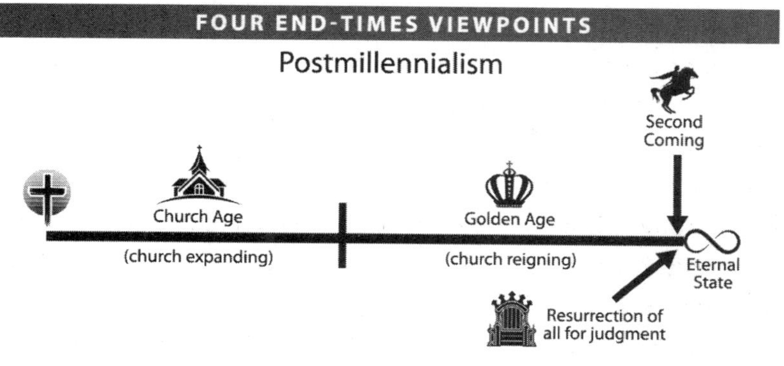

CHART 3

When it comes to providing a template for the kingdom of Christ according to the postmillennial timeline, Alexander Campbell developed his own unique four kingdoms concept.[85] He believed that, first, God initially ruled over the Kingdom of Nature—all creatures naturally born—which lasted during the patriarchal dispensation from the creation in Genesis 1 to the wilderness wanderings of Exodus 19. Second, the Kingdom of God, also known as the First Kingdom or the Kingdom of Law, covered the Old Testament Jewish dispensation from Sinai in Exodus 20 through Pentecost in Acts 1. Third, the Kingdom of Heaven, also known as the Second Kingdom, provided Christ's rule from heaven through the church over the world during the church age and subsequent millennium. And fourth, the Everlasting Kingdom of God, also known as the Third Kingdom and the eternal state, actually transcends the other three due to its ultimate eternality. Campbell interpreted the kingdom of Christ to be a constitutional monarchy through the church in the here and now, but conceded that it has existed within the bounds of a transcendent eschatological kingdom of God that remains eternal and unabated.[86]

Analysis

The strength of the postmillennial interpretive framework rests on incorporating some literal hermeneutics into its understanding of eschatology. The view has also long excited the evangelistic passions of Christians to leave the confines of their church buildings to fulfill the Great Commission, a fervor that had lasted uninterrupted for nearly two centuries. The revitalization of postmillennialism among Kingdom Now and Dominion theologies has once again enflamed their adherents' desire to see the kingdom of Christ reach its full potential, but in the present day.

The problems with postmillennialism, however, are legion. For one, the view was founded upon a fatally flawed assumption—that mankind is inherently good.[87] This assumption can be quickly dispelled by Scripture (Jeremiah 17:9; Romans 3:9-18).

Two, the motive to build the kingdom of Christ apart from the salvific work of the victoriously returned Messiah, thereby assigning His victory to the works of man through the church, is not only highly unbiblical but, as John Walvoord bull's-eyed it, "a dream."[88] After all, Christ's description of His return in Matthew 24–25 described a world in great rebellion and persecuting the Jews and the saints.

Three, reality demonstrates that the world is growing much worse, not better, just as the Bible prophesied.

Four, the three cornerstone scriptures most often used to justify the eschatology held by Kingdom Now and Dominion theology are misinterpreted due to their practice of spiritualizing Scripture.[89] The first misinterpreted passage, Acts 3:20-21, which reads, "Jesus Christ... whom heaven must receive until the times of restoration of all things," is paraphrased by postmillennialists as "Jesus must remain in heaven until all things have been restored." The verse clearly explains that Christ will remain in heaven until the time He comes to restore all things, not that He must stay in heaven until the church restores all things (see Isaiah 11:3-9).

The second misinterpreted verse, Matthew 24:14, reads, "This gospel of the kingdom will be preached in all the world as a witness to all the nations, and then the end will come." This is paraphrased by postmillennialists as, "The entire world must be converted to Christ before He will return." The nuance of this passage rests on the difference between the gospel being preached to the world versus the gospel having been accepted by the world. Revelation describes the ongoing evangelistic efforts that will continue during the tribulation, including God sending an "angel...having the everlasting gospel" (Revelation 14:6) just before Christ's triumphal return to Mount Zion (Revelation 19–20).

The third misinterpreted verse, Romans 8:19, reads, "The earnest expectation of the creation eagerly waits for the revealing of the sons of God." This is misinterpreted by postmillennialists as, "The creation will be redeemed while the church spreads the gospel." The context of Romans 8 instead points to how the resurrection of the saints will reveal who the sons of God truly are, and at that time, the curse over the creation will be lifted.

As with the amillennial view, when it comes to evaluating postmillennialism in light of the 12 litmus-test questions that evaluate whether this interpretive view lines up with the authority of Scripture, the answer to all 12 is a resounding no. Once more, when the Bible's plain-sense meaning is spiritualized or allegorized, the authority of Scripture is transferred from the inerrant, divine Godhead to fallen, mortal man. Therefore, any interpretation that spiritualizes Scripture over the Holy Spirit's literal and intended meaning can only fall short of the glory of God (Romans 3:23).

Has God washed His hands of the Jewish people, as postmillennialists claim? Romans 9–11 emphatically declares no, for God's gifts and calling are irrevocable (Romans 11:29).

Will the entire world be converted for Jesus by the church, as postmillennialists claim? Not according to Jesus, who taught, "Narrow is the gate and difficult is the way which leads to life, and there are few who find it" (Matthew 7:14).

Is it the mission of the church to convert all nations, as Dominionists claim? No, the church has only been ordered to preach the gospel (Mark 16:15).

Can the church possibly establish the kingdom of Christ without the King being physically present? According to Daniel, it is the other way around—the newly returned Davidic King will grant the resurrected saints the authority to rule under Him (Daniel 7:13-14, 18, 27; Revelation 3:21).

Can the church reign over the earth for 1,000 years in light of the aforementioned verses, which describe an imminent return of Jesus? Postmillennialism stumbles over the doctrine of imminency.

And can the church possibly replace the King in His kingdom? Reagan appropriately called this errant belief "blasphemy."[90] So, no, of course not. Postmillennialism is tragically the product of the Enlightenment's pride in man, and as the proverb says, for postmillennialism's adherents, such "pride will bring him low" (Proverbs 29:23).

4. Modern Premillennialism

History and Origins

Like historic premillennialism, the origins of the modern premillennial interpretive framework as it applies to the kingdom of Christ originated with the teachings of Jesus Christ and His disciples. These teachings became adopted and were espoused by the early church fathers, including Papias, Irenaeus, Justin Martyr, Tertullian, Hippolytus, Methodius, Commodianus, and Lactantius.[91]

As stated, premillennialism remained the dominant view for the first three centuries of church history, but with the rise of Augustinian amillennialism, the premillennial view not only fell out of favor, but the papacy made sure that those who held the view were suppressed. As Thomas Newton, the eighteenth-century Anglican bishop of Bristol explained:

> In short, the doctrine of the millennium was generally believed in the three first and purest [centuries]... Afterwards this doctrine grew into disrepute for various reasons...It hath suffered by misrepresentations of its enemies [who have] charged the millenarians with absurd and impious opinions which they never held...Besides wherever the influence and authority of the church of Rome have extended, she hath endeavoured by all means to discredit this doctrine [which] lay depressed for many ages, but it sprung up again at the Reformation, and will flourish together with the study of Revelation.[92]

Modern premillennialism, also called dispensational or futurist premillennialism, refined the historic premillennial framework. It's based on the teachings of Clement of Alexandria, who, in the third century, divided human history into seven ages or dispensations: Adam to Noah, Noah to Abraham, Abraham to Moses, Moses to Christ's first coming, Christ's first coming to His second coming, and the millennium.[93] Clement believed that when one followed a literal reading of the prophetic passages in the Bible, clear divisions could be discerned throughout history, during which the relationship between God and humanity changed.[94]

Joachim of Fiore, a twelfth-century Cistercian monk, who was branded by the Catholic Church as a heretic for holding to Clement's dispensational view, also divided history into different ages. He based them on how he saw God's grace being applied to His sovereignty over human affairs: a past age of the Father (Old Testament), the current age of the Son (from Christ to 1260), and a coming age of the Holy Spirit (when God's love would cover the earth).[95]

It wasn't until the sixteenth century, when the Protestant Reformation began challenging the supremacy of the Catholic Church, that premillennialism was able to be spoken aloud without recrimination.

Modern premillennialists credit premillennialism's true revival to German Calvinist theologian Johann Heinrich Alsted and his book *The Beloved City* (1627), as well as the teachings of Anglican scholar Joseph Mede.[96] These biblical scholars, along with seventeenth-century supporters such as J.H. Bengel, Isaac Newton, and Joseph Priestley, made it quite common for Protestant churches during the 1600s through the 1800s to recognize that historical periods could be identified throughout biblical history, and their view became cemented as a feature of historicism.[97]

Dispensational premillennialism was further refined over the last two centuries to delineate the ages as the patriarchal period (governed by pre-Mosaic law), a Torah period (when the law of Moses was in effect), the present church age (one of grace), a future tribulation (a seven-year period when the Antichrist rules), and the millennium (1,000 years of peace with the Messiah ruling on earth).[98] Some dispensationalists also separate the creation period before the Fall, from the Fall to the Flood, and after the millennial kingdom (the eternal state) as three additional ages, making for a total of eight dispensations.

Beliefs and Tenets

Modern premillennialism (in Latin, *premillennialism* means "before the millennium") is the theological interpretive framework that follows a consistent application of historical-grammatical hermeneutics based on a literal or plain-sense interpretation of Scripture while taking into account genre, literary structure, and the canonicity of the Bible.[99] As Moore noted, "A determination to interpret the Bible literally, for its plain-sense meaning, is the hallmark of the Premillennial viewpoint."[100]

While modern premillennialism holds to the essential doctrines and timeline of historic premillennialism, it does differ over two distinct aspects. One, in contrast to covenant theology, which divides human history into only two ages based on God's old and new covenants, dispensationalists see world history as being divided into five to eight different ages, or dispensations. In each subsequent age, God revealed more of Himself and His kingdom. As a result, mankind became more responsible for what it knew about the Lord and for its sins, though tempered by God's grace.

And two, modern premillennialists see the second coming of Christ occurring in two stages. They separate the rapture of the church, when Jesus calls believers both dead and alive up to heaven, from Christ's physical return with His saints to the earth to then sit upon the throne of David. The timing of the rapture coincides with the seven-year tribulation period, though premillennialists disagree over whether the rapture occurs before the tribulation (pre-tribulation rapture view), three-and-a-half years into the tribulation (mid-tribulation rapture view), three-quarters into the tribulation (pre-wrath rapture view), or a very short moment before the second coming, which ends the tribulation (post-tribulation rapture view).

Thus, the timeline of events for the kingdom of Christ as interpreted by modern premillennialists is as follows, taking into account the different timing views concerning the rapture, of course:[101]

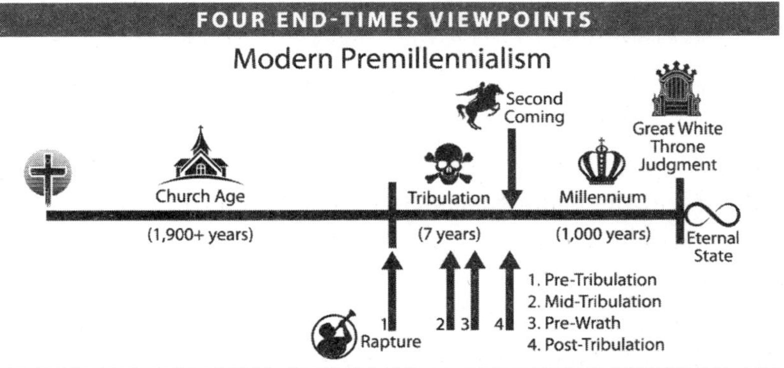

CHART 4

Traditional dispensationalists acknowledge that in the first century, Christ's disciples expected an immediate earthly kingdom (Luke 19:11; 24:21; Acts 1:6). Jesus kept to Himself the information about when exactly the kingdom would commence (Acts 1:7), ordering the disciples instead to labor toward the bringing of souls to salvation while He was away (Luke 19:12-26; Acts 1:8). The church would then act as the proverbial hands and feet of their Lord, building what Jesus Christ revealed to Pontius Pilate as "My kingdom is not of this world" (John 18:36). In prophesying both a spiritual and ecclesiastical kingdom through the church with Jesus ruling from heaven, but anticipating His bodily return to set up His earthly Davidic kingdom and ruling from Jerusalem, Jesus presented His kingdom as an "already but not yet" prophetic promise.[102]

An offshoot of modern premillennialism has surfaced in recent years, known as progressive dispensationalism. Progressive dispensationalism denies that there will be any exclusively future fulfillment of the Davidic kingdom. It rejects the traditional view that the church, in its present form, remains unrelated to and distinct from the Davidic kingdom.[103] Instead of anticipating that Jesus Christ will in the future take up His Davidic mantle over the earth and rule from the throne of David in Jerusalem, this view teaches that Christ, at His ascension, had already been inaugurated as the Davidic King, and so reigns over the Davidic kingdom from heaven during the church age.[104] So, while traditional dispensationalists see the millennial kingdom as the inaugural stage of the final fulfillment of the Davidic kingdom in the eternal state, progressive dispensationalists instead recognize the church as the inaugural stage of the final fulfillment of the Davidic kingdom in the millennium.[105] The difference may be subtle, but which view one holds concerning the exclusivity of the future fulfillment of the Davidic kingdom greatly influences how one interprets the kingdom of Christ, and so too the kingdom's impact on restraining the problem of evil as it pertains to failed human governments.

Analysis

The strength of the modern premillennial interpretive framework rests firmly on the fact it incorporates a literal hermeneutic to its understanding of the Bible, and especially biblical eschatology. Also, the timeline of this framework particularly harmonizes with the plethora of biblical passages that place the timing of Christ's earthly reign in concert with His second coming to the earth. As one modern premillennialist exhorted:

> Students of Bible prophecy must allow God's revelations in Scripture to guide our understanding. Doing so allows us to discern not only the "what" of end-time events, but the "why." It also provides us discernment regarding the "when" in that we should recognize that we are living in the season of the Lord's return.[106]

Where Israel Fits In

When it comes to the inauguration of the kingdom of Christ during the millennial age, traditional dispensational premillennialism can securely answer yes to all 12 of the litmus-test questions. We can therefore conclude that this interpretive view does indeed line up with the authority of Scripture.

For example, with regard to questions 1 through 3, if the world is now in the millennium, whether literally or figuratively, can we say that the Jewish people have all been regathered to the land of Israel? Or is a restored Israel even relevant to future history? As noted previously, according to Isaiah, a second and final worldwide regathering of the Jewish people in unbelief must happen to restore the remnants' hearts to their Messiah (Isaiah 11:11–12:6). This regathering has been occurring over the past century, culminating in the rebirth of the nation of Israel in 1948. Only the first 483 years of the prophesied 490-year period has been fulfilled in history, so there remains seven years of this prophetic time clock left for Israel to complete this restoration—the same seven years marked for the tribulation (Daniel 9:24-27).[107] As Fruchtenbaum pointed out, "Daniel 9:24-27 requires a Jewish State to be in existence before the Tribulation, and today there is one," and so "this is another way the modern State of Israel fits within Bible prophecy."[108]

The Binding of Satan

Likewise, concerning question 12, has Satan been bound, released, and then permanently defeated? Revelation 20:1-3 provides compelling evidence for a future millennium, and such a restriction of Satan would be incompatible with the breathtaking amount of evil the world has been experiencing throughout the church age.[109] Whatever can be construed as the binding of Satan, the present reality of heightened evil in our day proves otherwise. Likewise, the chronology of Revelation verifies Satan's imprisonment (20:1-3) as following the second coming of Christ (19:11-21). Thus the chronological progression between the two passages confirms that Satan's eviction to a physical abyss for 1,000 years remains future.[110] If Satan's banishment to the bottomless pit for a literal 1,000 years must indeed become a reality, then so, too, must all the other prophesies tied to the millennial kingdom as presented in questions 4 through 11.

The Rapture of the Church

Those who argue against modern premillennialism often focus on the fact the view presents the second coming as occurring in two stages—the rapture of the church up to heaven in relation to the tribulation, then at the end of the tribulation, Christ returning with His church back down to the earth.[111] Contenders point to Matthew 24, where Jesus presented a sweeping survey of the tribulation before declaring, "Immediately after the tribulation of those days," He will send forth His angels to "gather together His elect from the four winds" (verses 29, 31). At first read, this gathering appears to coincide with Christ's second coming, so either this teaching is omitting the rapture, or the post-tribulation rapture view should be assumed.

Dispensational premillennialists will parry by pointing out that in the book of Matthew, Jesus was addressing a Jewish audience, and so was prophesying a Jewish remnant having to endure the tribulation. Therefore, this particular gathering then would be comprised of those specifically who become saved during the tribulation. This gathering is separate and distinct from the earlier gathering of the church, as years later Paul would describe (1 Corinthians 15:50-58; 1 Thessalonians 4:13-18).[112]

Also in Matthew 24, Jesus addressed the doctrine of imminency. We learned that Christ returns exactly 2,520 days from the onset of the tribulation, which means He must have been referring to another event, one unexpected and imminent, and therefore separate from the second coming—i.e., the rapture.

Another challenge to modern premillennialism is aimed at the "modernness" of the view. Skeptics erroneously credit the origins of the belief in the rapture to the early 1800s in connection with a Plymouth Brethren preacher by the name of John Nelson Darby. As noted earlier, the dispensationalism aspect of premillennialism has been around since Clement of Alexandria in the third century. Therefore, the view is not "too new to be true."

As for the historic belief in the rapture occurring separate and apart from the second coming, or at least as an earlier phase of Christ's return, modern literary scholars such as William Watson and Lee Brainard and others have, in just the past decade, unearthed hundreds of ancient documents from early church history that reveal many of the early church fathers differentiated the rapture from the second coming because of the inherent imminency of Christ's return.[113] You'll find this differentiation in the writings of Clement of Rome and Ignatius of Antioch, as well as in early publications such as the *Didache* (60–100), the Epistle of Barnabas (130–131), and *The Shepherd of Hermas* (110). Brainard has recently added to the list his translation of the works of the sainted monk Ephraim the Syrian (306–373), revealing he also held a belief in the rapture, and particularly the pre-tribulation rapture.[114]

The modern premillennial aspects of dispensationalism and the rapture have been popularized in more recent times by William Blackstone, C.I. Scofield, Hal Lindsey, and Tim LaHaye. But these scholars are merely the most modern purveyors of academic teachings that have stretched back to the earliest beginnings of church history. This is understandable, for as Daniel prophesied, Bible prophecies would be more progressively revealed as the church enters the end of the end times (Daniel 12:9). But—and this is important—the historical underpinnings of any interpretive framework are altogether irrelevant to its validity, for the one essential as to whether or not a doctrine is deemed scriptural is whether it is actually found in Scripture.[115]

CHAPTER 23

THE FINAL REVIEW

How vast is eternity! It will swallow up all the human race; it will collect all the intelligent universe; it will open scenes and prospects wide enough, great enough, and various enough to fix the attention, and absorb the minds of all intelligent beings forever.[1]

Nathanael Emmons, eighteenth-century pastor and theologian

We began our study of the millennial kingdom by identifying God's purpose for human governments, as perceived by America's Founding Fathers: true and lasting security, equal and impartial justice, and happiness through virtue for its people. God has ordained human governments to function, to a limited extent, for the purpose of restraining evil and punishing evildoers.

RESTATING THE PROBLEM

Tragically, human governments have consistently failed to live up to their God-given purpose in a variety of unfortunate ways. Most often, they fail to protect their citizens from all forms of lawlessness, natural disasters, hunger, diseases, wars, and human suffering.

The reason why human governments continue to fail is because they are inherently evil, for mankind is inherently fallen and evil.

After all, human rights are quintessentially grounded in God-given inalienable freedoms, but making free, morally based decisions that contribute toward the common good of society requires an understanding of the Divine Lawgiver. Secular society has rejected God and His moral law. Therefore, it is no surprise that any efforts made by human governments to promote freedom are doomed to limited successes, and more often, disappointments. As a result, societies often crumble from within because they will, over time, lack a cohesively shared value system. When disintegration occurs, human governments yet again demonstrate their inability to create a unified belief system by which to hold their societies together, even when using force. The result? People inevitably lose their faith in both their governments and the God who ordained this system of government.

This ultimate failure of human governments to live up to humanity's longing for a perfect utopian system has created the problem of evil that we have been addressing. The failure of human governments has long caused a crisis of faith for both those who believe in God and those who don't. Unbelievers, in particular, face a major obstacle to their coming to saving faith in Jesus Christ. Practical atheists who have forsaken the Creator and a theistic worldview transfer onto governments the divine qualities of a maximally great being: omniscience, omnipotence, and omnibenevolence. Because no human or human organization can possibly possess all these qualities and abilities, governments will invariably let their people down, resulting in unbelievers' faith remaining misplaced and perpetually in crisis.

For those who believe in God and His Son Jesus Christ, we can at times find ourselves struggling with the inclination to blame the Almighty for not preventing everything bad that happens, while also projecting that same blame onto our God-ordained human governments. Many of us have seen Christians abandon their trust in God because they cannot find a satisfactory answer to this dilemma: *What happens when the God you believe in appears to have failed?* Left unanswered, this question can become an existential crisis, even leading some to deeply question their faith in Jesus Christ. We've identified this dilemma as the problem of evil as it relates to failed human governments.

RESTATING THE SOLUTION

Is there any hope that mankind will finally be freed from the failure that is flawed human government?

No longer are we to be left wondering, *Is humanity destined to forever suffer under its corrupted weight?* As we've joyously learned, the Bible does indeed respond to the problem of evil as it relates to failed human governments with an emphatic and consistent yes!

God articulated His answer most clearly in the vision He gave to King Nebuchadnezzar, interpreted by the prophet Daniel and recorded in Daniel 2. Daniel prophesied that after a succession of world empires, a divine ruler will break from the heavens to obliterate human governments once and for all. He will then establish His illustrious kingdom over the entire earth. Once Jesus Christ returns to the earth, He will "strike the nations" (Revelation 19:15) and at last establish His own eternal and universal kingdom (Revelation 20–22). On that glorious day, human governments will finally end, replaced by the kingdom of Christ forevermore. The Bible's response to the problem of evil as it concerns failed human governments can be found in the realization of the Davidic kingdom.

REVIEWING THE ARGUMENTS

Why Literal Interpretation Is Essential

Now that we have identified the solution to this existential problem, my hope is that this divine knowledge can help you and others remove any obstruction to your coming to, or remaining in, faith in Jesus Christ. You can trust in God's great plan, knowing that He will not leave us in this terrible predicament for very much longer.

I hope you've seen what tremendous value there is in adopting a plain-sense, literal methodology when interpreting the Bible, especially in the reading and evaluating the scores of kingdom-themed scriptures. In utilizing the golden rule of interpretation—"When the plain sense makes sense, look for no other sense, lest you end up with nonsense"—I have endeavored to argue a great truth. The Bible is indeed promising a literal kingdom, with an actual literal seed of David who will sit on a literal earthly throne that will last literally forever.[2]

Take the advice of the late esteemed scholar Paul Lee Tan, who championed, "The only dependable approach to prophecy is the literal method of interpretation."[3] He added that this "method assumes that Bible prophecy, written in regular human language, should be interpreted according to laws governing written communication," so that the student of the Bible will find "a trustworthy and God-honoring method of interpretation which takes the Bible at its word."[4]

When one utilizes the golden rule of interpretation, realization quickly dawns that the kingdom of Christ is not just rolled up in the initial three folds Cotton Mather defined—the Spiritual Kingdom, the Providential Kingdom, and the Ecclesiastical Kingdom. The kingdom also contains a fourth fold—the Davidical Kingdom. Jesus Christ's frequent use of the personal reference "Son of Man" was meant as a proclamation identifying Himself as the Davidic King who will fulfill Daniel's kingdom prophecy. Jesus Christ is indeed the very stone not cut out by human hands, the rock from Nebuchadnezzar's dream that will smash the world empires and will "break in pieces and consume all these kingdoms, and it shall stand forever" (Daniel 2:44). The Son of Man is the only being divinely authorized to reign from Israel over all of the world, and in doing so, He will fulfill all aspects of the Davidic covenant.

How unfortunate it is that the church, over the last 2,000 years, has gone through periods of confusion as to what constitutes the kingdom of Christ. Whatever interpretation was popular at the time often left out the fourth fold of the kingdom. Doing so has left the believers' understanding of the kingdom of Christ and God's response to failed human governments incomplete. Therefore, we took the time to explore the four main interpretive frameworks as they pertain to the kingdom of Christ—historic premillennialism, amillennialism, postmillennialism, and modern premillennialism. How one interprets the reign of Christ over the earth becomes key to truly understanding, or misunderstanding, the Bible's response to this problem of evil.

As Charles Ryrie exposed, "To build the kingdom on the first coming of Christ produces a theological error with many serious ramifications."[5] Doing so creates confusion between the church and the kingdom, which causes church and kingdom ethics to be intermixed, "usually with the result that kingdom ethics are promoted more than church ethics, thus Christians are urged to live the kingdom here and now."[6] Again, we wish to avoid a crisis of faith.

Armed with a literal interpretation, hopefully you realized while we explored the amillennial and postmillennial interpretive frameworks the error their adherents have made in placing the Davidic kingdom solely within the church age. Doing so merely relegates the earthly reign of King Jesus to a distant, celestial oversight through His church; which, in truth, is yet again another fallen form of human government. The rejection of the King and kingdom during Christ's first advent did indeed trigger the need for a second advent, where the church would serve as a spiritual form of the kingdom in the interim—the Ecclesiastical Kingdom.

But let us not stop there. The church was never meant to serve as the final form of the kingdom of Christ. Rather, the church age foreshadows an even greater kingdom to come—the millennial kingdom. The plethora of verses describing the nature and purpose of the Davidic kingdom that we have explored prove this greater coming kingdom to be true. As Kenneth Barker concluded:

> New Testament historical fulfillment falls dramatically short of Old Testament eschatological expectation. Therefore, only a future earthly kingdom could fulfill that of which the Old Testament prophets wrote.[7]

Israel Awaits Its Glorious Future

Another aspect of the kingdom of Christ that the amillennial and postmillennial interpretive frameworks failed to adequately address is God's remaining promises to the nation of Israel. The mistake of rejecting the covenants God made to the Jewish people has led Walter Kaiser to exhort:

> The Old Testament is not a patchwork of unconnected predictions; it is a single symphony with variations on the Promise Theme. And that man of promise is Jesus, the King of Glory![8]

God has been divinely orchestrating a second regathering of the Jewish people back to their Promised Land. This regathering has been culminating over the last century, and after 1,900 years of Diaspora exile, can only be viewed as a modern-day miracle. God is bringing His long-lost children back to fulfill His promise that they will be His people again, but a people who will be refined to love truth and righteousness, and so be committed at last to Messiah Yeshua.

This is key—God's plan to save a Jewish remnant so they can serve as a priestly people during His earthly reign coincides with Him putting an end to failed earthly human governments. The cry "Baruch haba b'Shem Adonai" from the united voices of the Jewish remnant will counter the nation's former rejection of their Messiah, and with this acceptance, Jesus Christ will return. As demonstrated, Christ's prophetic plan for His glorious return and the institution of His Davidic kingdom hinges on these promises made to the Jewish people coming to fruition.

The national salvation of the Jewish people upon Christ's return, as well as the nature of the rapture of the church before the second coming, in my opinion, causes historic premillennialism, amillennialism, and postmillennialism to fall short of providing a complete picture of the Davidic kingdom. Only modern/dispensational premillennialism fully recognizes the Lord's salvific plans for national Israel, as well as the redemption of the Jewish people and their place as a priesthood in the hierarchy of the millennial kingdom.

The Importance of the Rapture

Modern premillennialism also recognizes God's grace granted to us church-age Christians, in that we are promised never to have to endure the wrath of God (Romans 5:9; Ephesians 5:6; Colossians 3:4; 1 Thessalonians 1:10; 5:9; Revelation 3:10). This "snatching up" rescue by Jesus Christ before the wrath of God is poured out on the world—known as the rapture—will rescue the bride of Christ from having to endure the Almighty's wrath. While identifying the timing of the rapture stands outside the scope of our study, I want to firmly state my belief that the Bible provides many clues indicating that the rapture will occur pre, or before, the tribulation (read Isaiah 26:19-21; Malachi 3:17; Luke 21:36; John 14:1-14; 1 Corinthians 15:51-58; 1 Thessalonians 4:13-18).

The Lesson of the Millennial Kingdom

We who are modern premillennialists can make our claims with surety because, as author Charles Gieschen noted, we "do not come to that text *tabula rasa*—with a blank-slate mind—but we stand on the shoulders of close to two thousand years' worth of interpreters and interpretation."[9] The strength of the modern premillennial framework—a literal approach to the interpretation of Scripture—will invariably point one to the premillennial return of Christ to reign bodily on the earth.[10]

Criticisms have been leveled at premillennialists, claiming that due to Satan's release after 1,000 years, as well as the subsequent final rebellion of the children born during the millennium, the Davidic kingdom should be considered a failure. Therefore, it's not a truly biblical response to the problem of evil as it relates to failed human governments. In response, we have learned that if the millennial kingdom could be considered a failure, the fault definitely does not lie in its perfect Sovereign, Jesus Christ. Also, any apparent failure attributed to the millennial kingdom definitely does not lay with the glorified administrators of the kingdom, because they will rule in a sinless, glorified state.

The central fault with the millennial kingdom will lie with the subjects of that kingdom, for they will remain in their earthly, corrupted bodies. Our Lord Jesus, not wishing to force love and loyalty on anyone, will continue during that time to allow people to make their own choices, leaving them fully responsible for their actions. Choice has always been essential to God's plan of salvation, or humanity would be as mindless as robots who have no choice but to obey their programming to love and worship their Maker. God has always wanted to populate heaven with those who freely desire and so choose to be with Him.

We have learned that even in the long-sought-after utopian state that the millennium will provide, as long as there are humans who remain in a fallen state, problems will invariably arise. This is the central lesson that God has long been trying to teach humanity: that even in a utopian society with the perfect King and government, the destructive nature of sin will inevitably lead people to rebel. And when they do, a perfect society can no longer exist.

So, while the blissful millennial kingdom ruled by its exalted Davidic King will bring an end to human governments, living up to God's promise in Daniel 2, there will remain an element of evil within its earthly citizens to contend with. This is the last era of souls—a final harvest—that Christ wishes to save. Think of the millennial kingdom then as an intermediate kingdom, distinct from both this present evil age the church finds herself in and the coming perfect eternal state. The Davidic kingdom will at last achieve God's glorious goal of ending every problem of evil and bringing redeemed humanity back full circle to the perfect, sinless, Garden-of-Eden relationship, but it will be fully achieved at the onset of the eternal state.

We must remember that the Davidic King is promised an eternal reign, and that the millennial kingdom will last only 1,000 years. Scripture says the reign of Christ must extend into the eternal state. So the kingdom of Christ is not to be found in the church age, nor will it conclude at the end of the millennial kingdom, but it will live on and on and on in the eternal state.

God's solution to mankind's problem of evil as it relates to failed governments is to be found yet again in the concept of the Messiah, but under this new phase of the kingdom of Christ, the one that lays beyond the millennial kingdom, as soon as sin and death have finally been conquered (Revelation 20:14-15). The eternal destruction of Satan and his demons, the unredeemed, Hades, and death itself, means that the last vestiges of human rebellion against God will all have been defeated going into the eternal state. Jesus will then hand the kingdom over to the Father. And with that victorious act, the Davidic King and His faithful citizens will enter the final and ultimate phase of the kingdom.

In truth, the millennium will merely serve as the opening act for the eternal state. It is the eternal-state phase of the kingdom of Christ that will fully and finally cure mankind's problem of evil—that is, fallen humanity. Therefore, in conclusion, the biblical response to the problem of evil as it relates to failed human governments will at last be realized in this final and everlasting phase of the Davidic kingdom.

THE SIGNIFICANCE TO YOU

The significance of what we have learned is threefold.

1. Equipping Yourself to Better Share the Gospel

First, for those who proclaim the gospel—the Christian—I hope this book aids you in your evangelistic efforts. By applying Bible prophecy as an effective apologetic, particularly in the defense and proclamation of the concept of the kingdom of Christ, we become better equipped to serve as evangelists in our duty to lead the lost to salvation. Even the great evangelistic messages, such as given by the apostle Peter in Acts 2 and Justin Martyr's own defense of Christianity, were heavily based on the messianic prophecies from the Old Testament, and made a powerful case for the truthfulness of Christianity.[11] Likewise, God's use of revealed Bible prophecy as an evangelistic apologetic brings Him glory, leads the lost to salvation, and provides a defense of the Christian faith. Christ Himself set the example by using messianic prophecies as an evangelistic apologetic. I hope you will as well.

2. Strengthening Your Faith

If you are already saved, I pray that your hope has been renewed and your faith strengthened. For not only did I endeavor to equip you to become a better evangelist, but to spur you toward living a holy life. As one of our great modern-day evangelists pointed out:

> Holy living is connected to an awareness that the Lord may return at any moment, and so also is evangelism...The greater the awareness a person has of the Lord's imminent return, the greater will be that person's motivation to live a holy life and to share the Gospel with others.[12]

Theologian John DeGruchy commented that knowing the truth concerning the promised return of the Davidic King "calls us

[Christians] to faithfulness in the struggle for justice and peace," and "keeps the hope against hope alive without which we would give up the struggle."[13] Knowing with certainty that Jesus Christ will return to establish His kingdom inspires us to engage in evangelistic efforts, calls us to holy living, provides hope in these dark days, and encourages us to "keep fighting the good fight." In doing so, while we wait longingly for the return of the King to this earth, we can embody His kingdom here on earth.[14]

For those Christians struggling to "work out [their] own salvation with fear and trembling" (Philippians 2:12), God's prophetic Word is meant to provide us with hope. Prophecy demonstrates that God will be faithful to all His covenants. He will restore a remnant of devoted people who will dwell with Him in His everlasting kingdom. The world today may live perpetually in the pains and sufferings of a broken world, but Jesus promised that He will "overcome the world" by bringing in His perfect kingdom (John 16:33). As we wait for this promised earthly kingdom, we must not lose hope or let go of our faith. God's revealed prophecies are meant to point people to Jesus Christ as the faithful covenant-keeper. He will fulfill His promises in these last days. With that revelation, we Christians can take heart, shore up our faith, and not lose hope.

3. *Saving You from the Just Punishment of Hell*

And, finally, if you have not yet surrendered your life to Jesus Christ, then the message of the kingdom of Christ is meant to serve as your wake-up call.

You may find yourself asking, *How do I become a citizen of the millennial kingdom?*

A citizen of the kingdom is one who realizes they are a sinner and have fallen short of the glory of God (Romans 3:23). They will confess their sins and pray in faith for the risen Jesus Christ to forgive them for their rebellion against Him. In doing so, they will accept

Jesus as their personal Savior (Romans 10:9-10, 13). With great joy, they will recognize that their just sentence to hell due to their sinful rebellion was paid for by Jesus Christ when He died on the cross. Their damnable destiny to the second death was canceled by Christ's resurrection from the dead (Romans 5:8; 6:23).

Upon calling out for the Lord's grace and forgiveness, they will experience Jesus' washing away of their guilt and instilling their lives with hope for the future. They will have now become citizens of the kingdom. This means they can live their lives in great anticipation knowing that one day soon they will stand before the Father in new, glorified bodies that have been made holy and pure (Romans 5:1; 8:1). Through Christ, the relationship between Father and child has been restored, and so they can live forevermore in that promised loving relationship with their King (Romans 8:38-39).

I pray that in faith and repentance, you have surrendered your life to Jesus Christ. I am so looking forward to being a fellow citizen of the kingdom of Christ with you. Together we will reside in that great kingdom together, then and forevermore. May God bless you!

NOTES

CHAPTER 1—NATIONS IN FREEFALL

1. Stowe, Harriet Beecher, *Uncle Tom's Cabin* (Philadelphia, PA: H. Altemus Company, 1900), PDF download, https://www.loc.gov/item/00004791/.
2. Cory Price, "Greatest Empires In The History Of The World," *WorldAtlas*, https://www.worldatlas.com/ancient-world/greatest-empires-in-the-history-of-the-world.html.
3. Ibid.
4. Robbie Mitchell, "Naram-Sin: The Conqueror-King of Ancient Akkad," *Ancient Origins*, https://www.ancient-origins.net/history-famous-people/naram-sin-0019001.
5. "Best Xerxes Quotes," *The Narratologist*, https://www.thenarratologist.com/best-xerxes-quotes/.
6. Elizabeth Nix, "Did Caligula really make his horse a consul?," *History*, https://www.history.com/news/did-caligula-really-make-his-horse-a-consul.
7. Price, "Greatest Empires In The History Of The World."
8. Karen Danao, "50 Genghis Khan Quotes to Help You Conquer the World," *Quote Ambition*, https://www.quoteambition.com/genghis-khan-quotes/.
9. M. Edward Yapp and Stanford Jay Shaw, "Decline of the Ottoman Empire," *Encyclopedia Britannica*, January 11, 2024, https://www.britannica.com/place/decline-of-the-Ottoman-Empire-2230672.
10. University of Cambridge Faculty of History, "The Divine Right of Kings: 4," https://www.hist.cam.ac.uk/divine-right-kings-4.
11. Anthony Eden, *The Reckoning: The Memoirs of Anthony Eden, Earl of Avon* (Boston, MA: Houghton Mifflin, 1965), 427.
12. Daniel Immerwahr, "Should America Still Police the World?," *The New Yorker*, https://www.newyorker.com/books/under-review/should-america-still-police-the-world.
13. Thomas Paine, *Common Sense*, 1776.
14. Introductory note written by Thomas Jefferson, which appears in Destutt de Tracy, *A Treatise on Political Economy* (Georgetown: Joseph Milligan, 1817).
15. John Adams, *Thoughts on Government*, April 1776, https://founders.archives.gov/documents/Adams/06-04-02-0026-0004.
16. R.J. Behn, "America's Founding Drama," The Lehrman Institute, http://www.lehrmaninstitute.org/history/founders-optimism.html.

17. The John Birch Society, "The Constitution of the United States: Back to Basics," https://jbs.org/constitution/basics/.
18. Paine, *Common Sense.*
19. Price, "Greatest Empires In The History Of The World."
20. Ibid.
21. Bob Wenz, "Your Government Failed You: But Then, We Don't Want an All-Powerful Government Any More than We Want an All-Powerful God," *Christianity Today* 49, no. 2 (February 2005): 54, https://search.ebscohost.com/login.aspx?direct=true&db=rfh&AN=ATLA0001456894&site=ehost-live.
22. Murray Print, Carolina Ugarte, Concepción Naval, and Anja Mihr, "Moral and Human Rights Education: The Contribution of the United Nations," *Journal of Moral Education* 37, no. 1 (March 2008): 115, doi:10.1080/03057240701803726.
23. Vincent Williams, "The Purpose of Human Life According to Thomas Aquinas," *Curating Theology*, https://curatingtheology.org/blog/2019/5/17/the-purpose-of-human-life-according-to-thomas-aquinas. Note: As an organization promoting secular answers to the world's problems, the UN members have been, from the start, ill-equipped to truly understand how objective human rights are grounded. They continually act upon Aristotle's theory that purposes humans as being defined by their intellect, and so, the world governmental organization continues to place their messianic hope for humanity in educational programs. Thomas Aquinas, in his attempt to synthesize the teachings of Aristotle and Christ in his grand work *Summa Theologiae*, borrowed from Aristotle the same intellectual assertion, but pointed out that mere earthly understanding lacks the ultimate *telos* of humans—to know and understand God. Human rights are grounded in God-given inalienable freedoms and making free, morally based decisions that contribute toward the common good of all in society requires an understanding of the moral Lawgiver. Therefore, it is of no surprise that by leaving God out of the equation that any UN response to promoting freedom is doomed to limited successes and more often failure.
24. Print et al., "Moral and Human Rights Education: The Contribution of the United Nations."
25. Esther D. Reed, "Responsibility to Protect and Militarized Humanitarian Intervention: When and Why the Churches Failed to Discern Moral Hazard," *Journal of Religious Ethics* 40, no. 2 (June 2012): 309, https://search.ebscohost.com/login.aspx?direct=true&db=rfh&AN=ATLA0001899509&site=ehost-live.
26. Ibid., 309.
27. Wenz, "Your Government Failed You: But Then, We Don't Want an All-Powerful Government Any More than We Want an All-Powerful God," 52.
28. Ibid., 52.
29. Ibid., 54.
30. Ibid., 54.
31. William L. Rowe, "The Problem of Evil and Some Varieties of Atheism," in *The Evidential Argument from Evil*, ed. Daniel Howard-Snyder (Bloomington, IN: Indiana University Press, 1996), 1-2.
32. Ibid., 1-2.
33. Donna Robinson Divine, "The Gods That Failed in Israel," *Israel Studies* 23, no. 3 (Fall 2018): 42, doi:10.2979/israelstudies.23.3.07.
34. Ibid., 42.
35. Gloria L. Schaab, "Nebuchadnezzar's Dream or the End of a Medieval Catholic Church," *Theological Studies* 69, no. 4 (December 2008): 961, https://search.ebscohost.com/login.aspx?direct=true&db=rfh&AN=ATLA0001691623&site=ehost-live.

36. Ibid., 961.
37. Ana S. Iltis, "The Failed Search for the Neutral in the Secular: Public Bioethics in the Face of the Culture Wars," *Christian Bioethics: Non-Ecumenical Studies in Medical Morality* 15, no. 3 (December 2009): 221, doi:10.1093/cb/cbp018.
38. Nathan Jones and Steve Howell, *12 Faith Journeys of the Minor Prophets*, 1st ed. (McKinney, TX: Lamb & Lion Ministries, 2016), 151.
39. Josiah Derby, "A Fresh Look at Nebuchadnezzar," *Jewish Bible Quarterly* 28, no. 3 (July 2000): 185, https://search.ebscohost.com/login.aspx?direct=true&db=rfh&AN=ATLA0000910638&site=ehost-live.
40. Kenneth L. Barker, "Premillennialism in the Book of Daniel," *The Master's Seminary Journal* 4, no. 1 (Spr 1993): 27-28, https://search.ebscohost.com/login.aspx?direct=true&db=rfh&AN=ATLA0000864503&site=ehost-live.
41. Ibid., 27-28.
42. Arnold G. Fruchtenbaum, *The Footsteps of the Messiah: A Study of the Sequence of Prophetic Events* (San Antonio, TX: Ariel Ministry Publishers, 2004), 22-25.
43. Ibid., 22-25.
44. Fruchtenbaum, 21. He does not rule out the times of temporary Jewish control of Jerusalem, such as the Maccabbean Period (164–63 BC), the First Jewish Revolt against Rome (AD 66–70), the Second Jewish Revolt or Bar Kokhba Revolt against Rome (AD 132–135), or the modern state of Israel's control since the Six-Day War in 1967, but makes his definition based on the condition that the Gentiles are still capable of exerting influence over the city of Jerusalem and ends that time when they no longer can.
45. Barker, "Premillennialism in the Book of Daniel," 29.
46. Lit-Sen Chang, *What Is Apologetics?*, trans. Samuel Ling (Phillipsburg, NJ: P&R Publishing, 1999), 59-61.
47. Ibid., 59-61.
48. Ibid., 59-61.
49. Ibid., 11.
50. Sidney Greidanus, "Applying Daniel's Messages to the Church Today." *Calvin Theological Journal* 47, no. 2 (November 2012): 270-271, https://search.ebscohost.com/login.aspx?direct=true&db=rfh&AN=ATLA0001921266&site=ehost-live.
51. Ibid., 270-271.
52. Tim Moore, *Looking Forward to the Reign of Jesus Christ* (McKinney, TX: Lamb & Lion Ministries, 2020), 9.

CHAPTER 2—THE KINGDOM OF CHRIST

1. Mary B. Slade, *Good News*, ed. Rigdon McIntosh (Boston, MA: Oliver Ditson, 1876).
2. Cotton Mather, *Things to be look'd for. Discourses on the Glorious Characters, Conjectures...the Latter Dayes* (Boston, MA: 1691), 8-9.
3. Charles C. Ryrie, *Basic Theology* (Wheaton, IL: Victor Books, 1986), 397-399.
4. Mather, *Things to be look'd for. Discourses on the Glorious Characters, Conjectures...the Latter Dayes*, 8-9.
5. Ibid., 8-9.
6. Edward Viening, ed., *The Zondervan Topical Bible* (Grand Rapids, MI: Zondervan, 1969), 608-609.
7. Ibid., 608-609.

8. Frank S. Mead, *The Encyclopedia of Religious Quotations* (Old Tappan, NJ: Fleming H. Revell, 1965), 265.
9. Mather, *Things to be look'd for. Discourses on the Glorious Characters, Conjectures...the Latter Dayes*, 8-9.
10. The term *church* is not meant to denote the Roman Catholic or Orthodox churches, nor any Protestant denomination, but rather, the entirety of those who have placed their faith in Jesus Christ as their Lord and Savior from Pentecost on until the great snatching up (Acts 2; 1 Thessalonians 4:13-18).
11. Viening, *The Zondervan Topical Bible*, 122-125.
12. Wilbur M. Smith, "The Prophetic Literature of Colonial America," *Bibliotheca Sacra* 100, no. 398 (April 1943): 273-274, https://search.ebscohost.com/login.aspx?direct=true&db=rfh&AN=ATLA0001513840&site=ehost-live.
13. Ibid., 273-274.
14. Ibid., 273-274.
15. Ibid., 273-274.
16. Ibid., 273-274.
17. Cotton Mather, *Meditations upon the Ark as a Type of the Church; Delivered in a Sermon at Boston* (Boston, MA: 1689), 48.
18. Ibid., 48.
19. Mead, *The Encyclopedia of Religious Quotations*, 265.
20. Merrill F. Unger, *Unger's Guide to the Bible* (Wheaton, IL: Tyndale House, 1974), 528.
21. Ibid., 528.
22. Unger, *Unger's Guide to the Bible*, 28-29. First promised in Genesis 3:15.
23. Arthur W. Kac, *The Messianic Hope: A Divine Solution for the Human Problem* (Grand Rapids, MI: Baker Book House, 1975), 23-29.
24. Eugene W. Pond, "The Background and Timing of the Judgment of the Sheep and Goats," *Bibliotheca Sacra* 159, no. 634 (April 2002): 205, https://search.ebscohost.com/login.aspx?direct=true&db=rfh&AN=ATLA0001322859&site=ehost-live.
25. Hayyim Angel, "The Eternal Davidic Covenant in II Samuel Chapter 7 and Its Later Manifestations in the Bible," *Jewish Bible Quarterly* 44, no. 2 (April 2016): 83-86, https://search.ebscohost.com/login.aspx?direct=true&db=rfh&AN=ATLAn3859150&site=ehost-live.
26. Walter C. Kaiser Jr., "The Promise Doctrine and Jesus," *Trinity Journal* 4 (Spr 1975): 64, https://search.ebscohost.com/login.aspx?direct=true&db=rfh&AN=ATLA0001275813&site=ehost-live.
27. Hayyim Angel, "The Eternal Davidic Covenant in II Samuel Chapter 7 and Its Later Manifestations in the Bible," 83-86.
28. Kaiser, "The Promise Doctrine and Jesus," 64.
29. Sunwoo Hwang, "Coexistence of Unconditionality and Conditionality of the Davidic Covenant in Chronicles," *Heythrop Journal* 58, no. 2 (March 2017): 239, https://search.ebscohost.com/login.aspx?direct=true&db=rfh&AN=ATLAiBCB170327000584&site=ehost-live.
30. Ibid., 239.
31. John L. MacKay, *Isaiah*, vol. 1, chapters 1-39 (Faverdale North, UK: Evangelical Press, 2008), 288-295.
32. Ibid., 288-295.
33. Reference Psalms 2; 18; 20–21; 45; 72; 89; 101; 132; 144; Isaiah 11:24-25; 54; 60–61; Jeremiah

23:5-6; 30:8-9; 33:14-17, 20-21; Ezekiel 37:24-25; Daniel 7:13-14; Hosea 3:4-5; Amos 8:11; Zechariah. 14:4, 9.

34. Andrew E. Steinmann, "What Did David Understand about the Promises in the Davidic Covenant?," *Bibliotheca Sacra* 171, no. 681 (January 2014): 19, https://search.ebscohost.com/login.aspx?direct=true&db=rfh&AN=ATLA0001966888&site=ehost-live.
35. Ibid. References: Matthew 9:27; 12:23; 15:22; 20:30; 21:9; Mark 10:47-48; Luke 18:38-39.
36. Stephen J. Nichols, "The Dispensational View of the Davidic Kingdom: A Response to Progressive Dispensationalism," *The Master's Seminary Journal* 7, no. 2 (Fall 1996): 221, https://search.ebscohost.com/login.aspx?direct=true&db=rfh&AN=ATLA0001016694&site=ehost-live.
37. Geoffrey W. Bromiley, Everett F. Harrison, Roland K. Harrison, William Sanford LaSore, and Edgar W. Smith Jr., eds., *The International Standard Bible Encyclopedia*. vol. 1, A-D (Grand Rapids, MI: William B. Eerdmans, 1979), 876.
38. Nichols, "The Dispensational View of the Davidic Kingdom: A Response to Progressive Dispensationalism," 221.
39. Unger, *Unger's Guide to the Bible*, 528.
40. Ibid., 528.
41. Ibid., 31-32.
42. Ryrie, *Basic Theology*, 460.
43. Cleon Rogers, "The Davidic Covenant in Acts-Revelation," *Bibliotheca Sacra* 151 (January-March 1994): 84.
44. Ibid., 84.
45. L.S. Chafer, "Dispensationalism," *Bibliotheca Sacra* 93 (October-December 1936): 435. References: Matthew 25:31, 32. cf. 19:28; Acts 15:16; Luke 1:31-33; Matthew 2:2.
46. Charles Lee Feinberg, *The Prophecy of Ezekiel: The Glory of the Lord* (Chicago, IL: Moody Press, 1969), 219.

CHAPTER 3—THE PROMISED RETURN OF CHRIST

1. Frank S. Mead, *The Encyclopedia of Religious Quotations* (Old Tappan, NJ: Fleming H. Revell, 1965), 266.
2. David R. Reagan, *Christ in Prophecy* (McKinney, TX: Lamb & Lion Ministries, 2006), 94.
3. Tim LaHaye, Ed Hindson, Thomas Ice, and James Combs, eds., *Tim LaHaye Prophecy Study Bible* (Chattanooga, TN: AMG Publishers, 2001), 1576-1599.
4. Henry H. Halley, *Halley's Bible Handbook*, 24th ed. (Grand Rapids, MI: Zondervan, 1965), 387.
5. Walter C. Kaiser Jr., "The Promise Doctrine and Jesus," *Trinity Journal* 4 (Spr 1975): 59-60, https://search.ebscohost.com/login.aspx?direct=true&db=rfh&AN=ATLA0001275813&site=ehost-live.
6. Ibid., 59-60.
7. LaHaye et al., *Tim LaHaye Prophecy Study Bible*, 1576-1599.
8. Jamie Grant, "Christ Ascended for Us—'I Have Gone to Prepare a Place for You,'" *Evangel* 25, no. 2 (Summer 2007): 39-40, https://search.ebscohost.com/login.aspx?direct=true&db=rlh&AN=25012923&site=ehost-live.
9. Ibid., 39-40.
10. LaHaye et al., *Tim LaHaye Prophecy Study Bible*, 1576-1599.
11. Reagan, *Christ in Prophecy*, 94.

12. LaHaye et al., *Tim LaHaye Prophecy Study Bible*, 1576-1599.

13. John B. Metzger, *God in Eclipse: God Has Not Always Been Silent* (Keller, TX: JHouse Publishing, 2013), 178-179.

14. Ibid., 178-179.

15. Roger Liebi, *The Promised Redeemer: The Fulfillment and Historical Authenticity of Messianic Prophecy*, trans. Timothy Capes (Dusseldorf, Germany: Christlicher Medienvertrieb Hagedorn, 2014), 7.

16. Ibid., 7.

17. Jonathan Bernis, *A Rabbi Looks at the Last Days* (Minneapolis, MN: Chosen Books, 2013), 106-108.

18. Ibid., 106-108.

19. Liebi, *The Promised Redeemer: The Fulfillment and Historical Authenticity of Messianic Prophecy*, 7.

20. Metzger, *God in Eclipse: God Has Not Always Been Silent*, 178-179.

CHAPTER 4—THE JEWS REGATHERED IN ISRAEL

1. Amir Tsarfati and Rick Yohn, *Discovering Daniel* (Eugene, OR: Harvest House, 2024), 196.

2. Roger Liebi, *The Promised Redeemer: The Fulfillment and Historical Authenticity of Messianic Prophecy*, trans. Timothy Capes (Dusseldorf, Germany: Christlicher Medienvertrieb Hagedorn, 2014), 106.

3. Ibid., 106.

4. Thomas Newton, *Dissertations on the Prophecies* (1766, repr. Philadelphia: James Martin, 1813), 147.

5. Jonathan Bernis, *A Rabbi Looks at the Last Days* (Minneapolis, MN: Chosen Books, 2013), 46-47.

6. Ibid., 49.

7. Ibid., 49.

8. Étan Levine, "Toward a Logic of Aliyah Discourse," *The Reconstructionist* 34, no. 14 (November 1968): 8-10, https://search.ebscohost.com/login.aspx?direct=true&db=rfh&AN=ATLA0001522795&site=ehost-live.

9. Ibid., 8-10.

10. Ibid., 9.

11. Chosen People Ministries, *How to Introduce Your Jewish Friends to the Messiah* (Charlotte, NC: Chosen People Ministries, Inc., 1991), 43.

12. Ibid., 43-44.

13. Ibid., 43-44.

14. Merrill F. Unger, *Unger's Guide to the Bible* (Wheaton, IL: Tyndale House, 1974), 31.

15. David H. Stern, *Restoring the Jewishness of the Gospel* (Jerusalem, Israel: Jewish New Testament Publications, 1988), 39.

16. Ibid., 39.

17. Arnold G. Fruchtenbaum, "The Modern State of Israel in Bible Prophecy," *Pre-Trib Research Center*, accessed December 11, 2021, https://pre-trib.org/images/2021_Conference/2021-Pre-Trib-Fruchtenbaum-Modern_State_of_Israel-Paper.pdf.

18. Ibid.

19. John B. Taylor, *Ezekiel: An Introduction and Commentary* (Downers Grove, IL: InterVarsity Press, 1969), 249-250.
20. John L. MacKay, *Isaiah*, vol. 1, chapters 1-39 (Faverdale North, UK: Evangelical Press, 2008), 302-303.
21. Fruchtenbaum, "The Modern State of Israel in Bible Prophecy."
22. Ibid. Joseph presents his own situation as an ancient example of God's unchanging and still relevant to today *modus operandi*—"But as for you, you meant evil against me; but God meant it for good, in order to bring it about as it is this day, to save many people alive" (Genesis 50:20).
23. References: Isaiah 1:22; 48:10; Jeremiah 6:27-30; 9:7; Zechariah 13:9; Malachi 3:2-3.
24. Donna Robinson Divine, "The Gods That Failed in Israel," *Israel Studies* 23, no. 3 (Fall 2018): 42-43, doi:10.2979/israelstudies.23.3.07.
25. Ibid., 45-46.
26. Ibid., 48.
27. Hizky Shoham, "From 'Great History' to 'Small History': The Genesis of the Zionist Periodization," *Israel Studies* 18, no. 1 (Spring 2013): 33, doi:10.2979/israelstudies.18.1.31.
28. Nelly Elias and Adriana Kemp, "The New Second Generation: Non-Jewish Olim, Black Jews and Children of Migrant Workers in Israel," *Israel Studies* 15, no. 1 (Spring 2010): 73-76, doi:10.2979/ISR.2010.15.1.73.
29. Shoham, 31-32.
30. Ibid., 31-32.
31. Ibid., 31-32.
32. Elias and Kemp, "The New Second Generation: Non-Jewish Olim, Black Jews and Children of Migrant Workers in Israel," 73-76.
33. Ibid., 73-76.
34. Ibid., 73-76.
35. Increase Mather, *The Mystery of Christ* (1686), 57.
36. "Number of Jews in the World 2022," *World Population Review*, https://worldpopulationreview.com/country-rankings/number-of-jews-in-the-world.
37. Mather, *The Mystery of Christ*, 76-77.
38. Ibid., 76-77.
39. Ibid., 76-77.

CHAPTER 5—THE DAY OF THE LORD

1. Jeff Kinley, *God's Grand Finale: Wrath, Grace, and Glory in Earth's Final Days* (Eugene, OR: Harvest House, 2023), 188.
2. Richard L. Mayhue, "The Bible's Watchword: Day of the Lord," *The Master's Seminary Journal* 22, no. 1 (Spr 2011): 66, 69, https://search.ebscohost.com/login.aspx?direct=true&db=rfh&AN=ATLA0001842440&site=ehost-live.
3. Nicholas R. Werse, "Obadiah's 'Day of the Lord': A Semiotic Reading," *Journal for the Study of the Old Testament* 38, no. 1 (September 2013): 116-117, doi:10.1177/0309089213492818.
4. Ibid., 116-117.
5. Mayhue, "The Bible's Watchword: Day of the Lord," 67.
6. Ibid. References: Isaiah 2:12; 13:9; Joel 2:31; 3:14; Obadiah 15; Zechariah 14:1; Malachi 4:5.
7. A.T. Pierson, *Many Infallible Proofs*, vol. 1 (Grand Rapids, MI: Zondervan, n.d.), 98.

8. Ibid., 98.
9. Arthur W. Kac, *The Messianic Hope: A Divine Solution for the Human Problem* (Grand Rapids, MI: Baker Book House, 1975), vii.
10. David R. Reagan, *Christ in Prophecy* (McKinney, TX: Lamb & Lion Ministries, 2006), 44.
11. Ibid., 68.
12. Arnold G. Fruchtenbaum, *The Footsteps of the Messiah: A Study of the Sequence of Prophetic Events* (San Antonio, TX: Ariel Ministry, 2004), 179-180.
13. Herbert M. Wolf, *Interpreting Isaiah: The Suffering and Glory of the Messiah* (Grand Rapids, MI: Zondervan, 1985), 286.
14. Ibid., 285.
15. Ibid., 286.
16. Craig A. Blaising, "The Day of the Lord and the Seventieth Week of Daniel," *Bibliotheca Sacra* 169, no. 674 (April 2012): 135, https://search.ebscohost.com/login.aspx?direct=true&db=rfh&AN=ATLA0001892476&site=ehost-live.
17. Roger Liebi, *The Promised Redeemer: The Fulfillment and Historical Authenticity of Messianic Prophecy*, trans. Timothy Capes (Dusseldorf, Germany: Christlicher Medienvertrieb Hagedorn, 2014), 15.
18. Ibid., 20. The 360-day prophetic year will later be substantiated in Revelation 11:3 and 12:14 as 3.5 years equaling 1,260 days or seven years equaling 2,520 days.
19. Reagan, *Christ in Prophecy*, 44.
20. Arnold G. Fruchtenbaum, "The Modern State of Israel in Bible Prophecy," *Pre-Trib Research Center*, accessed December 11, 2021, https://pre-trib.org/images/2021_Conference/2021-Pre-Trib-Fruchtenbaum-Modern_State_of_Israel-Paper.pdf.
21. Ibid.
22. Blaising, "The Day of the Lord and the Seventieth Week of Daniel," 135.
23. Ibid., 135.
24. Henry H. Halley, *Halley's Bible Handbook*, 24th ed. (Grand Rapids, MI: Zondervan, 1965), 385-386.
25. Mayhue, "The Bible's Watchword: Day of the Lord," 65.
26. Ibid., 65.
27. Ryan Foley, "Only 6% of self-professed Christians hold biblical worldview amid increasing syncretism in the US: survey," *The Christian Post*, May 1, 2024, https://www.christianpost.com/news/only-6-percent-christians-hold-biblical-worldview-syncretism-rises.html.
28. Reagan, *Christ in Prophecy*, 115-116.

CHAPTER 6—THE AFTERMATH

1. Randy Alcorn, *50 Days of Heaven: Reflections that Bring Eternity to Light* (Carol Stream, IL: Tyndale House, 2006), 126.
2. Walter C. Kaiser Jr., *Toward an Old Testament Theology* (Grand Rapids, MI: Zondervan, 1978), 218-219.
3. Don Finto, *God's Promise and the Future of Israel* (Ventura, CA: Gospel Light, 2006), 133.
4. Charles H. Spurgeon, *Christ in the Old Testament* (1899; repr., Chattanooga, TN: AMG Publishers, 1994), 541.
5. Herbert M. Wolf, *Interpreting Isaiah: The Suffering and Glory of the Messiah* (Grand Rapids, MI: Zondervan, 1985), 291-293.

6. Charles A. Gieschen, "Antichrist in the Scriptures and the Lutheran Confessions: The Relevance of Reformation Exegesis of 2 Thessalonians 2:1-12 for the Church Today," *Concordia Theological Quarterly* 81, no. 3–4 (July 2017): 274, https://search.ebscohost.com/login.aspx?direct=true&db=rfh&AN=ATLAiC9Y180604000036&site=ehost-live.
7. David R. Reagan, *Christ in Prophecy* (McKinney, TX: Lamb & Lion Ministries, 2006), 60. References: Isaiah 10:12-19; 11:4; 14:12-17; 24:21-22; 26:21–27:1; 30:27-28; 41:11-13; 63:1-6; 66:15-16; Daniel 7:11, 26; 11:45; Joel 3:12-16; Habakkuk 3:12-15; Zechariah 14:3, 12-15.
8. Jeffrey A.D. Weima, "The Slaying of Satan's Superman and the Sure Salvation of the Saints: Paul's Apocalyptic Word of Comfort (2 Thessalonians 2:1-17)," *Calvin Theological Journal* 41, no. 1 (April 2006): 83, 87, https://search.ebscohost.com/login.aspx?direct=true&db=rfh&AN=ATLA0001504948&site=ehost-live.
9. Eugene W. Pond, "The Background and Timing of the Judgment of the Sheep and Goats," *Bibliotheca Sacra* 159, no. 634 (April 2002): 201-202, https://search.ebscohost.com/login.aspx?direct=true&db=rfh&AN=ATLA0001322859&site=ehost-live.
10. Ibid., 203.
11. Ibid., 206.
12. John F. Walvoord, "Christ's Olivet Discourse on the End of the Age: The Judgment of the Nations," *Bibliotheca Sacra* 129, no. 516 (October 1972): 310, https://search.ebscohost.com/login.aspx?direct=true&db=rfh&AN=ATLA0001508911&site=ehost-live.
13. Charles C. Ryrie, *Basic Theology* (Wheaton, IL: Victor Books, 1986), 494-495.
14. Walvoord, "Christ's Olivet Discourse on the End of the Age: The Judgment of the Nations," 312.
15. Ibid., 312.
16. Pond, "The Background and Timing of the Judgment of the Sheep and Goats," 220.
17. Ibid., 202.
18. A.H. McNeile, *The Gospel According to St. Matthew* (London, UK: 1915), 369.
19. Walvoord, "Christ's Olivet Discourse on the End of the Age: The Judgment of the Nations," 314.
20. Ryrie, *Basic Theology*, 494-495. The great white throne judgment will be explored in more detail in the chapter concerning final judgment.

CHAPTER 7—THE MESSIAH'S GOVERNMENT: THE CHARACTER OF HIS REIGN

1. Charles H. Spurgeon, *Christ in the Old Testament* (1899; repr., Chattanooga, TN: AMG Publishers, 1994), 547.
2. Dan Bruce, *He Is the One: Proofs from the Hebrew Scriptures that Jesus Was the Jewish Messiah* (Atlanta, GA: The Prophecy Society, 2015), 1.
3. Spurgeon, *Christ in the Old Testament,* 543-545.
4. Ibid., 543-545.
5. Charles C. Ryrie, *Basic Theology* (Wheaton, IL: Victor Books, 1986), 511.
6. Mark H. Heinemann, "An Exposition of Psalm 22," *Bibliotheca Sacra* 147, no. 587 (July 1990): 308, https://search.ebscohost.com/login.aspx?direct=true&db=rfh&AN=ATLA0000827911&site=ehost-live.
7. Ellen Van Wolde, "A Network of Conventional and Deliberate Metaphors in Psalm 22," *Journal for the Study of the Old Testament* 44, no. 4 (June 2020): 646, doi:10.1177/0309089219862816.

8. Heinemann, "An Exposition of Psalm 22," 286.
9. Richard Duane Patterson, "Psalm 22: From Trial to Triumph," *Journal of the Evangelical Theological Society* 47, no. 2 (June 2004): 226, https://search.ebscohost.com/login.aspx?direct=true&db=rfh&AN=ATLA0001457894&site=ehost-live.
10. Ibid., 226.
11. Other psalms that echo the assurance of Christ claiming His kingdom are Psalms 47; 67; 89:19-29; 110; 132:13-18.
12. K.R. Harriman, "The King Arrives, but for What Purpose?: The Christological Use of Zechariah 13–14 in Mark 13," *Journal of Theological Interpretation* 10, no. 2 (Fall 2016): 283-285, https://search.ebscohost.com/login.aspx?direct=true&db=rfh&AN=ATLAiEYD170206001927&site=ehost-live.
13. Don Finto, *God's Promise and the Future of Israel* (Ventura, CA: Gospel Light, 2006), 135.
14. Ibid., 138.
15. Tim Moore, *Looking Forward to the Reign of Jesus Christ* (McKinney, TX: Lamb & Lion Ministries, 2020), 25.
16. Kenneth L. Barker, "Premillennialism in the Book of Daniel," *The Master's Seminary Journal* 4, no. 1 (Spr 1993): 26, https://search.ebscohost.com/login.aspx?direct=true&db=rfh&AN=ATLA0000864503&site=ehost-live.
17. Ibid., 31-32.
18. Ibid., 35-36.
19. Otto Kaiser, *Isaiah 1–12 A Commentary*, 2d ed., trans. John Bowden (Philadelphia, PA: Westminster Press, 1981), 55.
20. Carl Umhau Wolf, "Luther on the Christmas Prophecy, Isaiah 9," *Lutheran Quarterly* 5, no. 4 (November 1953): 390, https://search.ebscohost.com/login.aspx?direct=true&db=rfh&AN=ATLA0000655348&site=ehost-live.
21. Ibid., 390.
22. Jake Stromberg, "The 'Root of Jesse' in Isaiah 11:10: Postexilic Judah, or Postexilic Davidic King?," *Journal of Biblical Literature* 127, no. 4 (Wint 2008): 655-657, https://search.ebscohost.com/login.aspx?direct=true&db=rfh&AN=ATLA0001696617&site=ehost-live.
23. Richard C. Brand Jr., "Either Or?," *The Expository Times* 116, no. 2 (November 2004): 56, https://search.ebscohost.com/login.aspx?direct=true&db=rfh&AN=ATLA0001548157&site=ehost-live.
24. Christopher M. Leighton and Adam Gregerman, "Between Text & Sermon: Isaiah 11:1-11," *Interpretation* 64, no. 3 (July 2010): 284, https://search.ebscohost.com/login.aspx?direct=true&db=rfh&AN=ATLA0001792576&site=ehost-live.
25. Ibid., 284.
26. Ibid., 284.
27. Brand, "Either Or?," 56.
28. Rick W. Byargeon, "The Relationship of Micah 4:1-3 and Isaiah 2:2-4: Implications for Understanding the Prophetic Message," *Southwestern Journal of Theology* 46, no. 1 (Fall 2003): 6-8, https://search.ebscohost.com/login.aspx?direct=true&db=rfh&AN=ATLA0001555792&site=ehost-live.
29. Ibid., 24.
30. J.J.M. Roberts, "The End of the War in the Zion Tradition: The Imperialistic Background of an Old Testament Vision of World Wide Peace," *Horizons in Biblical Theology* 26, no. 1 (June

2004): 4, https://search.ebscohost.com/login.aspx?direct=true&db=rfh&AN=ATLA0001980359&site=ehost-live.

31. Gene R. Smillie, "Isaiah 42:1-4 in Its Rhetorical Context," *Bibliotheca Sacra* 162, no. 645 (January 2005): 51, https://search.ebscohost.com/login.aspx?direct=true&db=rfh&AN=ATLA0001431958&site=ehost-live.

32. Jerome H. Neyrey, "The Thematic Use of Isaiah 42:1-4 in Matthew 12," *Biblica* 63, no. 4 (1982): 31, https://search.ebscohost.com/login.aspx?direct=true&db=rfh&AN=ATLA0000797522&site=ehost-live.

33. Smillie, "Isaiah 42:1-4 in Its Rhetorical Context," 56-58.

34. Kenneth D. Litwak, "The Use of Quotations from Isaiah 52:13–53:12 in the New Testament," *Journal of the Evangelical Theological Society* 26, no. 4 (December 1983): 393, https://search.ebscohost.com/login.aspx?direct=true&db=rfh&AN=ATLA0000941405&site=ehost-live.

35. Peter Dray, "Isaiah 52:13–53:12: Isaiah on the Suffering Servant," *Evangel* 26, no. 2 (Summer 2008): 33-34, https://search.ebscohost.com/login.aspx?direct=true&db=rlh&AN=31268707&site=ehost-live.

36. Gary V. Smith, "Isaiah 65–66: The Destiny of God's Servants in a New Creation," *Bibliotheca Sacra* 171, no. 681 (January 2014): 42, https://search.ebscohost.com/login.aspx?direct=true&db=rfh&AN=ATLA0001966890&site=ehost-live.

37. Paul Nadim Tarazi, "Israel and the Nations (According to Zechariah 14)," *St Vladimir's Theological Quarterly* 38, no. 2 (1994): 185, https://search.ebscohost.com/login.aspx?direct=true&db=rfh&AN=ATLA0000879688&site=ehost-live.

38. Ibid., 183.

CHAPTER 8—THE WORLD KNOWS THE LORD: THE CHARACTER OF ITS CITIZENS

1. Ron Rhodes, *Israel on High Alert* (Eugene, OR: Harvest House, 2023), 227.

2. Rick W. Byargeon, "The Relationship of Micah 4:1-3 and Isaiah 2:2-4: Implications for Understanding the Prophetic Message," *Southwestern Journal of Theology* 46, no. 1 (Fall 2003): 24-26, https://search.ebscohost.com/login.aspx?direct=true&db=rfh&AN=ATLA0001555792&site=ehost-live.

3. Ibid., 24-26.

4. Mark A. Hassler, "Isaiah 14 and Habakkuk 2: Two Taunt Songs against the Same Tyrant?," *The Master's Seminary Journal* 26, no. 2 (Fall 2015): 229, https://search.ebscohost.com/login.aspx?direct=true&db=rfh&AN=ATLAiBCA160705002050&site=ehost-live.

5. Ibid., 229.

6. Byargeon, "The Relationship of Micah 4:1-3 and Isaiah 2:2-4: Implications for Understanding the Prophetic Message," 24-26.

7. Mark H. Heinemann, "An Exposition of Psalm 22," *Bibliotheca Sacra* 147, no. 587 (July 1990): 306, https://search.ebscohost.com/login.aspx?direct=true&db=rfh&AN=ATLA0000827911&site=ehost-live.

8. Gary V. Smith, "Isaiah 65–66: The Destiny of God's Servants in a New Creation," *Bibliotheca Sacra* 171, no. 681 (January 2014): 50, https://search.ebscohost.com/login.aspx?direct=true&db=rfh&AN=ATLA0001966890&site=ehost-live.

9. G. Henry Waterman, "Sources of Paul's Teaching on the 2nd Coming of Christ in 1 and 2 Thessalonians," *Journal of the Evangelical Theological Society* 18, no. 2 (Spr 1975): 106, 111, https://search.ebscohost.com/login.aspx?direct=true&db=rfh&AN=ATLA0000751765&site=ehost-live.

10. Cletus Hull, "The Purpose of Suffering and Glory in the Pauline Eschatology of Christ's Parousia in 2 Thessalonians 1:5-10," *Conversations with the Biblical World* 36 (2016): 164, https://search.ebscohost.com/login.aspx?direct=true&db=rfh&AN=ATLAi9KZ180731002332&site=ehost-live.
11. Ibid., 183.
12. Hugo McCord, "The Meaning of YHWH Tsidkenu ('the Lord Our Righteousness') in Jeremiah 23:6 and 33:16," *Restoration Quarterly* 6, no. 3 (1962): 114, https://search.ebscohost.com/login.aspx?direct=true&db=rfh&AN=ATLA0001596830&site=ehost-live.

CHAPTER 9—JERUSALEM THE CAPITAL CITY: THE SEAT OF HIS AUTHORITY

1. Mark Robinson, "The Future of Jerusalem," *Israel My Glory*, June/July 1992, https://israelmyglory.org/article/the-future-of-jerusalem/.
2. Edward Viening, ed., *The Zondervan Topical Bible* (Grand Rapids, MI: Zondervan, 1969), 135-136.
3. Eugene W. Pond, "The Background and Timing of the Judgment of the Sheep and Goats," *Bibliotheca Sacra* 159, no. 634 (April 2002): 214, https://search.ebscohost.com/login.aspx?direct=true&db=rfh&AN=ATLA0001322859&site=ehost-live.
4. Gary V. Smith, "Isaiah 65–66: The Destiny of God's Servants in a New Creation," *Bibliotheca Sacra* 171, no. 681 (January 2014): 50-51, https://search.ebscohost.com/login.aspx?direct=true&db=rfh&AN=ATLA0001966890&site=ehost-live.
5. Tim LaHaye, Ed Hindson, Thomas Ice, and James Combs, eds., *Tim LaHaye Prophecy Study Bible* (Chattanooga, TN: AMG Publishers, 2001), 810.
6. Frank E. Gaebelein, ed., *The Expositor's Bible Commentary*, vol. 6, Isaiah–Jeremiah (Grand Rapids, MI: Zondervan, 1986), 996.
7. Ibid., 996.
8. Soo J. Kim, "YHWH Shammah: The City as Gateway to the Presence of YHWH," *Journal for the Study of the Old Testament* 39, no. 2 (December 2014): 188, doi:10.1177/0309089214567375.
9. Ibid., 188.
10. Kim, "YHWH Shammah: The City as Gateway to the Presence of YHWH," 205.
11. Jonathan Magonet, "Isaiah's Mountain or The Shape of Things to Come" *Prooftexts* 11, no. 2 (May 1991): 175, https://search.ebscohost.com/login.aspx?direct=true&db=rlh&AN=7157379&site=ehost-live.
12. Ibid., 179.
13. Paul Nadim Tarazi, "Israel and the Nations (According to Zechariah 14)," *St Vladimir's Theological Quarterly* 38, no. 2 (1994): 185-186, https://search.ebscohost.com/login.aspx?direct=true&db=rfh&AN=ATLA0000879688&site=ehost-live.
14. J.J.M. Roberts, "The End of the War in the Zion Tradition: The Imperialistic Background of an Old Testament Vision of World Wide Peace," *Horizons in Biblical Theology* 26, no. 1 (June 2004): 4-5, https://search.ebscohost.com/login.aspx?direct=true&db=rfh&AN=ATLA0001980359&site=ehost-live.
15. Peter G. Jarvis, "What Are We Looking Forward To?," *The Expository Times* 116, no. 1 (October 2004): 26, https://search.ebscohost.com/login.aspx?direct=true&db=rfh&AN=ATLA0001554656&site=ehost-live.
16. Harold R. Holmyard III, "Does Isaiah 33:23 Address Israel or Israel's Enemy?," *Bibliotheca Sacra* 152, no. 607 (July 1995): 275, https://search.ebscohost.com/login.aspx?direct=true&db=rfh&AN=ATLA0000897520&site=ehost-live.

17. Ibid., 276.
18. Roberts, "The End of the War in the Zion Tradition: The Imperialistic Background of an Old Testament Vision of World Wide Peace," 12.
19. Albert M. Wolters, "Targumic KRWBT (Zechariah 14:20) = Greek Koryphaia," *Journal of Biblical Literature* 115, no. 4 (Winter 1996): 710, https://search.ebscohost.com/login.aspx?direct=true&db=rfh&AN=ATLA0001016912&site=ehost-live.
20. Ibid., 710.
21. Joel Marcus, "No More Zealots in the House of the Lord: A Note on the History of Interpretation of Zechariah 14:21," *Novum Testamentum* 55, no. 1 (2013): 23-24, doi:10.1163/15685365-12341402.
22. Ibid., 23-24.
23. Zola Levitt, *The Seven Feasts of Israel* (Dallas, TX: Zola, 1979), 1-2.
24. Ibid., 1-2.
25. Alfred Edersheim, *The Temple: Its Ministry and Services as They Were at the Time of Christ* (Grand Rapids, MI: Wm. B. Eerdmans, 1975), 277.
26. Ibid., 286.
27. Ibid., 279.
28. Levitt, *The Seven Feasts of Israel*, 17-19.
29. Edersheim, *The Temple: Its Ministry and Services as They Were at the Time of Christ*, 279.
30. Peter Bynum, "Between Text and Sermon: Isaiah 2:1-4," *Interpretation* 71, no. 3 (2017): 311-312, doi:10.1177/0020964317698766.
31. Ibid., 311-312.
32. Ibid., 311-312.

CHAPTER 10—THE ROLE OF KING DAVID: THE SUB-REGENT

1. Jack Wellman, "Top 7 Bible Verses About David," *What Christians Want to Know*, https://www.whatchristianswanttoknow.com/top-7-bible-verses-about-david/.
2. Andrew E. Steinmann, "What Did David Understand about the Promises in the Davidic Covenant?," *Bibliotheca Sacra* 171, no. 681 (January 2014): 19, https://search.ebscohost.com/login.aspx?direct=true&db=rfh&AN=ATLA0001966888&site=ehost-live.
3. Orville J. Nave, *Nave's Topical Bible: A Digest of the Holy Scriptures* (Nashville, TN: The Southwestern Company, 1897), 278.
4. Ibid. References: Numbers 24:17, 19; 2 Samuel 7:11-16; 1 Chronicles 17:9-14; 22; 2 Chronicles 6:5-17; 13:5; 21:7; Psalm 89:19-37; Isaiah 9:7; 16:5; 22:20-25; Jeremiah 23:5; 33:15-26; Luke 1:32-33.
5. Geoffrey W. Bromiley, Everett F. Harrison, Roland K. Harrison, William Sanford LaSore, and Edgar W. Smith Jr., eds., *The International Standard Bible Encyclopedia*, vol. 1, A-D (Grand Rapids, MI: William B. Eerdmans, 1979), 876.
6. Charles F. Pfeiffer and Everett F. Harrison, eds. *The Wycliffe Bible Commentary* (Chicago, IL: Moody Press, 1962), 677.
7. Ibid., 763.
8. Ibid., 763.
9. George Albert Cooke, "Some Considerations on the Text and Teaching of Ezekiel 40–48: (A Paper Read before the Society for Old Testament Study, Meeting in London, January 3rd 1924)," *Zeitschrift Fur Die Alttestamentliche Wissenschaft* 42 (1924): 105, https://search.ebscohost.com/login.aspx?direct=true&db=rfh&AN=ATLAiFZK161121003006&site=ehost-live.

10. Pfeiffer and Harrison, *The Wycliffe Bible Commentary*, 755.
11. Adriane B. Leveen, "Returning the Body to Its Place: Ezekiel's Tour of the Temple," *Harvard Theological Review* 105, no. 4 (October 2012): 399-400, doi:10.1017/S0017816012000181.

CHAPTER 11—THE MILLENNIAL TEMPLE: THE HOUSE OF WORSHIP

1. Fred Hartman, "The Millennial Temple," *Israel My Glory*, August/September 1995, https://israelmyglory.org/article/the-millennial-temple/.
2. Charles H. Spurgeon, *Christ in the Old Testament* (1899; repr., Chattanooga, TN: AMG Publishers, 1994), 671, 677.
3. Ibid., 545.
4. Adam Kubis, "Zechariah 6:12-13 as the Referent of Γραφη in John 2:22 and 20:9: A Contribution to Johannine Temple-Christology," *The Biblical Annals* 2, no. 1 (March 2012): 153, https://search.ebscohost.com/login.aspx?direct=true&db=rfh&AN=CPLI0000536387&site=ehost-live.
5. Cecil Roth, "Cleansing of the Temple and Zechariah 14:21," *Novum Testamentum* 4, no. 3 (July 1960): 175-176, https://search.ebscohost.com/login.aspx?direct=true&db=rfh&AN=ATLA0000683451&site=ehost-live.
6. Ibid., 175-176.
7. John B. Taylor, *Ezekiel: An Introduction and Commentary* (Downers Grove, IL: InterVarsity Press, 1969), 251-252.
8. Tim LaHaye, Ed Hindson, Thomas Ice, and James Combs, eds., *Tim LaHaye Prophecy Study Bible* (Chattanooga, TN: AMG Publishers, 2001), 979.
9. Ibid., 979.
10. Taylor, *Ezekiel: An Introduction and Commentary*, 251-252.
11. LaHaye et al., *Tim LaHaye Prophecy Study Bible*, 979.
12. Feinberg, *The Prophecy of Ezekiel: The Glory of the Lord* (Chicago, IL: Moody, 1969), 233.
13. Adriane B. Leveen, "Returning the Body to Its Place: Ezekiel's Tour of the Temple," *Harvard Theological Review* 105, no. 4 (October 2012): 385, doi:10.1017/S0017816012000181.
14. George Albert Cooke, "Some Considerations on the Text and Teaching of Ezekiel 40–48: (A Paper Read before the Society for Old Testament Study, Meeting in London, January 3rd 1924)," *Zeitschrift Fur Die Alttestamentliche Wissenschaft* 42 (1924): 105, https://search.ebscohost.com/login.aspx?direct=true&db=rfh&AN=ATLAiFZK161121003006&site=ehost-live.
15. Ibid., 106.
16. The other three temples were the First or Solomon's Temple, the Second or Herod's Temple, and the Third Temple built during the tribulation but desecrated by the Antichrist and which clearly will not have survived beyond those seven years.
17. John Sietze Bergsma, "The Restored Temple as 'Built Jubilee' in Ezekiel 40–48," *Proceedings* 24 (2004): 75, https://search.ebscohost.com/login.aspx?direct=true&db=rfh&AN=ATLA0001494221&site=ehost-live.
18. Ibid., 76-78.
19. Ibid., 75.
20. Ibid., 79.
21. Leveen, "Returning the Body to Its Place: Ezekiel's Tour of the Temple," 387.
22. Kubis, "Zechariah 6:12-13 as the Referent of Γραφη in John 2:22 and 20:9: A Contribution to Johannine Temple-Christology," 164.

23. Walter A. Maier III, "The Divine Presence within the Cloud," *Concordia Theological Quarterly* 79, no. 1-2 (January 2015): 89, https://search.ebscohost.com/login.aspx?direct=true&db=rfh&AN=ATLAn3816524&site=ehost-live.
24. Ibid., 102.
25. References: Isaiah 2:2-3; 60:7, 13; 66:19-21; 56:6-7; Jeremiah 31:31-34; 32:38-40; 33:6-13; 33:15-18; 50:5; Ezekiel 37:26-28; 40:38-43; 42:13; 43:18-27; 45:15-25; 46:2-15; 20-24.
26. Jerry M. Hullinger, "The Problem of Animal Sacrifices in Ezekiel 40–48," *Bibliotheca Sacra* 152, no. 607 (July 1995): 279-280, https://search.ebscohost.com/login.aspx?direct=true&db=rfh&AN=ATLA0000897521&site=ehost-live.
27. Ibid., 279-280.
28. Ibid., 279-280.
29. Ibid., 281.
30. LaHaye et al., *Tim LaHaye Prophecy Study Bible*, 979.
31. Feinberg, *The Prophecy of Ezekiel: The Glory of the Lord*, 234.

CHAPTER 12—THE JEWS EXALTED: A PRIESTLY PEOPLE

1. Tzvi Freeman, "The Sixth Millennium and the Age of Moshiach," *Chabad*, https://www.chabad.org/library/article_cdo/aid/2057885/jewish/The-Sixth-Millennium-and-the-Age-of-Moshiach.htm.
2. Cotton Mather, *Things to be look'd for. Discourses on the Glorious Characters, Conjectures...the Latter Dayes* (Boston, MA: 1691), 9, 12.
3. William C. Watson, *Dispensationalism Before Darby: Seventeenth-Century and Eighteenth-Century English Apocalypticism* (Silverton, OR: Lampion Press, 2015), 203.
4. Heinrich Heine, *Ludwin Boerne* (1867), quoted in Ralph L. Woods, *The World Treasury of Religious Quotations* (New York: Hawthorn Books, 1966), 512.
5. Walter C. Kaiser Jr., "The Promise Doctrine and Jesus," *Trinity Journal* 4 (Spr 1975): 63, https://search.ebscohost.com/login.aspx?direct=true&db=rfh&AN=ATLA0001275813&site=ehost-live.
6. J. Duncan M. Derrett, "Mark's Technique: The Haemorrhaging Woman and Jairus' Daughter," *Biblica* 63, no. 4 (1982): 494-495, https://search.ebscohost.com/login.aspx?direct=true&db=rfh&AN=ATLA0000797523&site=ehost-live.
7. Greg A. King, "The Remnant in Zephaniah," *Bibliotheca Sacra* 151, no. 604 (October 1994): 424-425, https://search.ebscohost.com/login.aspx?direct=true&db=rfh&AN=ATLA0000885561&site=ehost-live.
8. Ibid., 424-425.
9. Ibid., 424-425.
10. John T. Willis, "Exclusivistic and Inclusivistic Aspects of the Concept of 'the People of God' in the Book of Isaiah," *Restoration Quarterly* 40, no. 1 (1998): 9-10, https://search.ebscohost.com/login.aspx?direct=true&db=rfh&AN=ATLA0000992062&site=ehost-live.
11. Randy Weiss, *Judaism Through the Eyes of Jesus* (Springfield, MO: 21st Century Press, 2016), 24.
12. Ibid., 24.
13. Ibid., 24.
14. David H. Stern, *Restoring the Jewishness of the Gospel* (Jerusalem, Israel: Jewish New Testament Publications, 1988), 37-38.
15. Ibid., 36.

16. Ibid., 37-38.
17. Tim LaHaye, Ed Hindson, Thomas Ice, and James Combs, eds., *Tim LaHaye Prophecy Study Bible* (Chattanooga, TN: AMG Publishers, 2001), 810.
18. David R. Reagan, *Christ in Prophecy* (McKinney, TX: Lamb & Lion Ministries, 2006), 44.
19. LaHaye et al., *Tim LaHaye Prophecy Study Bible*, 810.
20. Ibid., 810.
21. Ibid., 810.

CHAPTER 13—THE SAINTS REIGN: THE ADMINISTRATIVE BODY

1. John Piper, "One Day, We Will Rule with Christ," *Desiring God*, September 26, 2015, https://www.desiringgod.org/messages/one-day-we-will-rule-with-christ.
2. Edward Viening, ed., *The Zondervan Topical Bible* (Grand Rapids, MI: Zondervan, 1969), 131-135.
3. Tim Moore, *Looking Forward to the Reign of Jesus Christ* (McKinney, TX: Lamb & Lion Ministries, 2020), 28-29.
4. Shaye J.D. Cohen, *From the Maccabees to the Mishnah* (Philadelphia, PA: Westminster Press, 1989), 9.
5. Eleanor Doan, *Speaker's Sourcebook* (Grand Rapids, MI: Zondervan, 1978), 185.
6. Kenneth L. Barker, "Premillennialism in the Book of Daniel," *The Master's Seminary Journal* 4, no. 1 (Spr 1993): 32-33, https://search.ebscohost.com/login.aspx?direct=true&db=rfh&AN=ATLA0000864503&site=ehost-live.
7. Ibid., 32-33.
8. Eugene W. Pond, "The Background and Timing of the Judgment of the Sheep and Goats," *Bibliotheca Sacra* 159, no. 634 (April 2002): 210, https://search.ebscohost.com/login.aspx?direct=true&db=rfh&AN=ATLA0001322859&site=ehost-live.
9. Frank S. Mead, *The Encyclopedia of Religious Quotations* (Old Tappan, NJ: Fleming H. Revell, 1965), 267.
10. Timothy M. Willis, "Yahweh's Elders (Isa 24:23): Senior Officials of the Divine Court," *Zeitschrift Fur Die Alttestamentliche Wissenschaft* 103, no. 3 (1991): 384-385, https://search.ebscohost.com/login.aspx?direct=true&db=rfh&AN=ATLA0000851579&site=ehost-live.
11. Arnold G. Fruchtenbaum, *The Footsteps of the Messiah: A Study of the Sequence of Prophetic Events* (San Antonio, TX: Ariel Ministrries, 2004), 375.
12. Mike Stallard, "An Analysis of John Calvin's Criticism of Premillennialism in 'The Institutes,'" accessed December 11, 2021, https://pre-trib.org/images/2021_Conference/2021-Pre-Trib-Stallard-Calvin_and_Premillennialism-Paper.pdf.
13. Ibid.
14. Gary V. Smith, "Isaiah 65–66: The Destiny of God's Servants in a New Creation," *Bibliotheca Sacra* 171, no. 681 (January 2014): 288, https://search.ebscohost.com/login.aspx?direct=true&db=rfh&AN=ATLA0001966890&site=ehost-live.
15. Fruchtenbaum, *The Footsteps of the Messiah*, 375.
16. Ibid., 375.
17. Because this book approaches the subject of the Davidic kingdom using a literal hermeneutic, the same literal hermeneutic will be applied to the subject of the creation, taking into account the Hebrew word *yom* as meaning an actual 24-hour day as well as the six references in Genesis 1 to "evening and the morning" substantiating six literal 24-hour days of creation with a seventh literal 24-hour day of rest.

18. David R. Reagan, *Christ in Prophecy* (McKinney, TX: Lamb & Lion Ministries, 2006), 47.
19. Cotton Mather, *Things to be look'd for. Discourses on the Glorious Characters, Conjectures…the Latter Dayes* (Boston, MA: 1691), 34.
20. Reagan, *Christ in Prophecy*, 47.

CHAPTER 14—A TIME OF JOY: THE MOOD OF THE ERA

1. Isaac Watts, "Joy to the World," *Hymnary*, 1719, https://hymnary.org/text/joy_to_the_world_the_lord_is_come.
2. Gary V. Smith, "Isaiah 65–66: The Destiny of God's Servants in a New Creation," *Bibliotheca Sacra* 171, no. 681 (January 2014): 49, https://search.ebscohost.com/login.aspx?direct=true&db=rfh&AN=ATLA0001966890&site=ehost-live.
3. David Brickner, *Christ in the Feast of Tabernacles* (Chicago, IL: Moody Publishers, 2006), 128.
4. Ibid., 16.
5. Ibid., 16.

CHAPTER 15—A TIME OF PEACE AND NO WAR BETWEEN MEN: THE POLITICS OF THE NATIONS

1. William E. Gladstone, "Peace Not War Quotes," *AZ Quotes*, https://www.azquotes.com/quotes/topics/peace-not-war.html.
2. Chris Hedges, "What Every Person Should Know About War," *The New York Times*, https://skeptics.stackexchange.com/questions/31604/have-humans-been-entirely-at-peace-for-268-out-of-the-last-3400-years.
3. Ibid.
4. Bastian Herre, Lucas Rodés-Guirao, Max Roser, Joe Hasell, and Bobbie Macdonald, "War and Peace," *Our World In Data*, https://ourworldindata.org/war-and-peace.
5. Ibid.
6. Eleanor Doan, *Speaker's Sourcebook* (Grand Rapids, MI: Zondervan, 1978), 185.
7. Ibid., 185.
8. Frank S. Mead, *The Encyclopedia of Religious Quotations* (Old Tappan, NJ: Fleming H. Revell, 1965), 325.
9. Wilbur M. Smith, "The Prophetic Literature of Colonial America," *Bibliotheca Sacra* 100, no. 398 (April 1943): 273-274, https://search.ebscohost.com/login.aspx?direct=true&db=rfh&AN=ATLA0001513840&site=ehost-live.
10. Ehud Luz, "Utopia and Return: On the Structure of Utopian Thinking and Its Relation to Jewish-Christian Tradition," *Journal of Religion* 73, no. 3 (July 1993): 358, doi:10.1086/489187.
11. W. Sibley Towner, "Tribulation and Peace: The Fate of Shalom in Jewish Apocalyptic," *Horizons in Biblical Theology* 6, no. 2 (December 1984): 3-4, https://search.ebscohost.com/login.aspx?direct=true&db=rfh&AN=ATLA0000953754&site=ehost-live.
12. Ibid., 3-4.
13. Mead, *The Encyclopedia of Religious Quotations*, 325. Quoting from *The City of God*, XV.
14. Arthur W. Kac, *The Messianic Hope: A Divine Solution for the Human Problem* (Grand Rapids, MI: Baker Book House, 1975), 28-29.
15. Peter Bynum, "Between Text and Sermon: Isaiah 2:1-4," *Interpretation* 71, no. 3 (2017): 310, doi:10.1177/0020964317698766.
16. Ibid., 310.

17. Shira J. Golani, "Swords That Are Ploughshares: Another Case of (Bilingual) Wordplay in Biblical Prophecy?," *Biblica* 98, no. 3 (2017): 427, doi:10.2143/bib.98.3.3245515.
18. Bynum, "Between Text and Sermon: Isaiah 2:1-4," 310.
19. Marvin A. Sweeney, "Swords into Plowshares or Plowshares into Swords?: Isaiah and the Twelve in Intertextual Perspective on Zion," *Toronto Journal of Theology* 34, no. 1 (Spr 2018): 98, doi:10.3138/tjt.2017-0210.
20. Mead, *The Encyclopedia of Religious Quotations*, 325.

CHAPTER 16—ANIMALS AT PEACE WITH MANKIND: SERENITY IN THE ANIMAL KINGDOM

1. "Isaiah 11:1-9—The Peaceable Kingdom," *Enter the Bible*, https://enterthebible.org/passage/isaiah-111-9-the-peaceable-kingdom.
2. John L. MacKay, *Isaiah*, vol. 1, chapters 1-39 (Faverdale North, UK: Evangelical Press, 2008), 296-297.
3. Richard C. Brand Jr., "Either Or?," *The Expository Times* 116, no. 2 (November 2004): 56, https://search.ebscohost.com/login.aspx?direct=true&db=rfh&AN=ATLA0001548157&site=ehost-live.
4. Michael Jinkins, "Trouble in Paradise: Isaiah Berlin, the Prophet Isaiah, and the Recovery of a Non-Utopian Eschatological Claim for Christian Preaching," *International Journal of Practical Theology* 11, no. 1 (April 2007): 57-58, doi:10.1515/IJPT.2007.5.
5. MacKay, *Isaiah*, 296-297.
6. Jinkins, "Trouble in Paradise: Isaiah Berlin, the Prophet Isaiah, and the Recovery of a Non-Utopian Eschatological Claim for Christian Preaching," 57-58.
7. John Calvin, *Commentary on the Book of the Prophet Isaiah*, vol. 3, trans. William Fringle (Grand Rapids, MI: Baker Book House, 1984), 406.
8. Ibid., 406.
9. MacKay, *Isaiah*, 296-297.
10. Brand, "Either Or?," 56.
11. Edward L. Wheeler, "When Wolves and Lambs Dwell Together: Sermon Based on Isaiah 11:1-10," *The Journal of the Interdenominational Theological Center* 46 (Fall 2018): 118-119, https://search.ebscohost.com/login.aspx?direct=true&db=rfh&AN=ATLAiACO190909001087&site=ehost-live.
12. Ibid., 118-119.
13. Jinkins, "Trouble in Paradise: Isaiah Berlin, the Prophet Isaiah, and the Recovery of a Non-Utopian Eschatological Claim for Christian Preaching," 70.

CHAPTER 17—THE BOUNTIFUL LAND: THE RESTORATION OF THE PLANET

1. John F. Walvoord, "The Doctrine of the Millennium—Part I: The Righteous Government of the Millennium," *Theological Journal Library*, https://walvoord.com/book/export/html/333.
2. Richard Duane Patterson, "Psalm 22: From Trial to Triumph," *Journal of the Evangelical Theological Society* 47, no. 2 (June 2004): 225, https://search.ebscohost.com/login.aspx?direct=true&db=rfh&AN=ATLA0001457894&site=ehost-live.
3. Eleanor Doan, *Speaker's Sourcebook* (Grand Rapids, MI: Zondervan, 1978), 184.
4. Alfred Edersheim, *The Temple: Its Ministry and Services as They Were at the Time of Christ* (Grand Rapids, MI: Wm. B. Eerdmans, 1975), 268-269.

5. "Dead Sea," *Wikipedia*, https://en.wikipedia.org/wiki/Dead_Sea.
6. Frank E. Gaebelein, ed., *The Expositor's Bible Commentary*, vol. 6, Isaiah–Jeremiah (Grand Rapids, MI: Zondervan, 1986), 989-990.
7. Katheryn Pfisterer Darr, "The Wall around Paradise: Ezekielian Ideas about the Future," *Vetus Testamentum* 37, no. 3 (July 1987): 277-279, https://search.ebscohost.com/login.aspx?direct=true&db=rfh&AN=ATLA0000977138&site=ehost-live.
8. Ibid., 277-279.
9. Gaebelein, *The Expositor's Bible Commentary*, 989-990.
10. Klyne Snodgrass, "Streams of Tradition Emerging from Isaiah 40:1-5 and Their Adaptation in the New Testament," *Journal for the Study of the New Testament* 2, no. 8 (May 1980): 32, https://search.ebscohost.com/login.aspx?direct=true&db=rfh&AN=ATLA0000782785&site=ehost-live.
11. Terry W. Eddinger, "An Analysis of Isaiah 40:1-11 (17)," *Bulletin for Biblical Research* 9 (1999): 126-127, https://search.ebscohost.com/login.aspx?direct=true&db=rfh&AN=ATLA0001492393&site=ehost-live.
12. The Gog-Magog War (Ezekiel 38:19-23), the sixth seal judgment (Revelation 6:12-14), at the murder of the two witnesses (Revelation 11:13), and the sixth bowl judgment (Revelation 16:17-21) comprise the four prophetic earthquakes of the tribulation that cause every island to fly away and the mountains to no longer be found.
13. Eddinger, "An Analysis of Isaiah 40:1-11 (17)," 126-127.
14. John Goldingay, "The Breath of Yahweh Scorching, Confounding, Anointing: The Message of Isaiah 40-42," *Journal of Pentecostal Theology* 5, no. 11 (December 1997): 12, https://search.ebscohost.com/login.aspx?direct=true&db=rfh&AN=ATLA0001019936&site=ehost-live.
15. Snodgrass, "Streams of Tradition Emerging from Isaiah 40:1-5 and Their Adaptation in the New Testament," 28.
16. Ibid., 28.

CHAPTER 18—LONG LIFE: THE REJUVENATION OF HUMANITY

1. Gavin de Becker, *The Gift of Fear: Survival Signals That Protect Us from Violence* (Boston, MA: Little, Brown and Company, 2021).
2. Frank S. Mead, *The Encyclopedia of Religious Quotations* (Old Tappan, NJ: Fleming H. Revell, 1965), 267.
3. John W. DeGruchy, "A New Heaven and a New Earth: An Exposition of Isaiah 65:17-25," *Journal of Theology for Southern Africa* 105 (November 1999): 70, https://search.ebscohost.com/login.aspx?direct=true&db=rfh&AN=ATLA0000909509&site=ehost-live.
4. Eleanor Doan, *Speaker's Sourcebook* (Grand Rapids, MI: Zondervan, 1978), 148.
5. Gregory K. Beale, "An Amillennial Response to a Premillennial View of Isaiah 65:20," *Journal of the Evangelical Theological Society* 61, no. 3 (September 2018): 492, https://search.ebscohost.com/login.aspx?direct=true&db=rfh&AN=ATLAiGU0181031002225&site=ehost-live.
6. DeGruchy, "A New Heaven and a New Earth: An Exposition of Isaiah 65:17-25," 70.
7. Mead, *The Encyclopedia of Religious Quotations*, 267.

CHAPTER 19—SATAN BOUND

1. This quote is widely attributed to William Cowper, but its original source is unknown.
2. Frank S. Mead, *The Encyclopedia of Religious Quotations* (Old Tappan, NJ: Fleming H. Revell, 1965), 111.

3. Matt Waymeyer, "The Binding of Satan in Revelation 20," *The Master's Seminary Journal* 26, no. 1 (Spr 2015): 21, https://search.ebscohost.com/login.aspx?direct=true&db=rfh&AN=ATLAn3771734&site=ehost-live.
4. Ibid., 19.
5. Sydney H.T. Page, "Revelation 20 and Pauline Eschatology," *Journal of the Evangelical Theological* Society 23, no. 1 (March 1980): 31, https://search.ebscohost.com/login.aspx?direct=true&db=rfh&AN=ATLA0000777656&site=ehost-live.
6. Waymeyer, "The Binding of Satan in Revelation 20," 21.

CHAPTER 20—SATAN DEFEATED

1. A.W. Tozer, *The Devil Shall Not Prevail: Unshakable Confidence in God's Almighty Power* (Bloomington, MN: Bethany House, 2023).
2. Frank S. Mead, *The Encyclopedia of Religious Quotations* (Old Tappan, NJ: Fleming H. Revell, 1965), 107.
3. Gregory H. Harris, "Must Satan Be Released?: Indeed He Must Be: Toward a Biblical Understanding of Revelation 20:3," *The Master's Seminary Journal* 25, no. 1 (Spr 2014): 25, https://search.ebscohost.com/login.aspx?direct=true&db=rfh&AN=ATLAn3771677&site=ehost-live.
4. Ibid., 19.
5. Mead, *The Encyclopedia of Religious Quotations*, 327.
6. John S. Feinberg, *The Many Faces of Evil* (Wheaton, IL: Crossway, 2004), 118.
7. John Dryden, *Absalom and Achitophel*, Pt. I,l.79.
8. John Clarke, as cited in Mead, *The Encyclopedia of Religious Quotations*, 109.
9. G. Campbell Morgan, *The Analyzed Bible* (Old Tappan, NJ: Fleming H. Revell, 1964), 599.
10. Martin Luther, "A Mighty Fortress Is our God," 1529, https://hymnary.org/text/a_mighty_fortress_is_our_god_a_trusty_sh .
11. Morgan, *The Analyzed Bible*, 599.
12. Harris, "Must Satan Be Released?: Indeed He Must Be: Toward a Biblical Understanding of Revelation 20:3," 26.
13. Ibid., 26.
14. Ibid., 26.
15. Sydney H.T. Page, "Revelation 20 and Pauline Eschatology," *Journal of the Evangelical Theological* Society 23, no. 1 (March 1980): 32, https://search.ebscohost.com/login.aspx?direct=true&db=rfh&AN=ATLA0000777656&site=ehost-live.
16. Michael Jinkins, "Trouble in Paradise: Isaiah Berlin, the Prophet Isaiah, and the Recovery of a Non-Utopian Eschatological Claim for Christian Preaching," *International Journal of Practical Theology* 11, no. 1 (April 2007): 58, doi:10.1515/IJPT.2007.5.
17. Ibid., 61-62.
18. Ibid., 61-62
19. Ibid., 70.
20. John W. DeGruchy, "A New Heaven and a New Earth: An Exposition of Isaiah 65:17-25," *Journal of Theology for Southern Africa* 105 (November 1999): 66, https://search.ebscohost.com/login.aspx?direct=true&db=rfh&AN=ATLA0000909509&site=ehost-live.
21. Ibid., 68.

22. Ibid. 67.
23. Arthur W. Kac, *The Messianic Hope: A Divine Solution for the Human Problem* (Grand Rapids, MI: Baker Book House, 1975), 372.
24. Ibid., 372.
25. Ibid., 372.
26. Ibid., 372.
27. Mike Stallard, "An Analysis of John Calvin's Criticism of Premillennialism in 'The Institutes,'" accessed December 11, 2021, https://pre-trib.org/images/2021_Conference/2021-Pre-Trib-Stallard-Calvin_and_Premillennialism-Paper.pdf.
28. Ibid.

CHAPTER 21—FINAL JUDGMENT

1. Sam Storms, "10 Things You Should Know about the Great White Throne Judgment," July 9, 2018, https://www.samstorms.org/enjoying-god-blog/post/10-things-you-should-know-about-the-great-white-throne-judgment.
2. Gregory H. Harris, "Must Satan Be Released?: Indeed He Must Be: Toward a Biblical Understanding of Revelation 20:3," *The Master's Seminary Journal* 25, no. 1 (Spr 2014): 11, https://search.ebscohost.com/login.aspx?direct=true&db=rfh&AN=ATLAn3771677&site=ehost-live.
3. J.I. Packer, *Knowing God* (Downers Grove, IL: InterVarsity, 1973), 125, 127.
4. David J. MacLeod, "The Sixth 'Last Thing': The Last Judgment and the End of the World (Rev 20:11-15)," *Bibliotheca Sacra* 157, no. 627 (July 2000): 316, https://search.ebscohost.com/login.aspx?direct=true&db=rfh&AN=ATLA0000006311&site=ehost-live.
5. Ibid. The twelfth reference can be found in James 3:6.
6. Joe B. Fulton, "Mark Twain's New Jerusalem: Prophecy in the Unpublished Essay 'About Cities in the Sun,'" *Christianity and Literature* 55, no. 2 (Wint 2006): 187-188, https://search.ebscohost.com/login.aspx?direct=true&db=rfh&AN=ATLA0001530017&site=ehost-live. Note: Twain's manuscript "About Cities in the Sun" is housed in the Mark Twain Papers, The Bancroft Library, at the University of California at Berkeley (see microfilm edition of Mark Twain's Literary Manuscripts, Berkeley: The Bancroft Library, 2001: Reel 22).
7. MacLeod, "The Sixth 'Last Thing': The Last Judgment and the End of the World (Rev 20:11-15)," 318.
8. Ibid., 318.
9. The resurrection of the millennial saints remains a biblical mystery. Some theologians believe that no true believer will die during the millennial kingdom and so will live on into the eternal state in their earthly bodies. As nothing impure enters eternity, more than likely the millennial saints will receive their resurrected, glorified bodies sometime just before the great white throne judgment event. Again, the Bible does not say.
10. MacLeod, "The Sixth 'Last Thing': The Last Judgment and the End of the World (Rev 20:11-15)," 321.
11. Tim LaHaye, Ed Hindson, Thomas Ice, and James Combs, eds., *Tim LaHaye Prophecy Study Bible* (Chattanooga, TN: AMG Publishers, 2001), 1540.
12. MacLeod, "The Sixth 'Last Thing': The Last Judgment and the End of the World (Rev 20:11-15)," 322.
13. Ibid., 325.
14. This paragraph is the result of a discussion with biblical linguist and author Lee Brainard.

CHAPTER 22—MILLENNIAL VIEWPOINTS

1. William Faulkner, *The Sound and the Fury* (New York: Jonathan Cape and Harrison Smith, 1929).
2. William C. Watson, *Dispensationalism Before Darby: Seventeenth-Century and Eighteenth-Century English Apocalypticism* (Silverton, OR: Lampion Press, 2015), 3.
3. Philip Schaff, *History of the Christian Church*, vol. 2 (Grand Rapids, MI: Eerdmans, 1910), 614.
4. Ibid., 614.
5. Watson, *Dispensationalism Before Darby: Seventeenth-Century and Eighteenth-Century English Apocalypticism*, 5.
6. Ibid., 5.
7. Justin Martyr, *Dialogue with Trypho*, LXXX.
8. Ben Witherington, *The Problem with Evangelical Theology: Testing the Exegetical Foundations of Calvinism, Dispensationalism and Wesleyanism* (Waco, TX: Baylor Univeristy Press, 2005), 101.
9. Michael J. Vlach, "The Kingdom of God and the Millennium," *The Master's Seminary Journal* 23, no. 2 (Fall 2012): 227, https://search.ebscohost.com/login.aspx?direct=true&db=rfh&AN=ATLA0001924490&site=ehost-live.
10. Tim LaHaye, Ed Hindson, Thomas Ice, and James Combs, eds., *Tim LaHaye Prophecy Study Bible* (Chattanooga, TN: AMG Publishers, 2001), 1540.
11. Ibid., 1541.
12. Kenneth L. Barker, "Premillennialism in the Book of Daniel," *The Master's Seminary Journal* 4, no. 1 (Spr 1993): 29, https://search.ebscohost.com/login.aspx?direct=true&db=rfh&AN=ATLA0000864503&site=ehost-live.
13. Vlach, "The Kingdom of God and the Millennium," 225-226.
14. Craig A. Blaising, "The Day of the Lord and the Seventieth Week of Daniel," *Bibliotheca Sacra* 169, no. 674 (April 2012): 142, https://search.ebscohost.com/login.aspx?direct=true&db=rfh&AN=ATLA0001892476&site=ehost-live.
15. Vlach, "The Kingdom of God and the Millennium," 227.
16. Ibid., 226.
17. Mike Stallard, "An Analysis of John Calvin's Criticism of Premillennialism in 'The Institutes,'" accessed December 11, 2021, https://pre-trib.org/images/2021_Conference/2021-Pre-Trib-Stallard-Calvin_and_Premillennialism-Paper.pdf.
18. Chart designed by the author.
19. Stallard, "An Analysis of John Calvin's Criticism of Premillennialism in 'The Institutes.'"
20. Arnold G. Fruchtenbaum, "The Modern State of Israel in Bible Prophecy," *Pre-Trib Research Center*, accessed December 11, 2021, https://pre-trib.org/images/2021_Conference/2021-Pre-Trib-Fruchtenbaum-Modern_State_of_Israel-Paper.pdf.
21. Stallard, "An Analysis of John Calvin's Criticism of Premillennialism in 'The Institutes.'"
22. Vlach, "The Kingdom of God and the Millennium," 227.
23. David R. Reagan, *What's the Difference in a Millennium and a Millipede?* (McKinney, TX: Lamb & Lion Ministries, 2022), 23.
24. See also Mark 13:37; Romans 13:11-12; 1 Corinthians 1:7; Philippians 3:20; 1 Thessalonians 5:2, 6; Titus 2:11-13; Hebrews 9:28; James 5:8-9; 1 Peter 1:13; 4:7; Revelation 1:1; 3:11; 22:7, 10.
25. Reagan, *What's the Difference in a Millennium and a Millipede?*, 26-27.
26. Twenty differences in the accounts of Christ's return have been identified by the author. The five listed are merely a sampling.

27. Reagan, *What's the Difference in a Millennium and a Millipede?*, 20.
28. LeRoy Edwin Froom, *The Prophetic Faith of Our Fathers* (Washington, DC: Review and Herald, 1950), 465-466.
29. Ibid., 465-466.
30. Heinrich Heine, *Ludwin Boerne* (1867), quoted in Ralph L. Woods, *The World Treasury of Religious Quotations* (New York: Hawthorn Books, 1966), 527.
31. St. Augustine, *City of God* (426), quoted in Ralph L. Woods, *The World Treasury of Religious Quotations* (New York: Hawthorn Books, 1966), 527.
32. Watson, *Dispensationalism Before Darby: Seventeenth-Century and Eighteenth-Century English Apocalypticism*, 6.
33. Ben Witherington, *The Problem with Evangelical Theology: Testing the Exegetical Foundations of Calvinism, Dispensationalism and Wesleyanism* (Waco, TX: Baylor University Press, 2005), 101.
34. Froom, *The Prophetic Faith of Our Fathers*, 465-466.
35. Watson, *Dispensationalism Before Darby: Seventeenth-Century and Eighteenth-Century English Apocalypticism*, 5.
36. Ibid., 7.
37. Reagan, *What's the Difference in a Millennium and a Millipede?*, 6.
38. Ibid., 22.
39. LaHaye et al., *Tim LaHaye Prophecy Study Bible*, 1539.
40. Augustine, *The City of God*, 20.7.
41. George E. Ladd, *A Commentary on the Revelation of John* (Grand Rapids, MI: Eerdmans, 1971), 262.
42. Floyd E. Hamilton, *The Basis of Millennial Faith* (Grand Rapids, MI: Eerdmans, 1942), 110.
43. Chart designed by the author.
44. Hamilton, *The Basis of Millennial Faith*, 144.
45. Lorraine Boettner, *The Millennium* (Philadelphia, PA: Presbyterian & Reformed Publishing, 1964), 80.
46. Fruchtenbaum, "The Modern State of Israel in Bible Prophecy."
47. Ibid.
48. Ibid.
49. Stallard, "An Analysis of John Calvin's Criticism of Premillennialism in 'The Institutes.'"
50. Matt Waymeyer, "The Binding of Satan in Revelation 20," *The Master's Seminary Journal* 26, no. 1 (Spr 2015): 36, https://search.ebscohost.com/login.aspx?direct=true&db=rfh&AN=ATLAn3771734&site=ehost-live.
51. Ibid., 22.
52. Ibid., 23.
53. Sydney H.T. Page, "Revelation 20 and Pauline Eschatology," *Journal of the Evangelical Theological* Society 23, no. 1 (March 1980): 35, https://search.ebscohost.com/login.aspx?direct=true&db=rfh&AN=ATLA0000777656&site=ehost-live.
54. Watson, *Dispensationalism Before Darby: Seventeenth-Century and Eighteenth-Century English Apocalypticism*, 3.
55. Froom, *The Prophetic Faith of Our Fathers*, 477.
56. Ibid., 491.

57. Cotton Mather, *Things to be look'd for. Discourses on the Glorious Characters, Conjectures…the Latter Dayes* (Boston, MA: 1691), 6.
58. Ibid., 15-16.
59. Reagan, *What's the Difference in a Millennium and a Millipede?*, 35.
60. Ibid., 36.
61. Ibid., 44.
62. Ibid., 44.
63. Mark G. Toulouse, "Campbell and Postmillennialism: The Kingdoms of God," *Journal of Discipliana* 60, no. 3 (Fall 2000): 79, https://search.ebscohost.com/login.aspx?direct=true&db=rfh&AN=ATLA0001282044&site=ehost-live.
64. Ibid., 79.
65. Ibid., 79.
66. Ibid., 78.
67. Reagan, *What's the Difference in a Millennium and a Millipede?*, 44.
68. James H. Moorhead, "The Erosion of Postmillennialism in American Religious Thought, 1865–1925," *Church History* 53, no. 1 (March 1984): 61, https://search.ebscohost.com/login.aspx?direct=true&db=rfh&AN=ATLA0000939099&site=ehost-live.
69. Ibid., 61.
70. Ibid., 61.
71. Ibid., 77.
72. Reagan, *What's the Difference in a Millennium and a Millipede?*, 46.
73. Ibid., 46.
74. Ibid., 46.
75. LaHaye et al., *Tim LaHaye Prophecy Study Bible*, 1540.
76. Tim Moore, *Looking Forward to the Reign of Jesus Christ* (McKinney, TX: Lamb & Lion Ministries, 2020), 32, 38.
77. Clarence Larkin, *Dispensational Truth* (Philadelphia, PA: The Rev. Clarence Larkin Estate, 1920), 4.
78. Mark G. Toulouse, "Campbell and Postmillennialism: The Kingdoms of God," *Journal of Discipliana* 60, no. 3 (Fall 2000): 80, https://search.ebscohost.com/login.aspx?direct=true&db=rfh&AN=ATLA0001282044&site=ehost-live.
79. Ibid., 81, 83.
80. Ibid., 83.
81. Moorhead, "The Erosion of Postmillennialism in American Religious Thought, 1865–1925," 62, https://search.ebscohost.com/login.aspx?direct=true&db=rfh&AN=ATLA0000939099&site=ehost-live.
82. Gregory H. Harris, "Must Satan Be Released?: Indeed He Must Be: Toward a Biblical Understanding of Revelation 20:3," *The Master's Seminary Journal* 25, no. 1 (Spr 2014): 131, https://search.ebscohost.com/login.aspx?direct=true&db=rfh&AN=ATLAn3771677&site=ehost-live.
83. Toulouse, "Campbell and Postmillennialism: The Kingdoms of God," 83.
84. Chart designed by the author.
85. Toulouse, "Campbell and Postmillennialism: The Kingdoms of God," 85-88.
86. Ibid., 85.

87. It has been noted that while some who hold this viewpoint are at odds with the view's mainstream notion that mankind is inherently good, concluding that as evangelism increases so too will more and more Christians populate the earth, and because regenerate Christ-followers are considered inherently "good" then the world will become a much better place, they still fall into the fallacy that regenerate people can bring about the kingdom by their own works. Though saved and indwelt by the Holy Spirit, as long as unglorified Christians remain with two natures—sin and sanctified—they still remain incapable of bringing about the kingdom of Christ. This limitation should be evident to anyone who has been caught up in the divisiveness of church politics. Only the King of kings can bring about the kingdom, which stands as one of the main points God has been making all throughout human history.
88. John F. Walvoord, "Christ's Olivet Discourse on the End of the Age: The Judgment of the Nations," *Bibliotheca Sacra* 129, no. 516 (October 1972): 314-315, https://search.ebscohost.com/login.aspx?direct=true&db=rfh&AN=ATLA0001508911&site=ehost-live.
89. Reagan, *What's the Difference in a Millennium and a Millipede?*, 46-48.
90. Ibid., 49.
91. Robert G. Clouse, *The Meaning of the Millennium: Four Views* (Downers Grove, IL: InterVarsity Press, 1977), 7-9.
92. Thomas Newton, *An Abridgement of Doctor Newton, Bishop of Bristol's Dissertations on the Prophecies* (Kilkenny, 1789), 84-85.
93. Clement of Alexandria, *To Marcellinus*, CXXXVIII,5,7.
94. Watson, *Dispensationalism Before Darby: Seventeenth-Century and Eighteenth-Century English Apocalypticism*, 3.
95. Ibid., 8.
96. Clouse, *The Meaning of the Millennium: Four Views*, 7-9.
97. Watson, *Dispensationalism Before Darby: Seventeenth-Century and Eighteenth-Century English Apocalypticism*, 3.
98. Ibid.
99. Vlach, "The Kingdom of God and the Millennium," 227.
100. Moore, *Looking Forward to the Reign of Jesus Christ*, 29.
101. Chart designed by the author.
102. Moore, *Looking Forward to the Reign of Jesus Christ*, 16.
103. Stephen J. Nichols, "The Dispensational View of the Davidic Kingdom: A Response to Progressive Dispensationalism," *The Master's Seminary Journal* 7, no. 2 (Fall 1996): 215, https://search.ebscohost.com/login.aspx?direct=true&db=rfh&AN=ATLA0001016694&site=ehost-live.
104. Ibid., 236.
105. Ibid., 239.
106. Moore, *Looking Forward to the Reign of Jesus Christ*, 37.
107. Fruchtenbaum, "The Modern State of Israel in Bible Prophecy," 11. For those who believe the modern state of Israel to be a historical aberration, as if God is not sovereign, and so capable of annihilation, they have to look no farther than Amos 9:15, where God promises that once Israel has been re-established the Jewish people will never be uprooted from their land ever again. As detailed earlier, even Satan and the Antichrist are incapable of achieving Israel's total destruction. Thus, those who hold to dispensational premillennialism do not fear that the modern-day nation of Israel can ever be truly destroyed, for God divinely protects it.
108. Ibid., 13.

109. Waymeyer, "The Binding of Satan in Revelation 20," 19.
110. Harris, "Must Satan Be Released?: Indeed He Must Be: Toward a Biblical Understanding of Revelation 20:3," 14.
111. Reagan, *What's the Difference in a Millennium and a Millipede?*, 60.
112. Ibid., 60
113. Watson, *Dispensationalism Before Darby: Seventeenth-Century and Eighteenth-Century English Apocalypticism.*
114. Lee W. Brainard, "Recent Pre-Trib Rapture Findings in the Early Church," *Pre-Trib Research Center*, accessed December 11, 2021, https://www.pre-trib.org/images/2021_Conference/2021-Pre-Trib-Brainard-Recent_Pre-Trib_Rapture_Findings-Paper.pdf.
115. Reagan, *What's the Difference in a Millennium and a Millipede?*, 67.

CHAPTER 23—THE FINAL REVIEW

1. Frank S. Mead, *The Encyclopedia of Religious Quotations* (Old Tappan, NJ: Fleming H. Revell, 1965), 123.
2. Paraphrased from Kenneth L. Barker, "Premillennialism in the Book of Daniel," *The Master's Seminary Journal* 4, no. 1 (Spr 1993): 26, https://search.ebscohost.com/login.aspx?direct=true&db=rfh&AN=ATLA0000864503&site=ehost-live.
3. Paul Lee Tan, *The Interpretation of Prophecy* (Winona Lake, IN: Assurance Publishers, 2010), 26.
4. Ibid., 26
5. Charles C. Ryrie, *Basic Theology* (Wheaton, IL: Victor Books, 1986), 508.
6. Ibid., 508.
7. Kenneth L. Barker, "Premillennialism in the Book of Daniel," *The Master's Seminary Journal* 4, no. 1 (Spr 1993): 43, https://search.ebscohost.com/login.aspx?direct=true&db=rfh&AN=ATLA0000864503&site=ehost-live.
8. Walter C, Kaiser Jr., "The Promise Doctrine and Jesus," *Trinity Journal* 4 (Spr 1975): 66, https://search.ebscohost.com/login.aspx?direct=true&db=rfh&AN=ATLA0001275813&site=ehost-live.
9. Charles A. Gieschen, "Antichrist in the Scriptures and the Lutheran Confessions: The Relevance of Reformation Exegesis of 2 Thessalonians 2:1-12 for the Church Today," *Concordia Theological Quarterly* 81, no. 3–4 (July 2017): 263, https://search.ebscohost.com/login.aspx?direct=true&db=rfh&AN=ATLAiC9Y180604000036&site=ehost-live.
10. Tim LaHaye, Ed Hindson, Thomas Ice, and James Combs, eds., *Tim LaHaye Prophecy Study Bible* (Chattanooga, TN: AMG Publishers, 2001), 1605.
11. Braxton Hunter, *Evangelistic Apologetics: Compatibility and Integration* (Evansville, IN: Trinity Academic Press, 2014), 29.
12. David R. Reagan, *Christ in Prophecy* (McKinney, TX: Lamb & Lion Ministries, 2006), 126.
13. John W. DeGruchy, "A New Heaven and a New Earth: An Exposition of Isaiah 65:17-25," *Journal of Theology for Southern Africa* 105 (November 1999): 73, https://search.ebscohost.com/login.aspx?direct=true&db=rfh&AN=ATLA0000909509&site=ehost-live.
14. Don Finto, *God's Promise and the Future of Israel* (Ventura, CA: Gospel Light, 2006), 143.